CLASSICS IN PSYCHOLOGY

CLASSICS IN PSYCHOLOGY

.

A NOTE ABOUT THE AUTHOR

THÉODULE ARMAND RIBOT was born in Guingamp, France, in 1839. He graduated from the Ecole Normale Supérieure in 1865 and thereafter taught philosophy at a number of lycèes. He studied various types of mental abnormalities in Paris from 1872 to 1885, at which time he was placed in charge of a course in experimental psychology at the Sorbonne. In 1889 a chair of experimental and comparative psychology was created for Ribot at the Collège de France and scientific psychology had achieved respectability in French intellectual life. Ribot remained in this position, editing the *Revue Philosophique* until his death in 1916.

Ribot's scientific goal was to study normal mental processes by focusing on evolutionary considerations and pathological dissolution. Beginning with simpler psychological functions, he found himself increasingly concerned with more complex phenomena such as attention, generalization, and emotion. His pioneering work on the imagination reflected this preoccupation of his later years.

ESSAY

ON THE

CREATIVE IMAGINATION

BY

Th[eodule Armand] Ribot

ARNO PRESS
A New York Times Company
New York ★ 1973

Reprint Edition 1973 by Arno Press Inc.

Reprinted from a copy in
The Newark Public Library

Classics in Psychology
ISBN for complete set: 0-405-05130-1
See last pages of this volume for titles.

Manufactured in the United States of America

————◆————

Library of Congress Cataloging in Publication Data

Ribot, Théodule Armand, 1839-1916.
    Essay on the creative imagination.

    (Classics in psychology)
    Translation of Essai sur l'imagination créatrice.
    Reprint of the 1906 ed. published by Open Court Pub.
Co., Chicago.
    1. Creation (Literary, artistic, etc.) 2. Imagi-
nation. I. Title.   [DNLM: BF R486ea
1906F]
BF408.R3513 1973   153.3   73-2987
ISBN 0-405-05159-X

ESSAY

ON THE

CREATIVE IMAGINATION

BY

TH. RIBOT

TRANSLATED FROM THE FRENCH

BY

ALBERT H. N. BARON

FELLOW IN CLARK UNIVERSITY

———

CHICAGO

THE OPEN COURT PUBLISHING COMPANY

London: Kegan Paul, Trench, Trübner & Co., Ltd.

1906

To the Memory of My Teacher
and Friend,

Arthur Allin, Ph. D.,

PROFESSOR OF PSYCHOLOGY AND EDUCATION,
UNIVERSITY OF COLORADO,

WHO FIRST INTERESTED ME IN THE PROBLEMS OF PSYCHOLOGY,
THIS BOOK IS DEDICATED, WITH REVERENCE
AND GRATITUDE, BY
THE TRANSLATOR.

TRANSLATOR'S PREFACE.

The name of Th. Ribot has been for many years well known in America, and his works have gained wide popularity. The present translation of one of his more recent works is an attempt to render available in English what has been received as a classic exposition of a subject that is often discussed, but rarely with any attempt to understand its true nature.

It is quite generally recognized that psychology has remained in the semi-mythological, semi-scholastic period longer than most attempts at scientific formulization. For a long time it has been the "spook science" *per se,* and the imagination, now analyzed by M. Ribot in such a masterly manner, has been one of the most persistent, apparently real, though very indefinite, of psychological spooks. Whereas people have been accustomed to speak of the imagination as an entity *sui generis,* as a lofty something found only in long-haired, wild-eyed "geniuses," constituting indeed the center of a cult, our author, Prometheus-like, has brought it down from the heavens, and has clearly shown that *imagination is a function of mind common to all*

men in some degree, and that it is shown in as
highly developed form in commercial leaders and
practical inventors as in the most bizarre of romantic
idealists. The only difference is that the manifestation is not the same.

That this view is not entirely original with M.
Ribot is not to his discredit—indeed, he does not
claim any originality. We find the view clearly
expressed elsewhere, certainly as early as Aristotle,
that the greatest artist is he who actually embodies
his vision and will in permanent form, preferably
in social institutions. This idea is so clearly enunciated in the present monograph, which the author
modestly styles an essay, that when the end of the
book is reached but little remains of the great
imagination-ghost, save the one great mystery underlying all facts of mind.

That the present rendering falls far below the
lucid French of the original, the translator is well
aware; he trusts, however, that the indulgent reader
will take into account the good intent as offsetting
in part, at least, the numerous shortcomings of this
version.

I wish here to express my obligation to those
friends who encouraged me in the congenial task
of translation.   A. H. N. B.

AUTHOR'S PREFACE

Contemporary psychology has studied the purely reproductive imagination with great eagerness and success. The works on the different image-groups —visual, auditory, tactile, motor—are known to everyone, and form a collection of inquiries solidly based on subjective and objective observation, on pathological facts and laboratory experiments. The study of the creative or constructive imagination, on the other hand, has been almost entirely neglected. It would be easy to show that the best, most complete, and most recent treatises on psychology devote to it scarcely a page or two; often, indeed, do not even mention it. A few articles, a few brief, scarce monographs, make up the sum of the past twenty-five years' work on the subject. The subject does not, however, at all deserve this indifferent or contemptuous attitude. Its importance is unquestionable, and even though the study of the creative imagination has hitherto remained almost inaccessible to experimentation strictly so-called, there are yet other objective processes that permit of our approaching it with some likelihood of success, and of continuing the work of former psychologists, but with methods better adapted to the requirements of contemporary thought.

The present work is offered to the reader as an essay or first attempt only. It is not our intention here to undertake a complete monograph that would require a thick volume, but only to seek the underlying conditions of the creative imagination, showing that it has its beginning and principal source in the natural tendency of images to become objectified (or, more simply, in the motor elements inherent in the image), and then following it in its development under its manifold forms, whatever they may be. For I cannot but maintain that, at present, the psychology of the imagination is concerned almost wholly with its part in esthetic creation and in the sciences. We scarcely get beyond that; its other manifestations have been occasionally mentioned—never investigated. Yet invention in the fine arts and in the sciences is only a special case, and possibly not the principal one. We hope to show that in practical life, in mechanical, military, industrial, and commercial inventions, in religious, social, and political institutions, the human mind has expended and made permanent as much imagination as in all other fields.

The constructive imagination is a faculty that in the course of ages has undergone a reduction—or at least, some profound changes. So, for reasons indicated later on, the mythic activity has been taken in this work as the central point of our topic, as the primitive and typical form out of which the greater number of the others have arisen. The creative power is there shown entirely unconfined, freed from all hindrance, careless of the possible and the impossible; in a pure state, unadulterated by the opposing influence of imitation, of ratiocination, of the knowledge of natural laws and their uniformity.

In the first or analytical part, we shall try to resolve the constructive imagination into its constitutive factors, and study each of them singly.

The second or genetic part will follow the imagination in its development as a whole from the dimmest to the most complex forms.

Finally, the third or concrete part, will be no longer devoted to the imagination, but to imaginative beings, to the principal types of imagination that observation shows us.

May, 1900.

ANALYTICAL TABLE OF CONTENTS.

INTRODUCTION.

THE MOTOR NATURE OF THE CONSTRUCTIVE IMAGINATION.

FIRST PART.

ANALYSIS OF THE IMAGINATION.

CHAPTER I.

THE INTELLECTUAL FACTOR.

CHAPTER II.

THE EMOTIONAL FACTOR.

CHAPTER III.

THE UNCONSCIOUS FACTOR.

CHAPTER IV.

THE ORGANIC CONDITIONS OF THE IMAGINATION.

CHAPTER V.

LAW OF THE DEVELOPMENT OF THE IMAGINATION.

THIRD PART.

THE PRINCIPAL TYPES OF IMAGINATION.

PRELIMINARY.

CHAPTER I.

THE PLASTIC IMAGINATION.

CHAPTER IV.

THE SCIENTIFIC IMAGINATION.

CHAPTER V.

THE PRACTICAL AND MECHANICAL IMAGINATION.

CHAPTER VI.

THE COMMERCIAL IMAGINATION.

CHAPTER VII.

THE UTOPIAN IMAGINATION.

CONCLUSION.

I. *The foundations of the creative imagination.*

II. *The imaginative type.*

APPENDICES.

OBSERVATIONS AND DOCUMENTS.

INTRODUCTION

INTRODUCTION

The Motor Nature of the Constructive Imagination

I

It has been often repeated that one of the principal conquests of contemporary psychology is the fact that it has firmly established the place and importance of movements; that it has especially through observation and experiment shown the representation of a movement to be a movement begun, a movement in the nascent state. Yet those who have most strenuously insisted on this proposition have hardly gone beyond the realm of the passive imagination; they have clung to facts of pure reproduction. My aim is to extend their formula, and to show that it explains, in large measure at least, the origin of the creative imagination.

Let us follow step by step the passage from reproduction pure and simple to the creative stage, showing therein the persistence and preponderance of the motor element in proportion as we rise from mere repetition to invention.

First of all, do all representations include motor

elements? Yes, I say, because every perception presupposes movements to some extent, and representations are the remnants of past perceptions. Certain it is that, without our examining the question in detail, this statement holds good for the great majority of cases. So far as visual and tactile images are concerned there is no possible doubt as to the importance of the motor elements that enter into their composition. The eye is very poorly endowed with movements for its office as a higher sense-organ; but if we take into account its intimate connection with the vocal organs, so rich in capacity for motor combinations, we note a kind of compensation. Smell and taste, secondary in human psychology, rise to a very high rank indeed among many animals, and the olfactory apparatus thus obtains with them a complexity of movements proportionate to its importance, and one that at times approaches that of sight. There yet remains the group of internal sensations that might cause discussion. Setting aside the fact that the vague impressions bound up with chemical changes within the tissues are scarcely factors in representation, we find that the sensations resulting from changes in respiration, circulation, and digestion are not lacking in motor elements. The mere fact that, in some persons, vomiting, hiccoughs, micturition, etc., can be caused by perceptions of sight or of hearing proves that representations of this character have a tendency to become translated into acts.

Without emphasizing the matter we may, then,

say that this thesis rests on a weighty mass of facts; that the motor element of the image tends to cause it to lose its purely "inner" character, to objectify it, to externalize it, to project it outside of ourselves.

It should, however, be noted that what has just been said does not take us beyond the reproductive imagination—beyond memory. All these revived images are *repetitions;* but the creative imagination requires something *new*—this is its peculiar and essential mark. In order to grasp the transition from reproduction to production, from repetition to creation, it is necessary to consider other, more rare, and more extraordinary facts, found only among some favored beings. These facts, known for a long time, surrounded with some mystery, and attributed in a vague manner "to the power of the imagination," have been studied in our own day with much more system and exactness. For our purpose we need to recall only a few of them.

Many instances have been reported of tingling or of pains that may appear in different parts of the body solely through the effect of the imagination. Certain people can increase or inhibit the beating of their hearts at will, *i. e.,* by means of an intense and persistent representation. The renowned physiologist, E. F. Weber, possessed this power, and has described the mechanism of the phenomenon. Still more remarkable are the cases of vesication produced in hypnotized subjects by means of suggestion. Finally, let us recall the persistent story of

the stigmatized individuals, who, from the thirteenth
century down to our own day, have been quite
numerous and present some interesting varieties—
some having only the mark of the crucifix, others
of the scourging, or of the crown of thorns.[1] Let
us add the profound changes of the organism, results of the suggestive therapeutics of contemporaries; the wonderful effects of the "faith cure," *i. e.,*
the miracles of all religions in all times and in all
places; and this brief list will suffice to recall certain
creative activities of the human imagination that we
have a tendency to forget.

It is proper to add that the image acts not altogether in a positive manner.   Sometimes it has an
inhibitory power.   A vivid representation of a
movement arrested is the beginning of the stoppage
of that movement; it may even end in complete
arrest of the movement.   Such are the cases of
"paralysis by ideas" first described by Reynolds,
and later by Charcot and his school under the name
of "psychic paralysis."   The patient's inward conviction that he cannot move a limb renders him
powerless for any movement, and he recovers his
motor power only when the morbid representation
has disappeared.

These and similar facts suggest a few remarks.

First, that we have here creation in the strict
sense of the word, though it be limited to the organism.   What appears is *new*.   Though one may

---

[1] A. Maury, in his book *L'Astronomie et la Magie,* enumerates
fifty cases.

strictly maintain that from our own experience we have a knowledge of formication, rapid and slow beating of the heart, even though we may not be able ordinarily to produce them at will, this position is absolutely untenable when we consider cases of vesication, stigmata, and other alleged miraculous phenomena: *these are without precedent in the life of the individual.*

Second, in order that these unusual states may occur, there are required additional elements in the producing mechanism. At bottom this mechanism is very obscure. To invoke "the power of the imagination" is merely to substitute a word where an explanation is needed. Fortunately, we do not need to penetrate into the inmost part of this mystery. It is enough for us to make sure of the facts, to prove that they have a representation as the starting point, and to show that the representation by itself is not enough. What more then is needed? Let us note first of all that these occurrences are rare. It is not within the power of everybody to acquire stigmata or to become cured of a paralysis pronounced incurable. This happens only to those having an ardent faith, a strong desire *that it shall come to pass.* This is an indispensable psychic condition. What is concerned in such a case is not a single state, but a double one: an image followed by a particular emotional state (desire, aversion, etc.). In other words, there are two conditions: In the first are concerned the motor elements included in the image, the remains of previous perceptions; in the second, there are concerned the foregoing, *plus* affective states, tendencies that sum up the individual's energy. It is the latter fact that explains their power.

To conclude: This group of facts shows us the existence, beyond images, of another factor, instinctive or emotional in form, which we shall have to study later and which will lead us to the ultimate source of the creative imagination.

I fear that the distance between the facts here given and the creative imagination proper will seem to the reader very great indeed. And why so? First, because the creative activity here has as its only material the organism, and is not separated from the creator. Then, too, because these facts are extremely simple, and the creative imagination, in the ordinary sense, is extremely complex; here there is one operating cause, a single representation more or less complex, while in imaginative creation we have several co-operating images with combinations, coördination, arrangement, grouping. But it must not be forgotten that our present aim is simply to find *a transition stage*[1] between reproduction and production; to show the common origin of the two forms of imagination—the purely *re*presentative faculty and the faculty of creating by means of the intermediation of images;—and to show at the same time the work of separation, of severance between the two.

[1] There are still others, as we shall see later on.

II

Since the chief aim of this study is to prove that the basis of invention must be sought in motor manifestations, I shall not hesitate to dwell on it, and I take the subject up again under another, clearer, more precise, and more psychological form, in putting the following question: Which one among the various modes of mind-activity offers the closest analogy to the creative imagination? I unhesitatingly answer, *voluntary activity*: Imagination, in the intellectual order, is the equivalent of will in the realm of movements. Let us justify this comparison by some proof.

1. Likeness of development in the two instances. Growth of voluntary control is progressive, slow, crossed and checked. The individual has to become master of his muscles and by their agency extend his sway over other things. Reflexes, instinctive movements, and movements expressive of emotion constitute the primary material of voluntary movements. The will has no movements of its own as an inheritance: it must coördinate and associate, since it separates in order to form new associations. It reigns by right of conquest, not by right of birth. In like manner, the creative imagination does not rise completely armed. Its raw materials are images, which here correspond to muscular movements. It goes through a period of trial. It always is, at the start (for reasons indicated later on), an imitation; it attains its complex forms only through a process of growth.

2. But this first comparison does not go to the bottom of the matter; there are yet deeper analogies. First, the completely subjective character of both instances. The imagination is subjective, personal, anthropocentric; its movement is from within outwards toward an objectification. The understanding, *i. e.,* the intellect in the restricted sense. has opposite characteristics—it is objective, impersonal, receives from outside. For the creative imagination the inner world is the regulator; there is a preponderance of the inner over the outer. For the understanding, the outside world is the regulator; there is a preponderance of the outer over the inner. The world of my imagination is *my* world as opposed to the world of my understanding, which is the world of all my fellow creatures. On the other hand, as regards the will, we might repeat exactly, word for word, what we have just said of the imagination. This is unnecessary. Back of both, then, we have our true cause, whatever may be our opinion concerning the ultimate nature of causation and of will.

3. Both imagination and will have a teleological character, and act only with a view toward an end, being thus the opposite of the understanding, which, as such, limits itself to proof. We are always wanting something, be it worthless or important. We are always inventing for an end—whether in the case of a Napoleon imagining a plan of campaign, or a cook making up a new dish. In both instances there is now a simple end attained by im-

mediate means, now a complex and distant goal presupposing subordinate ends which are means in relation to the final end. In both cases there is a *vis a tergo* designated by the vague term "spontaneity," which we shall attempt to make clear later, and a *vis a fronte,* an attracting movement.

4. Added to this analogy as regards their nature, there are other, secondary likenesses between the abortive forms of the creative imagination and the impotent forms of the will. In its normal and complete form will culminates in an act; but with wavering characters and sufferers from abulia deliberation never ends, or the resolution remains inert, incapable of realization, of asserting itself in practice. The creative imagination also, in its complete form, has a tendency to become objectified, to assert itself in a work that shall exist not only for the creator but for everybody. On the contrary, with dreamers pure and simple, the imagination remains a vaguely sketched inner affair; it is not embodied in any esthetic or practical invention. Revery is the equivalent of weak desires; dreamers are the abulics of the creative imagination.

It is unnecessary to add that the similarity established here between the will and the imagination is only partial and has as its aim only to bring to light the rôle of the motor elements. Surely no one will confuse two aspects of our psychic life that are so distinct, and it would be foolish to delay in order to enumerate the differences. The characteristic of novelty should by itself suffice, since it is the special and indispensable mark of invention, and for volition is only accessory: The extraction of a tooth requires of the patient as much effort the second time as the first, although it is no longer a novelty.

After these preliminary remarks we must go on to the analysis of the creative imagination, in order to understand its nature in so far as that is accessible with our existing means. It is, indeed, a tertiary formation in mental life, if we assume a primary layer (sensations and simple emotions), and a secondary (images and their associations, certain elementary logical operations, etc.). Being composite, it may be decomposed into its constituent elements, which we shall study under these three headings, viz., the intellectual factor, the affective or emotional factor, and the unconscious factor. But that is not enough; the analysis should be completed by a synthesis. All imaginative creation, great or small, is organic, requires a unifying principle: there is then also a synthetic factor, which it will be necessary to determine.

PART ONE

ANALYSIS OF THE IMAGINATION

CHAPTER I

THE INTELLECTUAL FACTOR.

I

Considered under its intellectual aspect, that is, in so far as it borrows its elements from the understanding, the imagination presupposes two fundamental operations—the one, negative and preparatory, dissociation; the other, positive and constitutive, association.

Dissociation is the "abstraction" of the older psychologists, who well understood its importance for the subject with which we are now concerned. Nevertheless, the term "dissociation" seems to me preferable, because it is more comprehensive. It designates a genus of which the other is a species. It is a spontaneous operation and of a more radical nature than the other. Abstraction, strictly so-called, acts only on isolated states of consciousness; dissociation acts, further, on series of states of consciousness, which it sorts out, breaks up, dissolves, and through this preparatory work makes suitable for entering into new combinations.

Perception is a synthetic process, but dissociation (or abstraction) is already present in embryo in perception, just because the latter is a complex state. Everyone perceives after an individual fashion, according to his constitution and the impression of the moment. A painter, a sportsman, a dealer, and an uninterested spectator do not see a given horse in the same manner: the qualities that interest one are unnoticed by another.[1]

The image being a simplification of sensory data, and its nature dependent on that of previous perceptions, it is inevitable that the work of dissociation should go on in it. But this is far too mild a statement. Observation and experiment show us that in the majority of cases the process grows wonderfully. In order to follow the progressive development of this dissolution, we may roughly differentiate images into three categories—complete, incomplete, and schematic—and study them in order.

The group of images here termed *complete* comprises first, objects repeatedly presented in daily experience—my wife's face, my inkstand, the sound of a church bell or of a neighboring clock, etc. In this class are also included the images of things that we have perceived but a few times, but which, for additional reasons, have remained clean-cut in our memory. Are these images complete, in the strict sense of the word? They cannot be; and the contrary belief is a delusion of consciousness that, however, disappears when one confronts it with the

---

[1] Cf. the well-known aphorism, "*Apperception ist alles.*" (Tr.)

reality. The mental image can contain all the qualities of an object in even less degree than the perception; the image is the result of selection, varying with every case. The painter Fromentin, who
was proud that he found after two or three years
"an exact recollection" of things he had barely
noticed on a journey, makes elsewhere, however,
the following confession: "My memory of things,
although very faithful, has never the certainty ad-
missible as documentary evidence. The weaker it
grows, the more is it changed in becoming the property of my memory and the more valuable is it for
the work that I intend for it. In proportion as the
exact form becomes altered, another form, partly
real, partly imaginary, which I believe preferable,
takes its place." Note that the person speaking thus
is a painter endowed with an unusual visual memory; but recent investigations have shown that
among men generally the so-called complete and
exact images undergo change and warping. One
sees the truth of this statement when, after a lapse
of some time, one is placed in the presence of the
original object, so that comparison between the real
object and its image becomes possible.[1] Let us
note that in this group *the image always corresponds*

---

[1] See especially J. Philippe, "La déformation et les transfor-
mations des images" in *Revue Philosophique*, May and Novem-
ber, 1897. Although these investigations had in view only
visual representations, it is not at all doubtful that the results
hold good for others, especially those of hearing (voice, song,
harmony).

to certain individual objects; it is not the same with the other two groups.

The group of *incomplete* images, according to the testimony of consciousness itself, comes from two distinct sources—first, from perceptions insufficiently or ill-fixed; and again, from impressions of like objects which, when too often repeated, end by becoming confused. The latter case has been well described by Taine. A man, says he, who, having gone through an avenue of poplars wants to picture a poplar; or, having looked into a poultry-yard, wishes to call up a picture of a hen, experiences a difficulty—his different memories rise up. The experiment becomes a cause of effacement; the images canceling one another decline to a state of imperceptible tendencies which their likeness and unlikeness prevent from predominating. Images become blunted by their collision just as do bodies by friction.[2]

This group leads us to that of *schematic* images, or those entirely without mark—the indefinite image of a rosebush, of a pin, of a cigarette, etc. This is the greatest degree of impoverishment; the image, deprived little by little of its own characteristics, is nothing more than a shadow. It has become that transitional form between image and pure concept that we now term "generic image," or one that at least resembles the latter.

The image, then, is subject to an unending process of change, of suppression and addition, of dissocia-

[2] *On Intelligence,* Vol. I, Bk. ii, Chap. 2.

tion and corrosion. This means that it is not a dead thing; it is not at all like a photographic plate with which one may reproduce copies indefinitely. Being dependent on the state of the brain, the image undergoes change like all living substance,—it is subject to gains and losses, especially losses. But each of the foregoing three classes has its use for the inventor. They serve as material for different kinds of imagination—in their concrete form, for the mechanic and the artist; in their schematic form, for the scientist and for others.

Thus far we have seen only a part of the work of dissociation and, taking it all in all, the smallest part. We have, seemingly, considered images as isolated facts, as psychic atoms; but that is a purely theoretic position. Images are not solitary in actual life; they form part of a chain, or rather of a woof or net, since, by reason of their manifold relations they may radiate in all directions, through all the senses. Dissociation, then, works also upon *series,* cuts them up, mangles them, breaks them, and reduces them to ruins.

The ideal law of the recurrence of images is that known since Hamilton's time under the name of "law of redintegration,"[1] which consists in the pass-

---

[1] In his recent history of the theories of the imagination, *La psicologia dell' immaginazione, nella storia filosofia* (Rome, 1898) Ambrosi shows that this law is found already formulated in the *Psychologia Empirica* of Christian Wolff [d. 1754]: "*Perceptio præterita integra recurrit cujus præsens continet partem.*"

ing from a part to the whole, each element tending to reproduce the complete state, each member of a series the whole of that series. If this law existed alone, invention would be forever forbidden to us; we could not emerge from repetition; we should be condemned to monotony. But there is an opposite power that frees us—it is dissociation.

It is very strange that, while psychologists have for so long a time studied the laws of association, no one has investigated whether the inverse process, dissociation, also has not laws of its own. We can not here attempt such a task, which would be outside of our province; it will suffice to indicate in passing two general conditions determining the association of series.

First, there are the internal or subjective causes. The revived image of a face, a monument, a landscape, an occurrence, is, most often, only partial. It depends on various conditions that revive the essential part and drop the minor details, and this "essential" which survives dissociation depends on subjective causes, the principal ones of which are at first practical, utilitarian reasons. It is the tendency already mentioned to ignore what is of no value, to exclude that from consciousness. Helmholtz has shown that in the act of seeing, various details remain unnoticed because they are immaterial in the concerns of life; and there are many other like instances. Then, too, emotional reasons governing the attention orientate it exclusively in one direction—these will be studied in the course of this work. Lastly, there are logical or intellectual reasons, if we understand by this term the law of mental inertia or the law of least resistance by means of which the mind tends toward the simplification and lightening of its labor.

Secondly, there are external or objective causes which are variations in experience. When two or more qualities or events are given as constantly associated in experience we do not dissociate them. The uniformity of nature's laws is the great opponent of dissociation. Many truths (for example, the existence of the antipodes) are established with difficulty, because it is necessary to break up closely knit associations. The oriental king whom Sully mentions, who had never seen ice, refused to credit the existence of solid water. A total impression, the elements of which had never been given us separately in experience, would be unanalyzable. If all cold objects were moist, and all moist objects cold; if all liquids were transparent and all non-liquids opaque, we should find it difficult to distinguish cold from moisture and liquidity from transparency. On his part, James adds further that what has been associated sometimes with one thing and sometimes with another tends to become dissociated from both. This might be called a law of association by concomitant variations.[1]

In order to thoroughly comprehend the absolute necessity for dissociation, let us note that total

---

[1] Sully, *Human Mind*, I, p. 365; James, *Psychology*, I, p. 502.

redintegration is *per se* a hindrance to creation. Examples are given of people who can easily remember twenty or thirty pages of a book, but if they want a particular passage they are unable to pick it out— they must begin at the beginning and continue down to the required place. Excessive ease of retention thus becomes a serious inconvenience. Besides these rare cases, we know that ignorant people, those intellectually limited, give the same invariable story of every occurrence, in which all the parts—the important and the accessory, the useful and the useless— are on a dead level. They omit no detail, they cannot select. Minds of this kind are inapt at invention. In short, we may say that there are two kinds of memory: one is completely systematized, e. g., habits, routine, poetry or prose learned by heart, faultless musical rendering, etc. The acquisition forms a compact whole and cannot enter into new combinations. The other is not systematized; it is composed of small, more or less coherent groups. This kind of memory is plastic and capable of becoming combined in new ways.

We have enumerated the spontaneous, natural causes of association, omitting the voluntary and artificial causes, which are but their imitations. As a result of these various causes, images are taken to pieces, shattered, broken up, but made all the readier as materials for the inventor. This is a process analogous to that which, in geologic time, produces new strata through the wearing away of old rocks.

II

Association is one of the big questions of psychology; but as it does not especially concern our subject, it will be discussed in strict proportion to its use here. Nothing is easier than limiting ourselves. Our task is reducible to a very clear and very brief question: What are the forms of association that give rise to new combinations and under what influences do they arise? All other forms of association, those that are only repetitions, should be eliminated. Consequently, this subject can not be treated in one single effort; it must be studied, in turn, in its relations to our three factors —intellectual, emotional, unconscious.

It is generally admitted that the expression "association of ideas" is faulty.[1] It is not comprehensive enough, association being active also in psychic states other than ideas. It seems indicative rather of mere juxtaposition, whereas associated states modify one another by the very fact of their being connected. But, as it has been confirmed by long usage, it would be difficult to eliminate the phrase.

On the other hand, psychologists are not at all agreed as regards the determination of the principal laws or forms of association. Without taking sides in the debate, I adopt the most generally accepted classification, the one most suitable for our subject —the one that reduces everything to the two funda-

[1] For a good criticism of the term, consult Titchener, *Outlines of Phychology* (New York, 1896), p. 190.

mental laws of contiguity and resemblance. In recent years various attempts have been made to reduce these two laws to one, some reducing resemblance to contiguity; others, contiguity to resemblance. Putting aside the ground of this discussion, which seems to me very useless, and which perhaps is due to excessive zeal for unity, we must nevertheless recognize that this discussion is not without interest for the study of the creative imagination, because it has well shown that each of the two fundamental laws has a characteristic mechanism.

Association by contiguity (or continuity), which Wundt calls external, is simple and homogeneous. It reproduces the order and connection of things; it reduces itself to habits contracted by our nervous system.

Is association by resemblance, which Wundt calls internal, strictly speaking, an elementary law? Many doubt it. Without entering into the long and frequently confused discussions to which this subject has given rise, we may sum up their results as follows: In so-called association by resemblance it is necessary to distinguish three moments—(a) That of the presentation; a state A is given in perception or association-by-contiguity, and forms the starting point. (b) That of the work of assimilation; A is recognized as more or less like a state a previously experienced. (c) As a consequence of the coëxistence of A and a in consciousness, they can later be recalled reciprocally, although the two original occurrences A and a have previously never existed together, and sometimes, indeed, may not possibly have existed together. It is evident that the crucial moment is the second, and that it consists of an act of active assimilation. Thus James maintains that "it is a relation that the mind perceives after the fact, just as it may perceive the relations of superiority, of distance, of causality, of container and content, of substance and accident, or of contrast between an object, and some second object which the associative machinery calls up."

Association by resemblance presupposes a joint labor of association and dissociation—it is an active form. Consequently it is the principal source of the material of the creative imagination, as the sequel of this work will sufficiently show.

After this rather long but necessary preface, we come to the intellectual factor rightly so termed, which we have been little by little approaching. The essential, fundamental element of the creative imagination in the intellectual sphere is the capacity of thinking by analogy; that is, by partial and often accidental resemblance. By analogy we mean an imperfect kind of resemblance: like is a genus of which analogue is a species.

Let us examine in some detail the mechanism of

[1] For the discussions on the reduction to a unity, a detailed bibliography will be found in Jodl, *Lehrbuch der Psychologie* (Stuttgart, 1896), p. 490. On the comparison of the two laws, James, *op. cit.*, I, 590; Sully, *op. cit.*, I, 331 ff; Höffding, *Psychologie*, 213 ff. (Eng. ed. *Outlines of Psychology*, pp. 152 ff.).

this mode of thought in order that we may understand how analogy is, by its very nature, an almost
inexhaustible instrument of creation.

1. Analogy may be based solely on the *number of
attributes compared*. Let *a b c d e f* and *r s t u d v*
be two beings or objects, each letter representing
symbolically one of the constitutive attributes. It
is evident that the analogy between the two is very
weak, since there is only one common element, *d*.
If the number of the elements common to both increases, the analogy will grow in the same proportion. But the agreement represented above is not
infrequent among minds unused to a somewhat se-
vere discipline. A child sees in the moon and stars
a mother surrounded by her daughters. The aborigines of Australia called a book "mussel," merely
because it opens and shuts like the valves of a shell-
fish.[1]

2. Analogy may have for its basis the *quality* or
value of the compound attributes. It rests on a
variable element, which oscillates from the essential
to the accidental, from the reality to the appearance.
To the layman, the likeness between cetacians and
fishes are great; to the scientist, slight. Here,
again, numerous agreements are possible, provided
one take no account either of their solidity or their
frailty.

3. Lastly, in minds without power, there occurs

[1] Note here a characteristically naïve working of the primitive
intellect in explaining the unknown in terms of the known.
Cf. Part II, Chap. iii, below. (Tr.)

a semi-unconscious operation that we may call a transfer through the omission of the middle term. There is analogy between $a\ b\ c\ d\ e$ and $g\ h\ a\ i\ f$ through the common letter a; between $g\ h\ a\ i\ f$ and $x\ y\ f\ z\ q$ through the common letter f; and finally an analogy becomes established between $a\ b\ c\ d\ e$ and $x\ y\ f\ z\ q$ for no other reason than that of their common analogy with $g\ h\ a\ i\ f$. In the realm of the affective states, transfers of this sort are not at all rare.

Analogy, an unstable process, undulating and multiform, gives rise to the most unforeseen and novel groupings. Through its pliability, which is almost unlimited, it produces in equal measure absurd comparisons and very original inventions.

After these remarks on the mechanism of thinking by analogy, let us glance at the processes it employs in its creative work. The problem is, apparently, inextricable. Analogies are so numerous, so various, so arbitrary, that we may despair of finding any regularity whatever in creative work. Despite this it seems, however, reducible to two principal types or processes, which are personification, and transformation or metamorphosis.

Personification is the earlier process. It is radical, always identical with itself, but transitory. It goes out from ourselves toward other things. It consists in attributing life to everything, in supposing in everything that shows signs of life—and even in inanimate objects—desires, passions, and acts of will analogous to ours, acting like ourselves in view of definite ends. This state of mind is incomprehensible to an adult civilized man; but it must be admitted, since there are facts without number that show its existence. We do not need to cite them—they are too well known. They fill the works of ethnologists, of travelers in savage lands, of books of mythology. Besides, all of us, at the commencement of our lives, during our earliest childhood, have passed through this inevitable stage of universal animism. Works on child-psychology abound in observations that leave no possible room for doubt on this point. The child endows everything with life, and he does so the more in proportion as he is more imaginative. But this stage, which among civilized people lasts only a brief period, remains in the primitive man a permanent disposition and one that is always active. This process of personification is the perennial fount whence have gushed the greater number of myths, an enormous mass of superstitions, and a large number of esthetic productions. To sum up in a word, all things that have been invented *ex analogia hominis.*

Transformation or metamorphosis is a general, permanent process under many forms, proceeding not from the thinking subject towards objects, but from one object to another, from one thing to another. It consists of a transfer through partial resemblance. This operation rests on two fundamental bases—depending at one time on vague resemblances (a cloud becomes a mountain, or a

mountain a fantastic animal; the sound of the wind
a plaintive cry, etc.), or again, on a resemblance
with a predominating emotional element: A perception provokes a feeling, and becomes the mark,
sign, or plastic form thereof (the lion represents
courage; the cat, artifice; the cypress, sorrow; and
so on). All this, doubtless, is erroneous or arbitrary; but the function of the imagination is to invent, not to perceive. All know that this process
creates metaphors, allegories, symbols; it should
not, however, be believed on that account that it
remains restricted to the realm of art or of the development of language. We meet it every moment
in practical life, in mechanical, industrial, commercial, and scientific invention, and we shall, later,
give a large number of examples in support of this
statement.

Let us note, briefly, that analogy, as an imperfect
form of resemblance—as was said above, if we assume among the objects compared a totality of likenesses and differences in varying proportions—
necessarily allows all degrees. At one end of the
scale, the comparison is made between valueless or
exaggerated likenesses. At the other end, analogy
is restricted to exact resemblance; it approaches
cognition, strictly so called; for example, in mechanical and scientific invention. Hence it is not at all
surprising that the imagination is often a substitute
for, and as Goethe expressed it, "a forerunner of,"
reason. Between the creative imagination and rational investigation there is a community of nature

—both presuppose the ability of seizing upon likenesses. On the other hand, the predominance of the
exact process establishes from the outset a difference
between "thinkers" and imaginative dreamers ("visionaries").[1]

[1] It is yet, and will probably long remain, an open question
whether we can draw any clear distinction between the two
kinds of mind here discussed. The author is careful to base
his distinction on the "predominance" of the "rational" or
of the "imaginative" process. So-called "thinkers," who *do*
nothing, can not, certainly, be ranked with the persons of great
intellectual attainment through whose efforts the progress of the
world is made; on the other hand, the author seeks to make
results or accomplishments the crucial test of true imagination
(see Introduction).

As regards the relative value or rank of the two bents of
mind there has ever been, and probably forever will be, great
difference of opinion. Even in this intensely "practical" age
there is an undercurrent of feeling that the narrowly "practical" individual is not the final ideal, and the innermost conviction of many is the same as that of the poet who declares
that "a dreamer lives forever, but a thinker dies in a day."
(Tr.)

CHAPTER II

THE EMOTIONAL FACTOR.

The influence of emotional states on the working of the imagination is a matter of current observation. But it has been studied chiefly by moralists, who most often have criticised or condemned it as an endless cause of mistakes. The point of view of the psychologist is altogether different. He does not need at all to investigate whether emotions and passions give rise to mental phantoms—which is an indisputable fact—but *why* and *how* they arise. For, the emotional factor yields in importance to no other; it is the ferment without which no creation is possible. Let us study it in its principal forms, although we may not be able at this moment to exhaust the topic.

I

It is necessary to show at the outset that the influence of the emotional life is unlimited, that it penetrates the entire field of invention with no restriction whatever; that this is not a gratuitous assertion, but is, on the contrary, strictly justified by facts, and that we are right in maintaining the following two propositions:

1. *All forms of the creative imagination imply elements of feeling.*

This statement has been challenged by authoritative psychologists, who hold that "emotion is added to imagination in its esthetic aspect, not in its mechanical and intellectual form." This is an error of fact resulting from the confusion, or from the imperfect analysis, of two distinct cases. In the case of non-esthetic creation, the rôle of the emotional life is simple; in esthetic creation, the rôle of emotional element is double.

Let us consider invention, first, in its most general form. The emotional element is the primal, original factor; for all invention presupposes a want, a craving, a tendency, an unsatisfied impulse, often even a state of gestation full of discomfort. Moreover, it is concomitant, that is, under its form of pleasure or of pain, of hope, of spite, of anger, etc., it accompanies all the phases or turns of creation. The creator may, haphazard, go through the most diverse forms of exaltation and depression; may feel in turn the dejection of repulse and the joy of success; finally the satisfaction of being freed from a heavy burden. I challenge anyone to produce a solitary example of invention wrought out *in abstracto,* and free from any factors of feeling. Human nature does not allow such a miracle.

Now, let us take up the special case of esthetic creation, and of forms approaching thereto. Here again we find the original emotional element as at first motor, then attached to various aspects of creation, as an accompaniment. But, *in addition, affective states become material for the creative activity.* It is a well-known fact, almost a rule, that the poet, the novelist, the dramatist, and the musician—often, indeed, even the sculptor and the painter—experience the thoughts and feeling of their characters, become identified with them. There are, then, in this second instance, two currents of feeling —the one, constituting emotion as material for art, the other, drawing out creative activity and developing along with it.

The difference between the two cases that we have distinguished consists in this and nothing more than this. The existence of an emotion-content belonging to esthetic production changes in no way the psychologic mechanism of invention generally. Its absence in other forms of imagination does not at all prevent the necessary existence of affective elements everywhere and always.

2. *All emotional dispositions whatever may influence the creative imagination.*

Here, again, I find opponents, notably Oelzelt-Newin, in his short and substantial monograph on the imagination.[1] Adopting the twofold division of emotions as sthenic and asthenic, or exciting and depressing, he attributes to the first the exclusive privilege of influencing creative activity; but though the author limits his study exclusively to the esthetic

[1] *Ueber Phantasievorstellungen,* Graz, 1889, p. 48.

imagination, his thesis, even understood thus, is untenable. The facts contradict it completely, and it is easy to demonstrate that all forms of emotion, without exception, act as leaven for imagination.

No one will deny that fear is the type of asthenic manifestations. Yet is it not the mother of phantoms, of numberless superstitions, of altogether irrational and chimerical religious practices?

Anger, in its exalted, violent form, is rather an agent of destruction, which seems to contradict my thesis; but let us pass over the storm, which is always of short duration, and we find in its place milder intellectualized forms, which are various modifications of primitive fury, passing from the acute to the chronic state: envy, jealousy, enmity, premeditated vengeance, and so forth. Are not these dispositions of the mind fertile in artifices, stratagems, inventions of all kinds? To keep even to esthetic creation, is it necessary to recall the saying *facit indignatio versum?*

It is not necessary to demonstrate the fecundity of joy. As for love, everyone knows that its work consists of creating an imaginary being, which is substituted for the beloved object; then, when the passion has vanished, the disenchanted lover finds himself face to face with the bare reality.

Sorrow rightly belongs in the category of depressing emotions, and yet, it has as great influence on invention as any other emotion. Do we not know that melancholy and even profound sorrow has furnished poets, musicians, painters, and sculptors with their most beautiful inspirations? Is there not an art frankly and deliberately pessimistic? And this influence is not at all limited to esthetic creation. Dare we hold that hypochondria and insanity following upon the delirium of persecution are devoid of imagination? Their morbid character is, on the contrary, the well whence strange inventions incessantly bubble.

Lastly, that complex emotion termed "self-feeling," which reduces itself finally to the pleasure of asserting our power and of feeling its expansion, or to the pitiable feeling of our shackled, enfeebled power, leads us directly to the motor elements that are the fundamental conditions of invention. Above all, in this personal feeling, there is the satisfaction of being a casual factor, i. e., a creator, and every creator has a consciousness of his superiority over non-creators. However petty his invention, it confers upon him a superiority over those who have invented nothing. Although we have been surfeited with the repeated statement that the characteristic mark of esthetic creation is "being disinterested," it must be recognized, as Groos has so truly remarked,[1] that the artist does not create out of the simple pleasure of creating, but in order that he may behold a mastery over other minds.[2] Production is the

[1] *Die Spiele der Thiere*, Jena, 1896. The subject has been very well treated by this author, pp. 294-301.

[2] The "disinterested" view is found widely advocated or hinted at in literature. Cf. Goethe's "Der Sänger" (Tr.).

natural extension of "self-feeling," and the accompanying pleasure is the pleasure of conquest.

Thus, on condition that we extend "imagination" to its full sense, without limiting it unduly ˙to esthetics, there is, among the many forms of the emotional life, not one that may not stimulate invention. It remains to see this emotional factor at work,—to note how it can give rise to new combinations; and this brings us to the association of ideas.

II

We have said above that the ideal and theoretic law of the recurrence of images is that of "total redintegration," as e. g., recalling all the incidents of a long voyage in chronological order, with neither additions nor omissions. But this formula expresses what ought to be, not what actually occurs. It supposes man reduced to a state of pure intelligence, and sheltered from all disturbing influences. It suits the completely systematized forms of memory, hardened into routine and habit; but, outside of these cases, it remains an abstract concept.

To this law of ideal value, there is opposed the real and practical law that actually obtains in the revival of images. It is rightly styled the "law of interest" or the affective law, and may be stated thus : In every past event the interesting parts alone revive, or with more intensity than the others. "Interesting" here means *what affects us in some way under a pleasing or painful form.* Let us note that the importance of this fact has been pointed out not by the associationists (a fact especially worth remembering) but by less systematic writers, strangers to that school,—Coleridge, Shadworth Hodgson, and before them, Schopenhauer. William James calls it the "ordinary or mixed association."[1] The "law of interest" doubtless is less exact than the intellectual laws of contiguity and resemblance. Nevertheless, it seems to penetrate all the more in later reasoning. If, indeed, in the problem of association we distinguish these three things—facts, laws, causes—the practical law brings us near to causes.

Whatever the truth may be in this matter, the emotional factor brings about new combinations by several processes.

There are the ordinary, simple cases, with a natural, emotional foundation, depending on momentary dispositions. They exist because of the fact that representations that have been accompanied by the same emotional state tend later to become associated: the emotional resemblance reunites and links disparate images. This differs from association by contiguity, which is a repetition of experience, and from association by resemblance in the intellectual sense. The states of consciousness become combined, not because they have been previously given together, not because we perceive the agreement of resemblance between them, but because they have a common *emotional* note. Joy,

[1] *Psychology,* I, 571 ff.

sorrow, love, hatred, admiration, ennui, pride, fatigue, etc., may become a center of attraction that groups images or events having otherwise no rational relations between them, but having the same emotional stamp,—joyous, melancholy, erotic, etc. This form of association is very frequent in dreams and reveries, i. e., in a state of mind in which the imagination enjoys complete freedom and works haphazard. We easily see that this influence, active or latent, of the emotional factor, must cause entirely unexpected grouping to arise, and offers an almost unlimited field for novel combinations, the number of images having a common emotional factor being very great.

There are unusual and remarkable cases with an exceptional emotional base. Of such is "colored hearing." We know that several hypotheses have been offered in regard to the origin of this phenomenon. Embryologically, it would seem to be the result of an incomplete separation between the sense of sight and that of hearing, and the survival, it is said, from a distant period of humanity, when this state must have been the rule; anatomically, the result of supposed anastamoses between the cerebral centers for visual and auditory sensations; physiologically, the result of nervous irradiation; psychologically, the result of association. This latter hypothesis seems to account for the greater number of instances, if not for all; but, as Flournoy has observed, it is a matter of "affective" imagination. Two sensations absolutely unlike (for instance, the color blue and the sound i) may resemble one another through the equal retentive quality that they possess in the organism of some favored individuals, and this emotional factor becomes a bond of association. Observe that this hypothesis explains also the much more unusual cases of "colored" smell, taste, and pain; that is, an abnormal association between given colors and tastes, smells, or pains.

Although we meet them only as exceptional cases, these modes of association are susceptible to analysis, and seem clear, almost self-evident, if we compare them with other, subtle, refined, barely perceptible cases, the origin of which is a subejct for supposition, for guessing rather than for clear comprehension. It is, moreover, a sort of imagination belonging to very few people: certain artists and some eccentric or unbalanced minds, scarcely ever found outside the esthetic or practical life. I wish to speak of the forms of invention that permit only fantastic conceptions, of a strangeness pushed to the extreme (Hoffman, Poe, Baudelaire, Goya, Wiertz, etc.), or surprising, extraordinary thoughts, known of no other men (the symbolists and decadents that flourish at the present time in various countries of Europe and America, who believe, rightly or wrongly, that they are preparing the esthetics of the future). It must be here admitted that there exists an altogether special manner of *feeling*, dependent on temperament at first, which many cultivate and refine as though it were a precious rarity. There lies the true source of their invention. Doubtless, to assert this pertinently, it would be necessary to establish the direct relations between their physical and psychical constitution and that of their work; to note even the particular states at the moment of the creative act. To me at least, it seems evident that the novelty, the strangeness of combinations, through its deep subjective character, indicates an emotional rather than an intellectual origin. Let us merely add that these abnormal manifestations of the creative imagination belong to the province of pathology rather than to that of psychology.

Association by contrast is, from its very nature, vague, arbitrary, indeterminate. It rests, in truth, on an essentially subjective and fleeting conception, that of contrariety, which it is almost impossible to delimit scientifically; for, most often, contraries exist only by and for us. We know that this form of association is not primary and irreducible. It is brought down by some to contiguity, by most others to resemblance. These two views do not seem to me irreconcilable. In association by contrast we may distinguish two layers,—the one, superficial, consists of contiguity: all of us have in memory associated couples, such as large-small, rich-poor, high-low, right-left, etc., which result from repetition and habit; the other, deep, is resemblance; *contrast exists only where a common measure between two terms is possible.* As Wundt remarks, a wedding may be compared to a burial (the union and separation of a couple), but not to a toothache. There is contrast between two colors, contrast between sounds, but not between a sound and a color, at least in that there may not be a common basis to which we may relate them, as in the previously given instances of "colored" sound. In association by contrast, there are conscious elements opposed to one another, and below, an unconscious element, resemblance,—not clearly and logically perceived, but felt—that evokes and relates the conscious elements.

Whether this explanation be right or not, let us remark that association by contrast could not be left out, because its mechanism, full of unforeseen possibilities, lends itself easily to novel relations. Otherwise, I do not at all claim that it is entirely dependent upon the emotional factor. But, as Höffding observes,[1] the special property of the emotional life is moving among contraries; it is altogether determined by the great opposition between pleasure and pain. Thus, the effects of contrasts are much stronger than in the realm of sensation. This form of association predominates in esthetic and mythic creation, that is to say, in creation of the free fancy; it becomes dimmed in the precise forms of practical, mechanical, and scientific invention.

III

Hitherto we have considered the emotional factor under a single aspect only—the purely emotional— that which is manifested in consciousness under an

[1] Höffding, *Psychologie*, p. 219; *Eng. trans.*, p. 161.

agreeable or disagreeable or mixed form. But thoughts, feelings, and emotions include elements that are deeper—motor, i. e., impulsive or inhibitory —which we may neglect the less since it is in movements that we seek the origin of the creative imagination. This motor element is what current speech and often even psychological treatises designate under the terms "creative instinct," "inventive instinct;" what we express in another form when we say that creators are guided by instinct and "are pushed like animals toward the accomplishment of certain acts."

If I mistake not, this indicates that the "creative instinct" exists in all men to some extent—feeble in some, perceptible in others, brilliant in the great inventors.

For I do not hesitate to maintain that the creative instinct, taken in this strict meaning, compared to animal instinct, is a mere figure of speech, an "entity" regarded as a reality, an abstraction. There are needs, appetites, tendencies, desires, common to all men, which, in a given individual at a given moment can result in a creative act; but there is no special psychic manifestation that may be the "creative instinct." What, indeed, could it be? Every instinct has its own particular end:—hunger, thirst, sex, the specific instincts of the bee, ant, beaver, consist of a group of movements adapted for a determinate end that is always the same. Now, what would be a creative instinct *in general* which, by hypothesis, could produce in turn an opera, a machine, a metaphysical theory, a system of finance, a plan of military campaign, and so forth? It is a pure fancy. Inventive genius has not *a* source, but *sources*.

Let us consider from our present viewpoint the human duality, the *homo duplex*:

Suppose man reduced to a state of pure intelligence, that is, capable of perceiving, remembering, associating, dissociating, reasoning, and nothing else. All creative activity is then impossible, because there is nothing to solicit it.

Suppose, again, man reduced to organic manifestations; he is then no more than a bundle of wants, appetites, instincts,—that is, of motor activities, blind forces that, lacking a sufficient cerebral organ, will produce nothing.

The coöperation of both these factors is indispensable: without the first, nothing begins; without the second, nothing results. I hold that it is in needs that we must seek for the primary cause of all inventions; it is evident that the motor element alone is insufficient. If the needs are strong, energetic, they may determine a production, or, if the intellectual factor is insufficient, may spoil it. Many want to make discoveries but discover nothing. A want so common as hunger or thirst suggests to one some ingenious method of satisfying it; another remains entirely destitute.

In short, in order that a creative act occur, there is required, first, a need; then, that it arouse a com-

bination of images; and lastly, that it objectify and
realize itself in an appropriate form.

We shall try later (in the Conclusion) to answer
the question, *Why* is one imaginative?   In passing,
let us put the opposite question, Why is one *not*
imaginative?   One may possess in the mind an inexhaustible treasure of facts and images and yet
produce nothing: great travelers, for example, who
have seen and heard much, and who draw from their
experiences only a few colorless anecdotes; men
who were partakers in great political events or military movements, who leave behind only a few dry
and chilly memoirs; prodigies of reading, living
encyclopedias, who remain crushed under the load
of their erudition.   On the other hand, there are
people who easily move and act, but are limited,
lacking images and ideas.   Their intellectual poverty condemns them to unproductiveness; nevertheless, being nearer than the others to the imaginative type, they bring forth childish or chimerical
productions.   So that we may answer the question
asked above: The non-imaginative person is such
from lack of materials or through the absence of re-
sourcefulness.

Without contenting ourselves with these theoretical remarks, let us rapidly show that it is thus
that these things actually happen.   All the work of
the creative imagination may be classed under two
great heads—esthetic inventions and practical inventions; on the one hand, what man has brought
to pass in the domain of art, and on the other hand,

all else. Though this division may appear strange, and unjustifiable, it has reason for its being, as we shall see hereafter.

Let us consider first the class of non-esthetic creations. Very different in nature, all the products of this group coincide at one point:—they are of practical utility, they are born of a vital need, of one of the conditions of man's existence. There are first the inventions "practical" in the narrow sense— all that pertains to food, clothing, defense, housing, etc. Every one of these special needs has stimulated inventions adapted to a special end. Inventions in the social and political order answer to the conditions of collective existence; they arise from the necessity of maintaining the coherence of the social aggregate and of defending it against inimical groups. The work of the imagination whence have arisen the myths, religious conceptions, and the first attempts at a scientific explanation may seem at first disinterested and foreign to practical life. This is an erroneous supposition. Man, face to face with the higher powers of nature, the mystery of which he does not penetrate, has a *need* of acting upon it; he tries to conciliate them, even to turn them to his service by magic rites and operations. *His* curiosity is not at all theoretic; he does not aim to know for the sake of knowing, but in order to act upon the outside world and to draw profit therefrom. To the numerous questions that necessity puts to him his imagination alone responds, because his reason is shifting and his scientific knowledge *nil*. Here, then, invention again results from urgent needs.

Indeed, in the course of the nineteenth century and on account of growing civilization all these creations reach a second moment when their origin is hidden. Most of our mechanical, industrial and commercial inventions are not stimulated by the immediate necessity of living, by an urgent need; it is not a question of existence but of better existence. The same holds true of social and political inventions which arise from the increasing complexity and the new requirements of the aggregates forming great states. Lastly, it is certain that primitive curiosity has partially lost its utilitarian character in order to become, in some men at least, the taste for pure research—theoretical, speculative, disinterested. But all this in no way affects our thesis, for it is a well-known elementary psychological law that upon primitive wants are grafted acquired wants fully as imperative. The primitive need is modified, metamorphosed, adapted; there remains of it, nonetheless, the fundamental activity toward creation.

Let us now consider the class of esthetic creations. According to the generally accepted theory which is too well known for me to stop to explain it, art has its beginning in a superfluous, bounding activity, useless as regards the preservation of the individual, which is shown first in the form of play. Then, through transformation and complication, play becomes primitive art, dancing, music, and poetry at the same time, closely united in an apparently indissoluble unity. Although the theory of the absolute inutility of art has met some strong criticism, let us accept it for the present. Aside from the true or false character of inutility, the psychological mechanism remains the same here as in the preceding cases; we shall only say that in place of a vital need it is a need of *luxury* acting, but it acts only because it is in man.

Nevertheless, the inutility of play is far from proven biologically. Groos, in his two excellent works on the subject,[1] has maintained with much power the opposite view. According to him the theory of Schiller and Spencer, based on the expenditure of superfluous activity and the opposite theory of Lazarus, who reduces play to a relaxation—that is, a recuperation of strength—are but partial explanations. Play has a positive use. In man there exist a great number of instincts that are not yet developed at birth. An incomplete being, he must have education of his capacities, and this is obtained through play, *which is the exercise of the natural tendencies of human activities*. In man and in the higher animals plays are a preparation, a prelude to the active functions of life. *There is no instinct of play in general, but there are special instincts that are manifested under the forms of play.* If we admit this explanation, which does not lack potency, the work of the esthetic

[1] Groos, *Die Spiele der Thiere*, 1896, and *Die Spiele der Menschen*, 1899 (Eng. trans., Appletons, New York, 1898, 1901).

imagination itself would be reduced to a biological necessity, and there would be no reason for making a separate category of it. Whichever view we may adopt, it still remains established that any invention is reducible, directly or indirectly, to a particular, determinate need, and that to allow man a special instinct, the definite specific character of which should be stimulation to creative activity, is a fantastic notion.

Whence, then, comes this persistent and in some respects seductive idea that creation is an instinctive result? Because a happy invention has characteristics that evidently relate it to instinctive activity in the strict sense of the word. First, precocity, of which we shall later give numerous examples, and which resembles the innateness of instinct. Again, orientation in a single direction: the inventor is, so to speak, polarized; he is the slave of music, of mechanics, of mathematics; often inapt at everything outside his own particular sphere. We know the witticism of Madame du Deffant on Vaucanson, who was so awkward, so insignificant when he ventured outside of mechanics. "One should say that this man had manufactured himself." Finally, the ease with which invention often (not always) manifests itself makes it resemble the work of a pre-established mechanism.

But these and similar characteristics may be lacking. They are necessary for instinct, not for invention. There are great creators who have been neither precocious nor confined in a narrow field,

and who have given birth to their inventions painfully, laboriously.   Between the mechanism of instinct and that of imaginative creation there are
frequently great analogies but not identity of nature.   Every tendency of our organization, useful or hurtful, may become the beginning of a
creative act.   Every invention arises from a particular need of human nature, acting within its
own sphere and for its own special end.

If now it should be asked why the creative
imagination directs itself preferably in one line
rather than in another—toward poetry or physics,
trade or mechanics, geometry or painting, strategy
or music, etc.—we have nothing in answer.   It is a
result of the individual organization, the secret of
which we do not possess.   In ordinary life we
meet people visibly borne along toward love or good
cheer, toward ambition, riches or good works;
we say that they are "so built," that such is their
character.   At bottom the two questions are identical, and current psychology is not in a position to
solve them.

CHAPTER III

THE UNCONSCIOUS FACTOR

I

By this term I designate principally, not exclusively, what ordinary speech calls "inspiration." In spite of its mysterious and semi-mythological appearance, the term indicates a positive fact, one that is ill-understood in a deep sense, like all that is near the roots of creation. This concept has its history, and if it is permissible to apply a very general formula to a particular case we may say that it has developed according to the law of the three states assumed by the positivists.

In the beginning, inspiration is literally ascribed to the gods—among the Greeks to Apollo and the Muses, and in like manner under various polytheistic religions. Later, the gods become supernatural spirits, angels, saints, etc. In one way or another it is always regarded as external and superior to man. In the beginnings of all inventions—agriculture, navigation, medicine, commerce, legislation, fine arts—there is a belief in revelation; the human mind considers itself incapable of having discovered all that. Creation has arisen, we do not know how, in a total ignorance of the processes.

Later on these higher beings become empty formulas, mere survivals; there remain only the poets to invoke their aid, through the force of tradition, without believing in them. But side by side with these formal survivals there remains a mysterious ground which is translated by vague expressions and metaphors, such as "enthusiasm," "poetic frenzy," "possession by a spirit," "being overcome," "having the devil inside one," "the spirit whispers as it lists," etc. Here we have come out of the supernatural without, however, attempting a positive (i. e., a scientific) explanation.

Lastly, in the third stage, we try to sound this unknown. Psychology sees in it a special manifestation of the mind, a particular, semi-conscious, semi-unconscious state which we must now study.

At first sight, and considered in its negative aspect, inspiration presents a very definite character. It does not depend on the individual will. As in the case of sleep or digestion, we may try to call it forth, encourage it, maintain it; but not always with success. Inventors, great and small, never cease to complain over the periods of unproductiveness which they undergo in spite of themselves. The wiser among them watch for the moment; the others attempt to fight against their evil fate and to create despite nature.

Considered in its positive aspect, inspiration has two essential marks—suddenness and impersonality.

(a) It makes a sudden eruption into consciousness, but one presupposing a latent, frequently long, labor. It has its analogues among other well-known psychic states; for example, a passion that is forgotten, which, after a long period of incubation, reveals itself through an act; or, better, a sudden resolve after endless deliberation which did not seem able to come to a head. Again, there may be absence of effort and of appearance of preparation. Beethoven would strike haphazard the keys of a piano or would listen to the songs of birds. "With Chopin," says George Sand, "creation was spontaneous, miraculous; he wrought without foreseeing. It would come complete, sudden, sublime." One might pile up like facts in abundance. Sometimes, indeed, inspiration bursts forth in deep sleep and awakens the sleeper, and lest we may suppose this suddenness to be especially characteristic of artists we see it in all forms of invention. "You feel a little electric shock striking you in the head, seizing your heart at the same time—that is the moment of genius" (Buffon). "In the course of my life I have had some happy thoughts," says Du Bois Reymond, "and I have often noted that they would come to me involuntarily, and when I was not thinking of the subject." Claude Bernard has voiced the same thought more than once.

(b) Impersonality is a deeper character than the preceding. It reveals a power superior to the conscious individual, strange to him although acting through him: a state which many inventors have expressed in the words, "I counted for nothing in that." The best means of recognizing it would be to write down some observations taken from the inspired individuals themselves. We do not lack them, and some have the virtue of good observation.[1] But that would lead us too far afield. Let us only remark that this unconscious impulse acts variously according to the individual. Some submit to it painfully, striving against it just like the ancient pythoness at the time of giving her oracle. Others, especially in religious inspiration, submit themselves entirely with pleasure or else sustain it passively. Still others of a more analytic turn have noted the concentration of all their faculties and capacities on a single point. But whatever characteristics it takes on, remaining impersonal at bottom and unable to appear in a fully conscious individual, we must admit, unless we wish to give it a supernatural origin, that inspiration is derived from the unconscious activity of the mind. In order to make sure of its nature it would then be necessary to make sure first of the nature of the unconscious, which is one of the enigmas of psychology.

I put aside all the discussions on the subject as tiresome and useless for our present aim. Indeed, they reduce themselves to these two principal propositions: for some the unconscious is a purely physiological activity, a "cerebration"; for others it is a gradual diminution of consciousness which

[1] Several of them will be found in Appendix A at the end of this work.

exists without being bound to me—i. e., to the principal consciousness. Both these are full of difficulties and present almost insurmountable objections.[1]

Let us take the "unconscious" as a fact and let us limit ourselves to clearing it up, relating inspiration to mental states that have been judged worthy of explaining it.

1. Hypermnesia, or exaltation of memory, in spite of what has been said about it, teaches us nothing in regard to the nature of inspiration or of invention in general. It is produced in hypnotism, mania, the excited period of "circular insanity," at the beginning of general paralysis, and especially under the form known as "the gift of tongues" in religious epidemics. We find, it is true, some observations (among others one by Regis of an illiterate newspaper vender composing pieces of poetry of his own), indicating that a heightened memory sometimes accompanies a certain tendency toward invention. But hypermnesia, pure and simple, consists of an extraordinary flood of memories totally lacking that essential mark of creation—new combinations. It even appears that in the two instances there is rather an antagonism since heightened memory comes near to the ideal law of total redintegration, which is, as we know, a hindrance to invention. They are alike only with respect to the great mass of separable materials, but where the principle of unity is wanting there can be no creation.

[1] On this subject see Appendix B.

2. Inspiration has often been likened to the state of excitement preceding intoxication. It is a well-known fact that many inventors have sought it in wine, alcoholic liquors, toxic subtances like hashish, opium, ether, etc. It is unnecessary to mention names. The abundance of ideas, the rapidity of their flow, the eccentric spurts and caprices, novel ideas, strengthening of the vital and emotional tone, that brief state of bounding fancy of which novelists have given such good descriptions, make evident to the least observing that under the influence of intoxication the imagination works to a much greater extent than ordinarily. Yet how pale that is compared to the action of the intellectual poisons above mentioned, especially hashish. The "artificial paradise" of DeQuincy, Moreau de Tours, Théophile Gautier, Baudelaire and others have made known to all an enormous expansion of the imagination launched into a giddy course without limits of time and space.

Strictly, these are facts representing only a stimulated, artificial, temporary inspiration. They do not take us into its true nature; at the most they may teach us concerning some of their physiological conditions. It is not even an inspiration in the strict sense, but rather a beginning, an embryo, an outline, analogous to the creations produced in dreams which are found very incoherent when we awake. One of the essential conditions of creation, a principal element—the directing principle that organizes and unifies—is lacking. Under the influence of alcoholic drinks and of poisonous intoxicants attention and will always fall into exhaustion.

3. With greater reason it has been sought to explain inspiration by comparison with certain forms of somnambulism, and it has been said that "it is only the lowest degree of the latter state, somnambulism in a waking state. In inspiration it is as though a strange personality were speaking to the author; in somnambulism it is the stranger himself who talks or holds the pen, who speaks or writes—in a word, does the work."[1] It would thus be the modified form of a state that is the culmination of subconscious activity and a state of double personality. As this last explanatory expression is wonderfully abused, and is called upon to serve in all conditions, preciseness is indispensable.

The inspired individual is like an awakened dreamer—he lives in his dream. (Of this we might cite seemingly authentic examples: Shelly, Alfieri, etc.) Psychologically, this means that there is in him a double inversion of the normal state.

To begin with, consciousness monopolized by the number and intensity of its images is closed to the influences of the outside world, or else receives them only to make them enter the web of its dream. The internal life annihilates the external, which is just the opposite of ordinary life.

Further, the unconscious or subconscious activity

[1] Dr. Chabaneix, *Le subconscient sur les artistes, les savants, et les écrivains,* Paris, 1897, p. 87.

passes to the first plane, plays the first part, while preserving its impersonal character.

This much allowed, if we would go further, we are thrown into increasing difficulties. The existence of an unconscious working is beyond doubt; facts in profusion could be given in support of this obscure elaboration which enters consciousness only when all is done. But what is the nature of this work? Is it purely physiological? Is it psychological? We come to two opposing theses. Theoretically, we may say that everything goes on in the realm of the unconscious just as in consciousness, *only without a message to me;* that in clear consciousness the work may be followed up step by step, while in unconsciousness it proceeds likewise, but unknown to us. It is evident that all this is purely hypothetical.

Inspiration resembles a cipher dispatch which the unconscious activity transmits to the conscious process, which translates it. Must we admit that in the deep levels of the unconscious there are formed only fragmentary combinations and that they reach complete systematization only in clear consciousness, or, rather, is the creative labor identical in both cases? It is difficult to decide. It seems to be accepted that genius, or at least richness, in invention depends on the subliminal imagination,[1] not on

[1] The recent case, studied with so much ability by M. Flournoy in his book, *"Des Indes à la planète Mars"* (1900), is an example of the subliminal creative imagination, and of the work it is capable of doing by itself.

the other, which is superficial in nature and soon exhausted. The one is spontaneous, true; the other, artificial, feigned. "Inspiration" signifies unconscious imagination, and is only a special case of it. Conscious imagination is a kind of perfected state.

To sum up, inspiration is the result of an underhand process existing in men, in some to a very great degree. The nature of this work being unknown, we can conclude nothing as to the ultimate nature of inspiration. On the other hand, we may in a positive manner fix the value of the phenomenon in invention, all the more as we are inclined to overvalue it. We should, indeed, note that inspiration is not a cause but an effect—more exactly, a moment, a crisis, a critical stage; it is an *index*. It marks either the end of an unconscious elaboration which may have been very short or very long, or else the beginning of a conscious elaboration which will be very short or very long (this is seen especially in cases of creation suggested by chance). On the one hand, it never has an absolute beginning; on the other hand, it never delivers a finished work; the history of inventions sufficiently proves this. Furthermore, one may pass beyond it; many creations long in preparation seem without a crisis, strictly so called; such as Newton's law of attraction, Leonardo da Vinci's "Last Supper," and the "Mona Lisa." Finally, many have felt themselves

---

[1] We shall return to this point in another part of this work. See Part II, chapter iv.

really inspired without producing anything of value.[1]

II

What has been said up to this point does not exhaust the study of the unconscious factor as a source of new combinations. Its rôle can be studied under a simpler and more limited form. For this purpose we need to return for the last time to association of ideas. The final reason for association (outside of contiguity, in part at least) must be sought in the temperament, character, individuality of the subject, often even in the *moment;* that is, in a passing influence, hardly perceptible because it is unconscious or subconscious. These momentary dispositions in latent form can excite novel relations in two ways—through mediate association and through a special mode of grouping which has recently received the name "constellation."

1. Mediate association has been well known since the time of Hamilton, who was the first to determine its nature and to give a personal example that has become classic. Loch Lomond recalled to him the Prussian system of education because, when visiting the lake, he had met a Prussian officer who conversed with him on the subject. His general formula is this: A recalls $C,$ although there is between them neither contiguity nor resemblance, but because a middle term, $B,$ which does not enter consciousness, serves as a transition between A and $C.$ This mode of association seemed universally accepted when, lat-

terly, it has been attacked by Münsterberg and others. People have had recourse to experimentation, which has given results only in slight agreement.[1] For my own part, I count myself among those contemporaries who admit mediate association, and they are the greater number. Scripture, who has made a special study of the subject, and who has been able to note all the intermediate conditions between almost clear consciousness and the unconscious, considers the existence of mediate association as proven. In order to pronounce as an illusion a fact that is met with so often in daily experience, and one that has been studied by so many excellent observers, there is required more than experimental investigations (the conditions of which are often artificial and unnatural), some of which, moreover, conclude for the affirmative.

This form of association is produced, like the others, now by contiguity, now by resemblance. The example given by Hamilton belongs to the first type. In he experiments by Scripture are found some of

---

[1] Thus Howe (*American Journal of Psychology*, vi, 239 ff.), has published some investigations in the negative. One series of 557 experiments gave him eight apparently mediate associations; after examination, he reduced them to a single one, which seemed to him doubtful. Another series of 961 experiments gives 72 cases, for which he offers an explanation other than mediate association. On the other hand, Aschaffenburg admits them to the extent of four per cent.; the association-time is longer than for average associations (*Psychologische Arbeiten*, I and II). Consult especially Scripture, *The New Psychology*, chapter xiii, with experiments in support of his conclusion.

the second type—e. g., a red light recalled, through the vague memory of a flash of strontium light, a scene of an opera.

It is clear that by its very nature mediate association can give rise to novel combinations. Contiguity itself, which is usually only repetition, becomes the source of unforeseen relations, thanks to the elimination of the middle term. Nothing, moreover, proves that there may not sometimes be several latent intermediate terms. It is possible that A should call up D through the medium of b and c, which remain below the threshold of consciousness. It seems even impossible not to admit this in the hypothesis of the subconscious, where we see only the two end links of the chain, without being able to allow a break of continuity between them.

2. In his determination of the regulating causes of association of ideas, Ziehen designates one of these under the name of "constellation," which has been adopted by some writers. This may be enunciated thus: The recall of an image, or of a group of images, is in some cases the result of a sum of predominant tendencies.

An idea may become the starting point of a host of associations. The word "Rome" can call up a hundred. Why is one called up rather than another, and at such a moment rather than at another? There are some associations based on contiguity and on resemblance which one may foresee, but how about the rest? Here is an idea A; it is the center of a network; it can radiate in all directions—$B, C, D, E, F, etc.$ Why does it call up now B, later F?

It is because every image is comparable to a force, which may pass from the latent to the active condition, and in this process may be reinforced or checked by other images. There are simultaneous and inhibitory tendencies. B is in a state of tension and C is not; or it may be that D exerts an arresting influence on C. Consequently C cannot prevail. But an hour later conditions have changed and victory rests with C. This phenomenon rests on a physiological basis: the existence of several currents diffusing themselves through the brain and the possibility of receiving simultaneous excitations.[1]

A few examples will make plainer this phenomenon of reinforcement, in consequence of which an association prevails. Wahle reports that the Gothic *Hôtel de Ville,* near his house, had never suggested to him the idea of the Doges' Palace at Venice, in spite of certain architectural likenesses, until a certain day when this idea broke upon him with much clearness. He then recalled that two hours before he had observed a lady wearing a beautiful brooch in the form of a gondola. Sully rightly remarks that it is much easier to recall the words of a foreign language when we return from the country where it is spoken than when we have lived a long time in our own, because the tendency toward recollection is reinforced by the recent experience of the

[1] Ziehen, *Leitfaden der physiologischen Psychologie,* 4th edition, 1898, pp. 164, 174. Also, Sully, *Human Mind,* I, 343.

words heard, spoken, read, and a whole array of latent dispositions that work in the same direction.

In my opinion we would find the finest examples of "constellation," regarded as a creative element, in studying the formation and development of myths. Everywhere and always man has had for material scarcely anything save natural phenomena —the sky, land, water, stars, storms, wind, seasons, life, death, etc. On each of these themes he builds thousands of explanatory stories, which vary from the grandly imposing to the laughably childish. Every myth is the work of a human group which has worked according to the tendencies of its special genius under the influence of various stages of intellectual culture. No process is richer in resources, of freer turn, or more apt to give what every inventor promises—the novel and unexpected.

To sum up: The initial element, external or internal, excites associations that one cannot always foresee, because of the numerous orientations possible; an analogous case to that which occurs in the realm of the will when there are present reasons for and against, acting and not acting, one direction or another, now or later—when the final resolution cannot be predicted, and often depends on imperceptible causes.

In conclusion, I anticipate a possible question: "Does the unconscious factor differ in nature from the two others (intellectual and emotional)?" The answer depends on the hypothesis that one holds as to the nature of the unconscious itself. According to one view it would be especially physiological, consequently different; according to another, the difference can exist only *in the processes:* unconscious elaboration is reducible to intellectual or emotional processes the preparatory work of which is slighted, and which enters consciousness ready made. Consequently, the unconscious factor would be a special form of the other two rather than a distinct element in invention.

CHAPTER IV

THE ORGANIC CONDITIONS OF THE IMAGINATION

Whatever opinion we may hold concerning the nature of the unconscious, since that form of activity is related more than any other to the physiological conditions of the mental life, the present time is suitable for an exposition of the hypotheses that it is permissible to express concerning the organic bases of the imagination. What we may regard as positive, or even as probable, is very little.

I

First, the anatomical conditions. Is there a "seat" of the imagination? Such is the form of the question asked for the last twenty years. In that period of extreme and closely bounded localization men strained themselves to bind down every psychic manifestation to a strictly determined point of the brain. Today the problem presents itself no longer in this simple way. As at present we incline toward scattered localization, functional rather than properly anatomical, and as we often understand by "center" the synergic action of several centers differently grouped according to the individual case, our question becomes equivalent to: "Are there certain portions of the brain having an exclusive or preponderating part in the working of the creative imagination?" Even in this form the question is hardly acceptable. Indeed, the imagination is not a primary and relatively simple function like that of visual, auditory and other sensations. We have seen that it is a state of tertiary formation and very complex. There is required, then, (1) that the elements constituting imagination be determined in a rigorous manner, but the foregoing analysis makes no pretense of being definitive; (2) that each of these constitutive elements may be strictly related to its anatomic conditions. It is evident that we are far from possessing the secret of such a mechanism.

An attempt has been made to put the question in a more precise and limited form by studying the brains of men distinguished in different lines. But this method, in avoiding the difficulty, answers our question indirectly only. Most often great inventors possess qualities besides imagination indispensable for success (Napoleon, James Watt, etc.). How draw a dividing line so as to assign to the imagination only its rightful share? In addition, the anatomical determination is beset with difficulties.

A method flourishing very greatly about the middle of the nineteenth century consisted of weighing carefully a large number of brains and drawing various conclusions as to intellectual superiority or inferiority from a comparison of the weights. We find on this point numerous documents in the special works published during the period mentioned. But this method of weights has given rise to so many surprises and difficulties in the way of explanation that it has been quite necessary to give it up, since we see in it only another element of the problem.

Nowadays we attribute the greatest importance to the morphology of the brain, to its histological structure, the marked development of certain regions, the determination not only of centers but of connections and associations between centers. On this last point contemporary anatomists have given themselves up to eager researches, and, although the cerebral architecture is not conceived by all in the same way, it is proper for psychology to note that all with their "centers" or "associational system" try to translate into their own language the complex conditions of mental life. Since we must choose from among these various anatomical views let us accept that of Flechsig, one of the most renowned and one having also the advantage of putting directly the problem of the orᵍanic conditions of the imagination.

We know that Flechsig relies on the embryological method—that is, on the development—in the order of time, of nerves and centers. For him there exist on the one hand sensitive regions (sensory-motor), occupying about a third of the cortical surface; on the other hand, association-centers, occupying the remaining part.

So far as the sensory centers are concerned, development occurs in the following order: Organic sensations (middle of cerebral cortex), smell (base of the brain and part of the frontal lobes), sight (occipital lobe), hearing (first temporal). Whence it results that in a definite part of the brain the body comes to proper consciousness of its impulses, wants, appetites, pains, movements, etc., and that this part develops first—"knowledge of the body precedes that of the outside world."

In what concerns the associational centers, Flechsig supposes three regions: The great posterior center (parieto-occipito-temporal); another, much smaller, anterior or frontal; and a middle center, the smallest of all (the Island of Reil). Comparative anatomy proves that the associational centers are more important than those of sensation. Among the lower mammals they develop as we go up the scale: "That which makes the psychic man may be said to be the centers of association that he possesses." In the new-born child the sensitive centers are isolated, and, in the absence of connections between them, the unity of the self cannot be manifested; there is a plurality of consciousness.

This much admitted, let us return to our special question, which Flechsig asks in these words: "On what does genius rest? Is it based on a special structure in the brain, or rather on special irritability? that is, according to our present notions, on chemical factors? We may hold the first opinion with all possible force. Genius is always united to a special structure, to a particular organization of the brain." All parts of this organ do not have the same value. It has been long admitted that the frontal part may serve as a measure of intellectual capacity; but we must allow, contrariwise, that there are other regions, "principally a center located under the protuberance at the top of the head, which is very much developed in all men of genius whose brains have been studied down to our day. In Beethoven, and probably also in Bach, the enormous development of this part of the brain is striking. In great scientists like Gauss the centers of the posterior region of the brain and those of the frontal region are strongly developed. The scientific genius thus shows proportions of brain-structure other than the artistic genius."[1] There would then be, according to our author, a preponderance of the frontal and parietal regions—the former obtain especially among artists; the latter among scientists. Already, twenty years before Flechsig, Rüdinger had noted the extraordinary development of the parietal convolutions in eminent men after a study of eighteen brains. All the convolutions and fissures were so developed, said he, that the parieto-occipital region had an altogether peculiar character.

By way of summary we must bear in mind that, as regards anatomical conditions, even when depending on the best of sources, we can at present give only fragmentary, incomplete, hypothetical views.

Let us now go on to the physiology.

[1] Flechsig, *Gehirn und Seele*, 1896.

II

We might have rightly asked whether the physiological states existing along with the working of the creative imagination are the cause, effect, or merely the accompaniment of this activity. Probably all the three conditions are met with. First, concomitance is an accomplished fact, and we may consider it as an organic manifestation parallel to that of the mind. Again, the employment of artificial means to excite and maintain the effervescence of the imagination assigns a causal or antecedent position to the physiologic conditions. Lastly, the psychic activity may be initial and productive of changes in the organism, or, if these already exist, may augment and prolong them.

The most instructive instances are those indicated by very clear manifestations and profound modifications of the bodily condition. Such are the moments of inspiration or simply those of warmth from work which arise in the form of sudden impulses.

The general fact of most importance consists of changes in the blood circulation. Increase of intellectual activity means an increase of work in the cortical cells, dependent on a congested, sometimes a temporarily anæmic state. Hyperæmia seems rather the rule, but we also know that slight anæmia increases cortical excitability. "Weak, contracted pulse; pale, chilly skin; overheated head; brilliant, sunken, roving eyes," such is the classic, frequently quoted description of the physiological state during creative labor. There are numerous inventors who, of their own accord, have noted these changes—irregular pulse, in the case of Lagrange; congestion of the head, in Beethoven, who made use of cold douches to relieve it, etc. This elevation of the vital tone, this nervous tension, translates itself also into motor form through movements analogous to reflexes, without special end, mechanically repeated and always the same in the same man—e. g., movement of the feet, hands, fingers; whittling the table or the arms of a chair (as in the case of Napoleon when he was elaborating a plan of campaign), etc. It is a safety-valve for the excessive flow of nervous impulse, and it is admitted that this method of expenditure is not useless for preserving the understanding in all its clearness. In a word, increase of the cerebral circulation is the formula covering the majority of observations on this subject.

Does experimentation, strictly so called, teach us anything on this point? Numerous and well-known physiological researches, especially those of Mosso, show that all intellectual, and, most of all, emotional, work, produces cerebral congestion; that the brain-volume increases, and the volume of the peripheral organs diminishes. But that tells us nothing particularly about the imagination, which is but a special case under the rule. Latterly, indeed, it has been proposed to study inventors by an objective method through the examination of their several circulatory, respiratory, digestive apparatus; their general and special sensibility; the modes of their memory and forms of association, their intellectual processes, etc. But up to this time no conclusion has been drawn from these individual descriptions that would allow any generalization. Besides, has an experiment, in the strict sense of the word, ever been made at the "psychological moment"? I know of none. Would it be possible? Let us admit that by some happy chance the experimenter, using all his means of investigation, can have the subject under his hand at the exact moment of inspiration —of the sudden, fertile, brief creative impulse— would not the experiment itself be a disturbing cause, so that the result would be *ipso facto* vitiated, or at least unconvincing?

There still remains a mass of facts deserving summary notice—the oddities of inventors. Were we to collect only those that may be regarded as authentic we could make a thick volume. Despite their anecdotal character these evidences do not seem to be unworthy of some regard.

It is impossible to enter here upon an enumeration that would be endless. After having collected for my own information a large number of these strange peculiarities, it seems to me that they are reducible to two categories:

(1) Those inexplicable freaks dependent on the individual constitution, and more often probably also on experiences in life the memory of which has been lost. Schiller, for example, kept rotten apples in his work desk.

(2) The others, more numerous, are easy to explain. They are physiological means consciously or unconsciously chosen to aid creative work; they are auxiliary helpers of the imagination.

The most frequent method consists of artificially increasing the flow of blood to the brain. Rousseau would think bare-headed in full sunshine; Bossuet would work in a cold room with his head wrapped in furs; others would immerse their feet in ice-cold water (Grétry, Schiller). Very numerous are those who think "horizontally"—that is, lying stretched out and often flattened under their blankets (Milton, Descartes, Leibniz, Rossini, etc.)

Some require motor excitation; they work only when walking,[1] or else prepare for work by physical exercise (Mozart). For variety's sake, let us note those who must have the noise of the streets, crowds, talk, festivities, in order to invent. For others there must be external pomp and a personal part in the scene (Machiavelli, Buffon). Guido Reni would paint only when dressed in magnificent style, his pupils crowded about him and attending to his wants in respectful silence.

On the opposite side are those requiring retirement, silence, contemplation, even shadowy darkness, like Lamennais. In this class we find especially scientists and thinkers—Tycho-Brahé, who for twenty-one years scarcely left his observatory; Leib-

---

[1] Is it possible that this would explain the fact of Aristotle lecturing to his pupils while walking about, thus giving the name "peripatetic" to his school and system? (Tr.)

niz, who could remain for three days almost motionless in an armchair.

But most methods are too artificial or too strong not to become quickly noxious. Every one knows what they are—abuse of wine, alcoholic liquors, narcotics, tobacco, coffee, etc., prolonged periods of wakefulness, less for increasing the time for work than to cause a state of hyperesthesia and a morbid sensibility (Goncourt).

Summing up: The organic bases of the creative imagination, if there are any specially its own, remain to be determined. For in all that has been said we have been concerned only with some conditions of the general working of the mind—assimilation as well as invention. The eccentricities of inventors studied carefully and in a detailed manner would finally, perhaps, be most instructive material, because it would allow us to penetrate into their inmost individuality. Thus, the physiology of the imagination quickly becomes pathology. I shall not dwell on this, having purposely eliminated the morbid side of our subject. It will, however, be necessary to return thereto, touching upon it in another part of this essay.

III

There remains a problem, so obscure and enigmatic that I scarcely venture to approach it, in the analogy that most languages—the spontaneous expression of a common thought—establish between physiologic and psychic creation. Is it only a superficial likeness, a hasty judgment, a metaphor, or does it rest on some positive basis? Generally, the various manifestations of mental activity have as their precursor an unconscious form from which they arise. The sensitiveness belonging to living substance, known by the names heliotropism, chemotropism, etc., is like a sketch of sensation and of the reactions following it; organic memory is the basis and the obliterated form of conscious memory. Reflexes introduce voluntary activity; appetitions and hidden tendencies are the forerunners of effective psychology. Instinct, on several sides, is like an unconscious and specific trial of reason. Has the creative power of the human mind also analogous antecedents, a physiological equivalent?

One metaphysician, Froschammer, who has elevated the creative imagination to the rank of primary world-principle, asserts this positively. For him there is an objective or cosmic imagination working in nature, producing the innumerable varieties of vegetable and animal forms; transformed into subjective imagination it becomes in the human brain the source of a new form of creation. "The very same principle causes the living forms to appear—a sort of objective images—and the subjective images, a kind of living form."[1] However ingenious and attractive this philosophical theory may be, it is evidently of no positive value for psychology.

Let us stick to experience. Physiology teaches

---

[1] *Die Phantasie als Grundprincip der Weltprocesses*, München, 1877. For other details on the subject, see Appendix C.

that generation is a "prolonged nutrition," a sur-
plus, as we see so plainly in the lower forms of
agamous generation (budding, division). The
creative imagination likewise presupposes a super-
abundance of psychic life that might otherwise spend
itself in another way. Generation in the physical
order is a spontaneous, natural tendency, although
it may be stimulated, successfully or otherwise, by
artificial means. We can say as much of the other.
This list of resemblances it would be easy to prolong. But all this is insufficient for the establish-
ment of a thorough identity between the two cases
and the solution of the question.

It is possible to limit it, to put it into more precise
language. Is there a connection between the development of the generative function and that of the
imagination? Even in this form the question scarcely permits any but vague answers. In favor of a
connection we may allege:

(1) The well-known influence of puberty on the
imagination of both sexes, expressing itself in day-
dreams, in aspirations toward an unattainable ideal,[1]

[1] A passage from Chateaubriand (cited by Paulhan, *Rev.
Philos.*, March, 1898, p. 237) is a typical description of the
situation: "The warmth of my (adolescent) imagination, my
shyness, and solitude, caused me, instead of casting myself on
something without, to fall back upon myself. Wanting a real
object, I evoked through the power of my desires, a phantom,
which thenceforth never left me; I made a woman, composed
of all the women that I had already seen. That charming
idea followed me everywhere, though invisible; I conversed
with her as with a real being; she would change according to
my frenzy. Pygmalion was less enamored of his statue."

in the genius for invention that love bestows upon the least favored. Let us recall also the mental troubles, the psychoses designated by the name hebephrenia. With adolescence coincides the first flowering of the fancy which, having emerged from its swaddling-clothes of childhood, is not yet sophisticated and rationalized.

It is not a matter of indifference for the general thesis of the present work to note that this development of the imagination depends wholly on the first effervescence of the emotional life. That "influence of the feelings on the imagination" and of "the imagination on the feelings" of which the moralists and the older psychologists speak so often is a vague formula for expressing this fact—that the motor element included in the images is reinforced.

(2) *Per contra,* the weakening of the generative power and of the constructive imagination coincide in old age, which is, in a word, a decay of nutrition, a progressive atrophy. It is proper not to omit the influence of castration. According to the theory of Brown-Séquard, it produces an abatement of the nutritive functions through the suppression of an internal stimulus; and, although its relations to the imagination have not been especially studied, it is not rash to admit that it is an arresting cause.

However, the foregoing merely establishes, between the functions compared, a concomitance in the general course of their evolution and in their critical periods; it is insufficient for a conclusion.

There would be needed clear, authentic and sufficiently numerous observations proving that individuals bereft of imagination of the creative type have acquired it suddenly through the sole fact of their sexual influences, and, inversely, that brilliant imaginations have faded under the contrary conditions. We find some of these evidences in Cabanis,[1] Moreau de Tours and various alienists; they would seem to be in favor of the affirmative, but some seem to me not sure enough, others not explicit enough. Despite my investigations on this point, and inquiry of competent persons, I do not venture to draw a definite conclusion. I leave the question open; it will perhaps tempt another more fortunate investigator.

[1] Cabanis, *Rapports du Physique et du Moral*, édition Peisse, pp. 248-249, an anecdote that he relates after Buffon. Analogous, but less clear, facts may also be found in Moreau de Tours' *Psychologie morbide*.

CHAPTER V

THE PRINCIPLE OF UNITY

The psychological nature of the imagination would be very imperfectly known were we limited to the foregoing analytical study. Indeed, all creation whatever, great or small, shows an organic character; it implies a unifying, synthetic principle. Every one of the three factors—intellectual, emotional, unconscious—works not as an isolated fact on its own account; they have no worth save through their union, and no signification save through their common bearing. This principle of unity, which all invention demands and requires, is at one time intellectual in nature, i. e., as a fixed idea; at another time emotional, i. e., as a fixed emotion or passion. These terms—fixed idea, fixed emotion—are somewhat absolute and require restrictions and reservations, which will be made in what follows.

The distinction between the two is not at all absolute. Every fixed idea is supported and maintained by a need, a tendency, a desire; i. e., by an affective element. For it is idle fancy to believe in the *persistence* of an idea which, by hypothesis, would be a purely intellectual state, cold and dry. The principle of unity in this form naturally predominates in certain kinds of creation: in the practical imagination wherein the end is clear, where images are direct substitutes for things, where invention is subjected to strict conditions under penalty of visible and palpable check; in the scientific and metaphysical imagination, which works with concepts and is subject to the laws of rational logic.

Every fixed emotion should realize itself in an idea or image that gives it body and systematizes it, without which it remains diffuse; and all affective states can take on this permanent form which makes a unified principle of them. The simple emotions (fear, love, joy, sorrow, etc.), the complex or derived emotions (religious, esthetic, intellectual ideas) may equally monopolize consciousness in their own interests.

We thus see that these two terms—fixed idea, fixed emotion—are almost equivalent, for they both imply inseparable elements, and serve only to indicate the preponderance of one or the other element.

This principle of unity, center of attraction and support of all the working of the creative imagination—that is, a subjective principle tending to become objectified—is the ideal. In the complete sense of the word—not restrained merely to esthetic creation or made synonymous with perfection as in ethics—the ideal is a construction in images that should become a reality. If we liken imaginative creation to physiological generation, the ideal is the ovum awaiting fertilization in order to begin its development.

We could, to be more exact, make a distinction between the synthetic principle and the ideal conception which is a higher form of it. The fixation of an end and the discovery of appropriate means are the necessary and sufficient conditions for all invention. A creation, whatever it be, that looks only to present success, can satisfy itself with a unifying principle that renders it viable and organized, but we can look higher than the merely necessary and sufficient.

The ideal is the principle of unity in motion in its historic evolution; like all development, it advances or recedes according to the times. Nothing is less justified than the conception of a fixed archetype (an undisguised survival of the Platonic Ideas), illuminating the inventor, who reproduces it as best he can. The ideal is a nonentity; it arises in the inventor and through him; its life is a *becoming*.

Psychologically, it is a construction in images belonging to the merely sketched or outlined type.[1] It results from a double activity, negative and positive, or dissociation and association, the first cause and origin of which is found in a *will that it shall be so;* it is the motor tendency of images in the

---

[1] For the distinction between this form of imagination and the two others (fixed, objectified), I refer the reader to the Conclusion of this work, where the subject will be treated in detail.

nascent state engendering the ideal. The inventor
cuts out, suppresses, sifts, according to his temperament, character, taste, prejudices, sympathies and
antipathies—in short, his *interest*. In this separation, already studied, let us note one important particular. "We know nothing of the complex psychic
production that may simply be the sum of component
elements and in which they would remain with their
own characters, with no modification. The nature
of the components disappears in order to give birth
to a novel phenomenon that has its own and particular features. The construction of the ideal is
not a mere grouping of past experiences; in its totality it has its own individual characteristics, among
which we no more see the composing lines than we
see the components, oxygen and hydrogen, in water.
In no scientific or artistic production, says Wundt,
does the whole appear as made up of its parts, like
a mosaic."[1] In other words, it is a case of mental
chemistry. The exactness of this expression, which
is due, I believe, to J. Stuart Mill, has been questioned. Still it answers to positive facts; for example, in perception, to the phenomena of contrast
and their analogues; juxtaposition or rapid succession of two different colors, two different sounds,
of tactile, olfactory, gustatory impressions different in quality, produces a particular state of consciousness, similar to a combination. Harmony or
discord does not, indeed, exist in each separate

[1] Colozza, *L'immaginazione nella Scienza,* Rome, 1900, pp.
111 ff.

sound, but only in the relations and sequence of sounds—it is a *tertium quid*. We have heretofore, in the discussion of association of ideas, very frequently represented the states of consciousness as fixed elements that approach one another, cohere, separate, come together anew, but always unalterable, like atoms. It is not so at all. Consciousness, says Titchener, resembles a fresco in which the transition between colors is made through all kinds of intermediate stages of light and shade. . . . The idea of a pen or of an inkwell is not a stable thing clearly pictured like the pen or inkwell itself. More than any one else, William James has insisted on this point in his theory of "fringes" of states of consciousness. Outside of the given instances we could find many others among the various manifestations of the mental life. It is not, then, at all chimerical to assume in psychology an equivalent of chemical combination. In a complex state there is, in addition to the component elements, the result of their reciprocal influences, of their varying relations. Too often we forget this resultant.

At bottom the ideal is an individual concept. If objection is offered that an ideal common to a large mass of men is a fact of common experience (e. g., idealists and realists in the fine arts, and even more so religious, moral, social and political concepts, etc.), the answer is easy: There are families of minds. They have a common ideal because, in certain matters, they have the same way of feeling and thinking. It is not a transcendental idea that unites them; but this result occurs because from their common aspirations the collective ideal becomes disengaged; it is, in scholastic terminology, a *universale post rem.*

The ideal conception is the first moment of the creative act, which is not yet battling with the conditions of the actual. It is only the internal vision of an individual mind that has not yet been projected externally with a form and body. We know how the passage from the internal to the external life has given rise among inventors to deceptions and complaints. Such was the imaginative construction that could not, unchanged, enter into its mould and become a reality.

Let us now examine the various forms of this coagulating[1] principle in advancing from the lowest to the highest, from the unity vaguely anticipated to the absolute and tyrannical masterful unity. Following a method that seems to me best adapted for these ill-explained questions I shall single out only the principal forms, which I have reduced to three —the unstable, the organic or middle, and the extreme or semi-morbid unity.

(1) The unstable form has its starting point directly and immediately in the reproductive imagi-

---

[1] This unifying, organizing, creative principle is so active in certain minds that, placed face to face with any work whatever—novel, picture, monument, scientific or philosophic theory, financial or political institution—while believing that they are merely considering it, they spontaneously remake it. This characteristic of their psychology distinguishes them from mere critics.

nation without creation. It assembles its elements somewhat by chance and stitches together the bits of our life; it ends only in beginnings, in attempts. The unity-principle is a momentary disposition, vacillating and changing without cessation according to the external impressions or modifications of our vital conditions and of our humor. By way of example let us recall the state of the day-dreamer building castles in the air; the delirious constructions of the insane, the inventions of the child following all the fluctuations of chance, of its caprice; the half-coherent dreams that seem to the dreamer to contain a creative germ. In consequence of the extreme frailty of the synthetic principle the creative imagination does not succeed in accomplishing its task and remains in a condition intermediate between simple association of ideas and creation proper.

(2) The organic or middle form may be given as the type of the unifying power. Ultimately it reduces itself to attention and presupposes nothing more, because, thanks to the process of "localization," which is the essential mark of attention, it makes itself a center of attraction, grouping about the leading idea the images, associations, judgments, tendencies and voluntary efforts. "Inspiration," the poet Grillparzer used to say, "is a concentration of which, for the time being, should represent the all the forces and capacities upon a single point world rather than enclose it. The reinforcement of the state of the mind comes from the fact that its several powers, instead of spreading themselves

over the whole world, are contained within the bounds of a single object, touch one another, reciprocally help and reinforce each other."[1] What the poet here maintains as regards esthetics only is applicable to all the *organic* forms of creation—that is to those ruled by an immanent logic, and, like them, resembling works of Nature.

In order to leave no doubt as to the identity of attention and imaginative synthesis, and in order to show that it is normally the true unifying principle, we offer the following remarks:

Attention is at times spontaneous, natural, without effort, simply dependent on the interest that a thing excites in us—lasting as long as it holds us in subjection, then ceasing entirely. Again, it is voluntary, artificial, an imitation of the other, precarious and intermittent, maintained with effort—in a word, laborious. The same is true of the imagination. The moment of inspiration is ruled by a perfect and spontaneous unity; its impersonality approaches that of the forces of Nature. Then appears the personal moment, the detailed working and long, painful, intermittent resumptions, the miserable turns of which so many inventors have described. The analogy between the two cases seems to me incontestable.

Next let us note that psychologists always adduce the same examples when they wish to illustrate on the one hand, the processes of the persistent, tenacious attention, and, on the other hand, the develop-

[1] Oelzelt-Newin, *op. cit.*, p. 49.

mental labor without which creative work does not come to pass: "Genius is only long patience," the saying of Newton; "always thinking of it," and like expressions of d'Alembert, Helmholtz and others, because in the one case as in the other the fundamental condition is the existence of a fixed, ever-active idea, notwithstanding its relaxations and its incessant disappearances into the unconscious with return to consciousness.

(3) The extreme form, which from its nature is semi-morbid, becomes in its highest degree plainly pathological; the unifying principle changes to a condition of obsession.

The normal state of our mind is a plurality of states of consciousness (polyideism). Through association there is a radiation in every direction. In this totality of coexisting images no one long occupies first place; it is driven away by others, which are displaced in turn by still others emerging from the penumbra. On the contrary, in attention (relative monoideism) a single image retains first place for a long time and tends to have the same importance again. Finally, in a condition of obsession (absolute monoideism) the fixed idea defies all rivalry and rules despotically. Many inventors have suffered painfully this tyranny and have vainly struggled to break it. The fixed idea, once settled, does not permit anything to dislodge it save for the moment and with much pain. Even then it is displaced only apparently, for it persists in the unconscious life where it has thrust its deep roots.

At this stage the unifying principle, although it can act as a stimulus for creation, is no longer normal. Consequently, a natural question arises: Wherein is there a difference between the obsession of the inventor and the obsession of the insane, who most generally destroys in place of creating?

The nature of fixed ideas has greatly occupied contemporary alienists. For other reasons and in their own way they, too, have been led to divide obsession into two classes, the intellectual and emotional, according as the idea or the affective state predominates. Then they have been led to ask: Which of these two elements is the primitive one? For some it is the idea. For others, and it seems that these are the more numerous, the affective state is in general the primary fact; the obsession always rests on a basis of morbid emotion and in a retention of impressions.[1]

But whatever opinion we may hold on this point, the difficulty of establishing a dividing line between the two forms of obsession above mentioned remains the same. Are there characters peculiar to each one?

It has been said: "The physiologically fixed idea is normally longed for, often sought, in all cases accepted, and it does not break the unity of the self." It does not impose itself fatally on consciousness; the individual knows the value thereof, knows

[1] Pitres et Régis, *Séméiologie des obsessions et des idées fixes*, 1878. Séglas, *Leçons cliniques sur les maladies mentales*, 1895. Raymond et Janet, *Névroses et idées fixes*, 1898

where it leads him, and adapts his conduct to its requirements. For example, Christopher Columbus.

The pathological fixed idea is "parasitic," automatic, discordant, irresistible. Obsession is only a special case of psychic disintegration, a kind of doubling of consciousness. The individual becomes a person "possessed," whose self has been confiscated for the sake of the fixed idea, and whose submission to his situation is wrought with pain.

In spite of this parallel the distinguishing criterion between the two is very vague, because from the sane to the delirious idea the transitions are very numerous. We are obliged to recognize "that with certain workers—who are rather taken up with the elaboration of their work, and not masters directing it, quitting it, and resuming it at their pleasure—an artistic, scientific, or mechanical conception succeeds in haunting the mind, imposing itself upon it even to the extent of causing suffering." In reality, pure psychology is unable to discover a positive difference between obsession leading to creative work and the other forms, because in both cases the mental mechanism is, at bottom, the same. The criterion must be sought elsewhere. For that we must go out of the internal world and proceed objectively. We must judge the fixed idea not in itself but by its effects. What does it produce in the practical, esthetic, scientific, moral, social, religious field? It is of value according to its fruits. If objection be made to this change of front we may, in order to stick to a strictly psychological point of view, state that it is certain that as soon as it passes beyond a middle point, which it is difficult to determine, the fixed idea profoundly troubles the mechanism of the mind. In imaginative persons this is not rare, which partly explains why the pathological theory of genius (of which we shall speak later) has been able to rally so many to its support and to allege so many facts in its favor.

SECOND PART

THE DEVELOPMENT OF THE
IMAGINATION.

CHAPTER I

IMAGINATION IN ANIMALS

Up to this point the imagination has been treated analytically only. This process alone would give us but a very imperfect idea of its essentially concrete and lively nature were we to stop here. So this part continues the subject in another shape. I shall attempt to follow the imagination in its ascending development from the lowest to the most complex forms, from the animal to the human infant, to primitive man, thence to the highest modes of invention. It will thus be exhibited in the inexhaustible variety of its manifestations which the abstract and simplifying process of analysis does not permit us to suspect.

I

I shall not dwell at length on the imagination of animals, not only because the question is much involved but also because it is hardly liable to a positive solution. Even eliminating mere anecdotes and doubtful observations, there is no lack of verified and authentic material, but it still remains to interpret them. As soon as we begin to conjecture we know how difficult it is to divest ourselves of all anthropomorphism.

The question has been formulated, even if not treated, with much system by Romanes in his *Mental Evolution in Animals.*[1] Taking "imagination" in its broadest sense, he recognizes four stages:

1. Provoked revival of images. For example, the sight of an orange reminds one of its taste. This is a low form of memory, resting on association by contiguity. It is met with very far down in the animal scale, and the author furnishes abundant proof of it.

2. Spontaneous revival. An object present calls up an absent object. This is a higher form of memory, frequent in ants, bees, wasps, etc., which fact explains the mistrustful sagacity of wild animals. At night, the distant baying of a hound stops the fox in his course, because all the dangers he has undergone are represented in his mind.

These two stages do not go beyond memory pure and simple, i. e., reproductive imagination. The other two constitute the higher imagination.

3. The capacity of associating absent images, without suggestion derived from without, through an internal working of the mind. It is the lower and primitive form of the creative imagination, which may be called a passive synthesis. In order to establish its existence, Romanes reminds us that dreams have been proven in dogs, horses, and a

[1] Chapter X.

large number of birds; that certain animals, especially in anger, seem to be subject to delusions and
pursued by phantoms; and lastly, that in some
there is produced a condition resembling nostalgia,
expressing itself in a violent desire to return to
former haunts, or in a wasting away resulting from
the absence of accustomed persons and things. All
these facts, especially the latter, can hardly be
explained without a vivid recollection of the images
of previous life.

4. The highest stage consists of intentionally
reuniting images in order to make novel combinations from them. This may be called an active
synthesis, and is the true creative imagination. Is
this sometimes found in the animal kingdom?
Romanes very clearly replies, no; and not without
offering a plausible reason. For creation, says he,
there must first be capacity for abstraction, and,
without speech, abstraction is very weak. One of
the conditions for creative imagination is thus
wanting in the higher animals.

We here come to one of those critical moments,
so frequent in animal psychology, when one asks,
Is this character exclusively human, or is it found
in embryo in lower forms? Thus it has been possible to support a theory opposing that of Romanes.
Certain animals, says Oelzelt-Newin, fulfill all the
conditions necessary for creative imagination—
subtle senses, good memory, and appropriate emotional states.[1] This assertion is perhaps true, but

[1] *Op. cit.,* Appendix.

it is purely dialectic. It is equivalent to saying that the thing is possible; it does not establish it as a fact. Besides, is it very certain that all the conditions for creative imagination are present here, since we have just shown that there is lack of abstraction? The author, who voluntarily limits his study to birds and the construction of their nests, maintains, against Wallace and others, that nest-building requires "the mysterious synthesis of representations." We might with equal reason bring the instances of other building animals (bees, wasps, white ants, the common ants, beavers, etc.). It is not unreasonable to attribute to them an anticipated representation of their architecture. Shall we say that it is "instinctive," consequently unconscious? At least, may we not group under this head, changes and adaptations to new conditions which these animals succeed in applying to the typical plans of their construction? Observations and even systematic experiments (like those of Huber, Forel, *et al.*) show that, reduced to the alternative of the impossibility of building or the modification of their habits, certain animals modify them. Judging from this, how refuse them invention altogether? This contradicts in no way the very just reservation of Romanes. It is sufficient to remark that abstraction or dissociation has stages, that the simplest are accessible to the animal intelligence. If, in the absence of words, the logic of concepts is forbidden it, there yet remains the logic of images,[2] which is sufficient for slight innovations. In a word, animals can invent according to the extent that they can dissociate.

In our opinion, if we may with any truthfulness attribute a creative power to animals, we must seek it elsewhere. Generally speaking, we attribute only a mediocre importance to a manifestation that might very well be the proper form of animal fancy. It is purely motor, and expresses itself through the various kinds of play.

Although play may be as old as mankind, its psychology dates only from the nineteenth century. We have already seen that there are three theories concerning its nature—it is "expenditure of superfluous activity," "a mending, restoring of strength, a recuperation," "an apprenticeship, a preliminary exercise for the active functions of life and for the development of our natural gifts."[1] The last position, due to Groos, does not rule out the other two; it holds the first valid for the young, the second for adults; but it comprehends both in a more general explanation.

[2] For a more detailed study of this subject, the reader is referred to the author's *Evolution of General Ideas* (English trans., Open Court Publishing Co., Chicago), chapter I, section I.

[1] A rather extended study of the subject by H. A. Carr will be found in the *Investigations of the Department of Psychology and Education of the University of Colorado*, vol. I, Number 2, 1902. The late Professor Arthur Allin devoted much time to the investigation of play. See his brief article entitled "Play" in the *University of Colorado Studies*, vol. I, 1902, pp. 58-73. (Tr.)

Let us leave this doctrinal question in order to call attention to the variety and richness of form of play in the animal world. In this respect the aforementioned book of Groos is a rich mine of evidence to which I would refer the reader. I limit myself to summing up his classification. He distinguishes nine classes of play, viz.: (1) Those that are at bottom experimental, consisting of trials at hazard without immediate end, often giving the animal a certain knowledge of the properties of the external world. This is the introduction to an experimental physics, optics, and mechanics for the brood of animals. (2) Movements or changes of place executed of their own accord—a very general fact as is proven by the incessant movements of butterflies, flies, birds, and even fishes, which often appear to play in the water rather than to seek prey; the mad running of horses, dogs, etc., in free space. (3) Mimicry of hunting, i. e., playing with a living or dead prey: the dog and cat following moving objects, a ball, feather, etc. (4) Mimic battles, teasing and fighting without anger. (5) Architectural art, revealing itself especially in the building of nests: certain birds ornament them with shining objects (stones, bits of glass), by a kind of anticipation of the esthetic feeling. (6) Doll-play is universal in mankind, whether civilized or savage. Groos believes he has found its equivalent in certain animals. (7) Imitation through pleasure, so familiar in monkeys (grimaces); singing-birds which counterfeit the voices of a large number of beasts. (8) Curiosity, which is the only mental play one meets in animals—the dog watching, from a wall or window, what is going on in the street. (9) Love-plays, "which differ from the others in that they are not mere exercises, but have in view a real object." They have been well-known since Darwin's time, he attributing to them an esthetic value which has been denied by Wallace, Tylor, Lloyd Morgan, Wallaschek, and Groos.

Let us recapitulate in thought the immense quantity of motor expressions included in these nine categories and let us note that they have the following characters in common: They are grouped in combinations that are often new and unforeseen; they are not a repetition of daily life, acts necessary for self-preservation. At one time the movements are combined simultaneously (exhibition of beautiful colors), again (and most often) successively (amorous parades, fights, flight, dancing, emission of noises, sounds or songs); but, under one form or another, there is *creation, invention*. Here, the imagination acts in its purely motor character; it consists of a small number of images that become translated into actions, and serve as a center for their grouping; perhaps even the image itself is hardly conscious, so that all is limited to a spontaneous production and a collection of motor phenomena.

It will doubtless be said that this form of imagination belongs to a very shallow, poor psychology. It cannot be otherwise. It is necessary that imagi-

native production be found reduced to its simplest
expression in animals, and the motor form must be
its special characteristic mark. It cannot have any
others for the following reasons: incapacity for
the work that necessarily precedes abstraction or
dissociation, breaking into bits the data of experience, making them raw material for the future
construction; lack of images, and especially fewness
of possible combinations of images. This last point
is proven alike from the data of animal psychology
and of comparative anatomy. We know that the
nervous elements in the brain serving as connections
between sensory regions—whether one conceive of
them as centers (Flechsig), or as bundles of com-
misural fibers (Meynert, Wernicke)—are hardly
outlined in the lower mammalia and attain only a
mediocre development in the higher forms.

By way of corroboration of the foregoing, let us
compare the higher animals with young children:
this comparison is not based on a few far-fetched
analogies, but in a thorough resemblance in nature.
Man, during the first years of his life, has a brain
but slightly differentiated, especially as regards
connections, a very poor supply of images, a very
weak capacity for abstraction. His intellectual
development is much inferior to that of reflex,
instinctive, impulsive, and imitative movements. In
consequence of this predominance of the motor
system, the simple and imperfect images, in children as in animals, tend to be immediately changed
into movements. Even most of their inventions in

play are greatly inferior to those enumerated above under nine distinct heads.

A serious argument in favor of the prevalence of imagination of the motor type in the child is furnished by the principal part taken by movements in infantile insanity: a remark made by many alienists. The first stage of this madness, they say, is found in the convulsions that are not merely a physical ailment, but "a muscular delirium." The disturbance of the automatic and instinctive functions of the child is so often associated with muscular disturbances that at this age the mental disorders correspond to the motor ganglionic centers situated below those parts that later assume the labor of analysis and of imagination. The disturbances are in the primary centers of organization and according to the symptoms lack those analytic or constructive qualities, those ideal forms, that we find in adult insanity. If we descend to the lowest stage of human life—to the baby—we see that insanity consists almost entirely of the activity of a muscular group acting on external objects. The insane baby bites, kicks, and these symptoms are the external measure of the degree of its madness.[1] Has not chorea itself been called a muscular insanity?

Doubtless, there likewise exists in the child a sensorial madness (illusions, hallucinations); but by reason of its feeble intellectual development the

---

[1] Hack Tuke, "Insanity of Children," in *Dictionary of Psychological Medicine.*

delirium causes a disorder of movements rather than of images; its insane imagination is above all a motor insanity.

To hold that the creative imagination belonging to animals consists of new combinations of movements is certainly an hypothesis. Nevertheless, I do not believe that it is merely a mental form without foundation, if we take into account the foregoing facts. I consider it rather as a point in favor of the motor theory of invention. It is a singular instance in which the original form of creation is shown bare. If we wanted to discover it, it would be necessary to seek it where it is reduced to the greatest simplicity—in the animal world.

CHAPTER II

THE CREATIVE IMAGINATION IN THE CHILD

At what age, in what form, under what conditions does the creative imagination make its appearance? It is impossible to answer this question, which, moreover, has no justification. For the creative imagination develops little by little out of pure reproduction by an evolutionary process, not by sudden eruption. Nevertheless, its evolution is very slow on account of causes both organic and psychological.

We could not dwell long on the organic causes without falling into tiresome repetitions. The newborn infant is a spinal being, with an unformed diffluent brain, composed largely of water. Reflex life itself is not complete in him, and the corticomotor system only hinted at; the sensory centers are undifferentiated, the associational systems remain isolated for a long time after birth. We have given above Flechsig's observation on this point.

The psychological causes reduce themselves to the necessity for a consolidation of the primary and secondary operations of the mind, without which the creative imagination cannot take form. To be precise, we might distinguish, as does Baldwin, four epochs in the mental development of the child: (1) affective (rudimentary sensory processes, pleasures and pains, simple motor adaptations); (2) and (3) objective, in which the author establishes two grades, (a) appearance of special senses, of memory, instincts primarily defensive, and imitation; (b) complex memory, complicated movements, offensive activities, rudimentary will; (4) subjective or final (conscious thought, constitutive will, ideal emotions). If we accept this scheme as approximately correct, the *moment* of imagination must be assigned to the third period (the second stage of the objective epoch) which fulfills all the sufficient and necessary conditions for its origination and for its rise above pure reproduction.

Whatever the propitious age may be, the study of the child-imagination is not without difficulties. In order to enter into the child-mind, we must become like a child; as it is, we are limited to an interpretation of it in terms of the adult, with much false interpretation possible, agreeing too much or too little with the facts. Furthermore, the children studied live and grow up in a civilized environment. The result is that the development of their imagination is rarely unhampered and complete; for as soon as their fancy passes the middle level, the rationalizing education of parents and teachers is eager to master and control it. In truth it gives its full measure and reveals itself in the fulness of growth only among primitive peoples. With us it is checked in its flight by an antagonistic power, which treats it as a harbinger of insanity. Finally, children are not equally well-suited for this study; we must make a distinction between the imaginative and non-imaginative, and the latter should be eliminated.

When we have thus chosen suitable subjects, observation shows from the start sufficiently distinct varieties, different orientations of the imagination depending on intellectual causes, such as the predominance of visual or acoustic or tactile-motor images making for mechanical invention; or dependent on emotional causes, that is, of character, according as the latter is timid, joyous, exuberant, retired, healthy, sickly, etc.

If we now attempt to follow the development of the child-imagination, we may distinguish four principal stages, without assigning them, otherwise, a rigorous chronological order.

1. The first stage consists of the passage from passive to creative imagination. Its history would be long were we to include all the hybrid forms that are made up partly of memories, partly of new groupings, being at the same time repetition and construction. Even in the adult, they are very frequent. I know a person who is always afraid of being smothered, and for this reason urgently asks that in his coffin his shirt be not tight at the neck: this odd prepossession of the mind belongs neither

to memory nor to imagination. This particular case illustrates in a very clear form the nature of the first flights of the mind attempting to exercise its imaginative powers. Without enumerating other facts of this kind, it is more desirable to follow the imagination's development, limiting ourselves to two forms of the psychic life—perception and illusion. The necessary presence of the image in these two forms has been so often proven by contemporary psychology that a few words to recall this to mind will be sufficient.

There seems to be a radical difference between perception, which seizes reality, and imagination. Nevertheless, it is generally admitted that in order to rise above sensation to perception, there must be a synthesis of images. To put it more simply, two elements are required—one, coming from without, the physiological stimulus acting on the nerves and the sensory centers, which becomes translated in consciousness through the vague state that goes by the name "sensation"; the other, coming from within, adds to the sensations present appropriate images, remnants of former experiences. So that perception requires an apprenticeship; we must feel, then imperfectly perceive, in order to finally perceive well. The sensory datum is only a fraction of the total fact; and in the operation we call "perceiving," that is, apprehending an object directly, a part only of the object is represented.

This, however, does not go beyond reproductive imagination. The decisive step is taken in illusion.

We know that illusion has as a basis and support a modification of the external senses which are meta-morphosed, amplified by an immediate construction of the mind: a branch of a tree becomes a serpent, a distant noise seems the music of an orchestra. Illusion has as broad a field as perception, since there is no perception but may undergo this erron-eous transformation, and it is produced by the same mechanism, but with interchange of the two terms. In perception, the chief element is the sensory, and the representative element is secondary; in illusion, we have just the opposite condition: what one takes as perceived is merely imagined—the imagination assumes the principal rôle. Illusion is the type of the transitional forms, of the mixed cases, that con-sist of constructions made up of memories, without being, in the strict sense, creations.

2. The creative imagination asserts itself with its peculiar characteristics only in the second stage, in the form of animism or the attributing of life to everything. This turn of the mind is already known to us, though mentioned only incidentally. As the state of the child's mind at that period resembles that which in primitive man creates myths, we shall return to it in the next chapter. Works on psychology abound in facts demonstrat-ing that this primitive tendency to attribute life and even personality to everything is a necessary phase that the mind must undergo—long or short in dura-tion, rich or poor in inventions, according to the level of the child's imagination. His attitude to-

wards his dolls is the common example of this state, and also the best example, because it is universal, being found in all countries without exception, among all races of men. It is needless to pile up facts on an uncontroverted point.[1] Two will suffice; I choose them on account of their extravagance, which shows that at this particular moment animism, in certain minds, can dare anything. "One little fellow, aged one year eight months, conceived a special fondness for the letter W, addressing it thus: 'Dear old boy W.' Another little boy well on in his fourth year, when tracing a letter L, happened to slip, so that the horizontal limb formed an angle, thus: ⌐ He instantly saw the resemblance to the sedentary human form, and said: "Oh, he's sitting down." Similarly, when he made an F turn the wrong way and then put the correct form to the left, thus, ℲℲ, he exclaimed, 'They're talking together!'" One of Sully's correspondents says: "I had the habit of attributing intelligence not only to all living creatures . . . but even to stones and manufactured articles. I used to feel how dull it must be for the pebbles in the causeway to lie still and only see what was round about. When I walked out with a basket for putting flowers in, I used sometimes to pick up a pebble or two and carry them out to have a change."

[1] One will find a large number of examples in Sully's work, *Studies of Childhood*, Chapter ii, entitled "The Age of Imagination." Most of the observations given in the present chapter have been borrowed from this author.

Let us stop a moment in order to try to determine the nature of this strange mental state, all the more as we shall meet it again in primitive man, and since it presents the creative imagination at its beginning.

a. The first element is a fixed idea, or rather, an image, or group of images, that takes possession of consciousness to the exclusion of everything else:— it is the analogue of the state of suggestion in the hypnotized subject, with this sole difference—that the suggestion does not come from without, from another, but from the child itself—it is auto-suggestion. The stick that the child holds between his legs becomes for him an imaginary steed. The poverty of his mental development makes all the easier this contraction of the field of his consciousness, which assures the supremacy of the image.

b. This has as its basis a reality that it includes. This is an important detail to note, because this reality, however tiny, gives objectivity to the imaginary creation and incorporates it with the external world. The mechanism is like that which produces illusion, but with a stable character excluding correction. The child transforms a bit of wood or paper into another self, because he perceives only the phantom he has created; that is, the images, not the material exciting them, haunt his brain.

c. Lastly, this creative power investing the image with all its attributes of real existence is derived from a fundamental fact—the state of belief, i. e., adherence of the mind founded on purely subjective conditions. It does not come within my province to treat incidentally such a large question. Neglected by the older physiology, whose faculty-method inclined it toward this omission, belief or faith has recently become the object of numerous studies.[1] I necessarily limit myself to remarking that but for this psychic state, the nature of the imagination is totally incomprehensible. The peculiarity of the imagination is the production of a reality of human origin, and it succeeds therein only because of the faith accompanying the image.

Representation and belief are not completely separated; it is the nature of the image to appear at first as a real object. This psychological truth, though proven through observation, has made itself acceptable only with great difficulty. It has had to struggle on the one hand against the prejudices of common-sense for which imagination is synonymous with sham and vain appearance and opposed to the real as non-being to being; on the other hand, against a doctrine of the logicians who maintain that the idea is at first merely conceived with no affirmation of existence or non-existence (*apprehensio simplex*). This position, legitimate in logic, which is an abstract science, is altogether unacceptable in psychology, a concrete science. The psychological viewpoint giving the true nature of the image has prevailed little by little. Spinoza already asserts "that representations considered by them-

---

[1] Apropos of this subject compare especially the recent studies by William James, *Varieties of Religious Experience.* (Tr.)

selves contain no errors," and he "denies that it is possible to perceive [represent] without affirming." More explicitly, Hume assigns belief to our subjective dispositions: Belief does not depend on the nature of the idea, but on the manner in which we conceive it. Existence is not a quality added to it by us; it is founded on habit and is irresistible. The difference between fiction and belief consists of a feeling added to the latter but not to the former. Dugald Stewart treats the question purely as a psychologist following the experimental method. He enumerates very many facts whence he concludes that imagination is always accompanied by an act of belief, but for which fact the more vivid the image, the less one would believe it; but just the contrary happens—the strong representation commands persuasion like sensation itself. Finally, Taine treats the subject methodically, by studying the nature of the image and its primitive character of hallucination.[1] At present, I think, there is no psychologist who does not regard as proven that the image, when it enters consciousness, has two moments. During the first, it is objective, appearing as a full and complete reality; during the second, which is definitive, it is deprived of its objectivity, reduced to a completely internal event, through the effect of other states of consciousness

---

[1] Spinoza, *Ethics*, II, 49, *Scholium;* Hume, *Human Understanding*, Part III, Section VII ff.; Dugald Stewart, *Elements of the Philosophy of the Human Mind*, Vol. I, Ch. III; Taine, *On Intelligence*. Part II.

which oppose and finally annihilate its objective character. There is an affirmation, then negation; impulse, then inhibition.

Faith, being only a mode of existence, an attitude of the mind, owes its creative and vivifying power to general dispositions of our constitution. Besides the intellectual element which is its content, its material—the thing affirmed or denied—there are tendencies and other affective factors (desire, fear, love, etc.) giving the image its intensity, and assuring it success in the struggle against other states of consciousness. There are active faculties that we sometimes designate by the name "will," understanding by the term, as James says, not only deliberate volition, but all the factors of belief (hope, fear, passions, prejudices, sectarian feeling, and so forth),[1] and this has justly given rise to the truthful saying that the test of belief is action.[2] This explains how in love, religion, in the moral life, in politics, and elsewhere, belief can withstand the logical assaults of the rationalizing intelligence—its power is found everywhere. It lasts as long as the mind waits and consents; but, as soon as these affective and active dispositions disappear in life's experience, faith falls with them, leaving in its place a formless content, an empty and dead representation.

After this, is it necessary to remark that belief

[1] James, *The Will to Believe and Other Essays*, p. 10.

[2] Payot, *De la croyance*, 139 ff.

depends peculiarly on the motor elements of our organization and not on the intellectual? As there is no imagination without belief, nor belief without imagination, we return by another route to the thesis supported in the first part of this essay, that creative activity depends on the motor nature of images.

Insofar as concerns the special case of the child, the first of the two moments (the affirming) that the image undergoes in consciousness is all in all for him, the second (the rectifying) is nothing: there is hypertrophy of one, atrophy of the other. For the adult the contrary is true—in many cases, indeed, in consequence of experience and habit, the first moment, wherein the image should be affirmed as a reality, is only virtual, is literally atrophied. We must, however, remark that this applies only partially to the ignorant and even less to the savage.

We might, nevertheless, ask ourselves if the child's belief in his phantoms is complete, entire, absolute, unreserved. Is the stick that he bestrides perfectly identified with a horse? Was Sully's child, that showed its doll a series of engravings to choose from, completely deceived? It seems that we must rather admit an intermittence, an alteration between affirmation and negation. On the one hand, the skeptical attitude of those who laugh at it displeases the child, who is like a devout believer whose faith is being broken down. On the other hand, doubt must indeed arise in him from time to time, for without this, rectification could never occur—one belief opposes the other or drives it away. This second work proceeds little by little, but then, under this form, imagination retreats.

3. The third stage is that of play, which, in chronological order, coincides with the one just preceding. As a form of creation it is already known to us, but in passing from animals to children, it grows in complexity and becomes intellectualized. It is no longer a simple combination of images.

Play serves two ends—for experimenting: as such it is an introduction to knowledge, gives certain vague notions concerning the nature of things; for creating: this is its principal function.

The human child, like the animal, expends itself in movements, forms associations new to it, simulates defence, flight, attack; but the child soon passes beyond this lower stage, in order to construct by means of images (ideally). He begins by imitating: this is a physiological necessity, reasons for which we shall give later (see chapter iv. *infra*). He constructs houses, boats, gives himself up to large plans; but he imitates most in his own person and acts, making himself in turn soldier, sailor, robber, merchant, coachman, etc.

To the period of imitation succeed more serious attempts—he acts with a "spirit of mastery," he is possessed by his idea which he tends to realize. The personal character of creation is shown in that he is really interested only in a work that emanates from himself and of which he feels himself the cause. B. Perez relates that he wanted to give a lesson to his nephew, aged three and a half years, whose inventions seemed to him very poor. Perez scratched in the sand a trench resembling a river, planted little branches on both banks, and had water flow through it; put a bridge across, and launched boats. At each new act the child would remain cool, his admiration would always have to be waited for. Out of patience, he remarked shortly that "this isn't at all entertaining." The author adds: "I believed it useless to persist, and I trampled under foot, laughing at myself, my awkward attempt at a childish construction."[1] "I had already read it in many a book, but this time I had learned from experience that the free initiative of children is always superior to the imitations we pretend to make for them. In addition, this experience and others like it have taught me that their creative force is much weaker than has been said."

4. At the fourth stage appears romantic invention, which requires a more refined culture, being a purely internal, wholly imaginative (i. e., cast in images) creation. It begins at about three or four years of age. We know the taste of imaginative children for stories and legends, which they have repeated to them until surfeited: in this respect they resemble semi-civilized people, who listen greedily to rhapsodies for hours at a time, experiencing all the emotions appropriate to the

[1] B. Perez, *Les trois premières années de l'enfant*, p. 323.

incidents of the tale. This is the prelude to creation, a semi-passive, semi-active state, an apprentice period, which will permit them to create in their own turn. Thus the first attempts are made with reminiscences, and imitated rather than created.

Of this we find numerous examples in the special works. A child of three and a half saw a lame man going along a road, and exclaimed: "Look at that poor ole man, mamma, he has dot [got] a bad leg." Then the romance begins: He was on a high horse; he fell on a rock, struck his poor leg; he will have to get some powder to heal it, etc. Sometimes the invention is less realistic. A child of three often longed to live like a fish in the water, or like a star in the sky. Another, aged five years nine months, having found a hollow rock, invented a fairy story: the hole was a beautiful hall inhabited by brilliant mysterious personages, etc.[1]

This form of imagination is not as common as the others. It belongs to those whom nature has well endowed. It forecasts a development of mind above the average. It may even be the sign of an inborn vocation and indicate in what direction the creative activity will be orientated.

[1] Sully, *op. cit.*, pp. 59-61. Compayré, *L'évolution intellectuelle et morale de l'enfant*, p. 145.

(Some time ago the writer was riding on a train, when the engine, for some reason or other, began to slow up, jerking, puffing, almost groaning, until it finally came to a full stop. The groaning continued. A little girl of about three called to her mother, "Too-too sick, too-too sick," and when finally the train started on again, the child was overjoyed that "too-too" was well again. (Tr.))

Let us briefly recall the creative rôle of the imagination in language, through the intervening of a factor already studied—thinking by analogy, an abundant source of often picturesque metaphors. A child called the cork of a bottle "door;" a small coin was called by a little American a "baby dollar;" another, seeing the dew on the grass, said, "The grass is crying."

The extension of the meaning of words has been studied by Taine, Darwin, Preyer, and others. They have shown that its psychological mechanism depends sometimes on the perception of resemblance, again on association by contiguity, processes that appear and intermingle in an unforeseen manner. Thus, a child applies the word "mambro" at first to his nurse, then to a sewing machine that she uses, then by analogy to an organ that he sees on the street adorned with a monkey, then to his toys representing animals.[1] We have elsewhere given more similar cases, where we perceive the fundamental difference between thought by imagery and rational thought.

To conclude: At this period the imagination is the master-faculty and the highest form of intellectual development. It works in two directions, one principal—it creates plays, invents romances, and extends language; the other secondary—it contains a germ of thought and ventures a fanciful explanation of the world which can not yet be conceived according to abstract notions and laws.

[1] Sully, *op. cit.*, p. 164.

CHAPTER III

PRIMITIVE MAN AND THE CREATION OF MYTHS

We come now to a unique period in the history of the development of the imagination—its golden age. In primitive man, still confined in savagery or just starting toward civilization, it reaches its full bloom in the creation of myths; and we are rightly astonished that psychologists, obstinately attached to esthetics, have neglected such an important form of activity, one so rich in information concerning the creative imagination. Where, indeed, find more favorable conditions for knowing it?

Man, prior to civilization, is a purely imaginative being; that is, the imagination marks the summit of his intellectual development. He does not go beyond this stage, but it is no longer an enigma as in animals, nor a transitory phase as in the civilized child who rapidly advances to the age of reason; it is a fixed state, permanent and lasting throughout life.[1] It is there revealed to us in its entire spon-

[1] Primitive man has been defined as "he for whom sensuous data and images surpass in importance rational concepts." From this standpoint, many contemporary poets, novelists, and artists would be primitive. The mental state of the human

taneity: it has free rein; it can create without imitation or tradition; it is not imprisoned in any conventional form; it is sovereign. As primitive man has knowledge neither of nature nor of its laws, he does not hesitate to embody the most senseless imaginings flitting through his brain. The world is not, for him, a totality of phenomena subject to laws, and nothing limits or hinders him.

This working of the pure imagination, left to itself and unadulterated by the intrusion and tyranny of rational elements, becomes translated into one form—the creation of myths; an anonymous, unconscious work, which, as long as its rule lasts, is sufficient in every way, comprehends everything—religion, poetry, history, science, philosophy, law.

Myths have the advantage of being the incarnation of pure imagination, and, moreover, they permit psychologists to study them objectively. Thanks to the labors of the nineteenth century, they offer an almost inexhaustible content. While past ages forgot, misunderstood, disfigured, and often despised myths as aberrations of the human mind, as unworthy of an hour's attention, it is no longer necessary in our time to show their interest and importance, even for psychology, which, however, has not as yet drawn all the benefit possible from them.

individual is not enough for such a determination; we must also take account of the (comparative) simplicity of the social environment.

But before commencing the psychological study of the genesis and formation of myths considered as an objective emanation of the creative imagination, we must briefly summarize the hypotheses at present offered for their origin. We find two principal ones—the one, etymological, genealogical, or linguistic; the other, ethno-psychological, or anthropological.[1]

The first, whose principal though not sole champion is Max Müller, holds that myths are the result of a disease of language—words become things, "nomina numina." This transformation is the effect of two principal linguistic causes—(a) Polynomy; several words for one thing. Thus the sun is designated by more than twenty names in the Vedas; Apollo, Phaethon, Hercules are three personifications of the sun; *Varouna* (night) and *Yama* (death) express at first the same conception, and have become two distinct deities. In short, every word tends to become an entity having its attributes and its legends. (b) Homonomy, a single word for several things. The same adjective, "shining," refers to the sun, a fountain, spring, etc. This is another source of confusion. Let us also add metaphors taken literally, plays upon words, wrong construction, etc.

The opponents of this doctrine maintain that in

[1] Let us mention the euhemeristic theory of Herbert Spencer, taken up recently by Grant Allen *(The Evolution of the Idea of God*, 1897), who brings down all religious and mythic concepts from a single origin—the worship of the dead.

the formation of myths, words represent scarcely five per cent. Whatever may be the worth of this assertion, the purely philological explanation remains without value for psychology: it is neither true nor false—it does not solve the question; it merely avoids it. The word is only an occasion, a vehicle; without the working of the mind exciting it, nothing would change. Moreover, Max Müller himself has recently recognized this.[1]

The anthropological theory, much more general than the foregoing, penetrates further to psychological origins—it leads us to the first advances of the human mind. It regards the myth not as an accident of primitive life, but as a natural function, a mode of activity proper to man during a certain period of his development. Later, the mythic creations seem absurd, often immoral, because they are survivals of a distant epoch, cherished and consecrated through tradition, habits, and respect for antiquity. According to the definition that seems to me best adapted for psychology, the myth is "the psychological objectification of man in all the phenomena that he can perceive."[2] It is a humanization of nature according to processes peculiar to the imagination.

---

[1] "When I tried to briefly characterize mythology in its inner nature, I called it a disease of language rather than a disease of thought. The expression was strange but intentionally so, meant to arouse attention and to provoke opposition. For me, language and thought are inseparable." *Nouvelles études de Mythologie*, p. 51.

[2] Vignoli, *Mito e Scienza*, p. 27.

Are these two views irreconcilable? It does not seem so to me, provided we accept the first as only a partial explanation. In any event, both schools agree on one point important for us—that the material for myths is furnished by the observation of natural phenomena, including the great events of human life: birth, sickness, death, etc. This is the objective factor. The creation of myths has its explanation in the nature of human imagination— this is the subjective factor. We can not deny that most works on mythology have a very decided tendency to give the greater importance to the first factor; in which respect they need a little psychology. The periodic returns of the dawn, the sun, the moon and stars, winds and storms, have their effect also, we may suppose, on monkeys, elephants, and other animals supposedly the most intelligent. Have they inspired myths? Just the opposite: "the surprising monotony of the ideas that the various races have made final causes of phenomena, of the origin and destiny of man, whence it results that the numberless myths are reduced to a very small number of types,"[1] shows that it is the human imagination that takes the principal part and that it is on the whole perhaps not so rich as we are pleased to say—that it is even very poor, compared to the fecundity of nature.

Let us now study the psychology of this creative activity, reducing it to these two questions: How

[1] Marillier, Preface to the French translation of Andrew Lang's *Myth, Ritual, and Religion.*

are myths formed? What line does their evolution follow?

I

The psychology of the origin of the myth, of the work that causes its rise, may theoretically, and for the sake of facilitating analysis, be regarded as two principal moments—that of creation proper, and that of romantic invention.

a. The moment of creation presupposes two inseparable operations which, however, we have to describe separately. The first consists of attributing life to all things, the second of assigning qualities to all things.

Animating everything, that is attributing life and action to everything, representing everything to one's self as living and acting—even mountains, rocks, and other objects (seemingly) incapable of movement. Of this inborn and irresistible tendency there are so many facts in proof that an enumeration is needless: it is the rule. The evidence gathered by ethnologists, mythologists, and travelers fill large volumes. This state of mind does not particularly belong to long-past ages. It is still in existence, it is contemporary, and if we would see it with our own eyes it is not at all necessary to plunge into virgin countries, for there are frequent reversions even in civilized lands. On the whole, says Tylor, it must be regarded as conceded that to the lower races of humanity the sun and stars, the trees and rivers, the winds and clouds, become

animated creatures living like men and beasts, ful-
filling their special function in creation—or rather
that what the human eye can reach is only the
instrument or the matter of which some gigantic
being, like a man, hidden behind the visible things,
makes use. The grounds on which such ideas are
based cannot be regarded as less than a poetic fancy
or an ill-understood metaphor; they depend on a
vast philosophy of nature, certainly rude and primitive, but coherent and serious.

The second operation of the mind, inseparable,
as we have said, from the first, attributes to these
imaginary beings various qualities, but all important to man. They are good or bad, useful or
hurtful, weak or powerful, kind or cruel. One
remains stupefied before the swarming of these
numberless genii whom no natural phenomenon, no
act of life, no form of sickness escapes, and these
beliefs remain unbroken even among the tribes that
are in contact with old civilizations.[1] Primitive
man lives and moves among the ceaseless phantoms
of his own imagination.[2]

[1] On this point consult a work very rich in information,
W. Crooke's book, *Popular Religion and Folk-lore of Northern
India*, 1897.

[2] "The Indian traversing the Montaña never feels himself
alone. Legions of beings accompany him. All of the nature
to whom he owes his soul speaks to him through the noise of
the wind, in the roaring of the waterfall. The insect like the
bird—everything, even to the bending twig wet with dew—for
him has language, distinct personality. The forest is alive in
its depths, has caprices, periods of anger; it avoids the thicket

Lastly, the psychological mechanism of the creative moment is very simple. It depends on a single factor previously studied—thinking by analogy. It is a matter first of all—and this is important—of conceiving beings analogous to ourselves, cast in our mould, cut after our pattern; that is, feeling and acting; then qualifying them and determining them according to the attributes of our own nature. But the logic of images, very different from that of reason, concludes an objective resemblance; it regards as alike, what seem alike; it attributes to an internal linking of images, the validity of an objective connection between things. Whence arises the discord between the imagined world and the world of reality. "Analogies that for us are only fancies were for the man of past ages real" (Tylor).

b. In the genesis of myths, the second moment is that of fanciful invention. Entities take form; they have a history and adventures: they become the stuff for a romance. People of poor and dry imagination do not reach the second period. Thus, the religion of the Romans peopled the universe with an innumerable quantity of genii. No object, no act, no detail, but had its own presiding genius. There was one for germinating grain, for sprouting grain, for grain in flower, for blighted grain; for

under the tread of the huntsman, or again presses him more closely, drags him into infected swamps, into closed bogs, where miserable goblins exhaust all their witchcraft upon him, drink his blood by attaching their lips to the wounds made by briers. The Indian knows all that; he knows those dread genii by name." Monnier, *Des Andes au Para*, p. 300.

the door, its hinges, its lock, etc. There was a
myriad of misty, formless entities. This is animism
arrested at its first stage; abstraction has killed
imagination.

Who created those legends and tales of adventure
constituting the subject-matter of mythology?
Probably inspired individuals, priests or prophets.
They came perhaps from dreams, hallucinations,
insane attacks—they are derived from several
sources. Whatever their origin, they are the work
of imaginative minds *par excellence* (we shall study
them later) who, confronted with any event whatever, must, because of their nature, construct a
romance.

Besides analogy, this imaginative creation has as
its principal source the associational form already
described under the name "constellation." We
know that it is based on the fact that, in certain
cases, the arousing of an image-group is the result
of a tendency prevailing at a given instant over
several that are possible. This operation has already been expounded theoretically with individual
examples in support.[1] But in order to gauge its
importance, we must see it act in large masses.
Myths allow us to do this. Ordinarily they have
been studied in their historical development according to their geographical distribution or ethnic character. If we proceed otherwise, if we consider only
their content—i. e., the very few themes upon which
the human imagination has labored, such as celestial

[1] See Part I, Chapter IV.

phenomena, terrestrial disturbances, floods, the
origin of the universe, of man, etc.—we are sur-
prised at the wonderful richness of variety. What
diversity in the solar myths, or those of creation,
of fire, of water! These variations are due to
multiple causes, which have orientated the imagination now in one direction, now in another. Let
us mention the principal ones: Racial characteristics—whether the imagination is clear or mobile,
poor or exuberant; the manner of living—totally
savage, or on a level of civilization; the physical
environment—external nature cannot be reflected
in the brain of a Hindoo in the same way as in
that of a Scandinavian; and lastly, that assemblage
of considerable and unexpected causes grouped
under the term "chance."

The variable combinations of these different
factors, with the predominance of one or the other,
explain the multiplicity of the imaginative conceptions of the world, in contrast to the unity and
simplicity of scientific conceptions.

II

The form of imagination now occupying our
attention by reason of its non-individual, anonymous, collective character, attains a long development that we may follow in its successive phases
of ascent, climax, and decline. To begin with, is it
necessarily inherent in the human mind? Are there
races or groups of men totally devoid of myths?
which is a slightly different question from that

usually asked, "Are there tribes totally devoid of religious thoughts?" Although it is very doubtful that there are such now, it is probable that there were in the beginning, when man had scarcely left the brute level—at least if we agree with Vignoli[1] that we already find in the higher animals embryonic forms of animism.

In any event, mythic creation appears early. We can infer this from the signs of puerility of certain legends. Savages who could not know themselves —the Iroquois, the Australian aborigines, the natives of the Andaman Islands—believed that the earth was at first sterile and dry, all the water having been swallowed by a gigantic frog or toad which was compelled, by queer stratagems, to regurgitate it. These are little children's imaginings. Among the Hindoos the same myth takes the form of an alluring epic—the dragon watching over the celestial waters, of which he has taken possession, is wounded by Indra after a heroic battle, and restores them to the earth.

Cosmogonies, Lang remarks, furnish a good example of the development of myths; it is possible to mark out stages and rounds according to the degree of culture and intelligence. The natives of Oceania believe that the world was created and organized by spiders, grasshoppers, and various birds. More advanced peoples regard powerful animals as gods in disguise (such are certain Mexican divinities). Later, all trace of animal worship

[1] *Op. cit.*, pp. 23-24.

disappears, and the character of the myth is purely anthropomorphic.[1] Kühn, in a special work, has shown how the successive stages of social evolution express themselves in the successive stages of mythology—myths of cannibals, of hunters, of herders, land-tillers, sailors. Speaking of pure savagery, Max Müller[2] admits at least two periods—pan-Aryan and Indo-Iranian—prior to the Vedic period. In the course of this slow evolution the work of the imagination passes little by little from infancy, becomes more and more complex, subtle and refined.

In the Aryan race, the Vedic epoch, despite its sacerdotal ritualism, is considered as the period *par excellence* of mythic efflorescence. "The myth," says Taine, "is not here (in the Vedas) a disguise, but an expression; no language is more true and more supple: it permits a glimpse of, or rather causes us to discern, the forms of mist, the movements of the air, change of seasons, all the accidents of sky, fire, storm: external nature has never found a mode of thought so graceful and flexible for reflecting itself thereby in all the inexhaustible variety of her appearances. However changeable nature may be, the imagination is equally so."[3] It animates everything—not only fire in general, *Agni,* but also the seven forms of flame, the wood that lights it, the ten fingers of the sacrificing priest, the

[1] Lang, *op. cit.,* I, 162, and *passim.*

[2] Max Müller, *op cit.,* p. 12.

[3] *Nouveaux Essais,* p. 320.

prayer itself, and even the railing surrounding the altar. This is one example among many others. The partisans of the linguistic theory have been able to maintain that at this moment every word is a myth, because every word is a name designating a quality or an act, transformed by the imagination into substance. Max Müller has translated a page of Hesiod, substituting the analytic, abstract, rational language of our time for the image-making names. Immediately, all the mythical material vanishes. Thus, "Selene kisses the sleeping Endymion" becomes the dry formula, "It is night." The most skilled linguists often declare themselves unable to change the pliant tongue of the imaginative age into our algebraic idioms.[2] Thought by imagery cannot remain itself and at the same time take on a rational dress.

The mental state that marks the zenith of the free development of the imagination, is at present met with only in mystics and in some poets. Language has, however, preserved numerous vestiges of it in current expressions, the mythic signification of which has been lost—the sun rises, the sea is treacherous, the wind is mad, the earth is thirsty, etc.

To this triumphant period there succeeds among the races that have made progress in evolution, i. e., that have been able to rise above the age of (pure)

[2] See Lang, *Myth, Ritual and Religion*, I, p. 234, a passage from the *Rig-Veda*, with four very different translations by Max Müller, Wilson, Benfrey, and Langlois.

imagination, the period of waning, of regression, of decline. In order to understand it and perceive the how and why of it, let us first note that myths are reducible to two great categories:

a. The explicative myths, arising from utility, from the necessity of knowing. *These undergo a radical transformation.*

b. The non-explicative myths, resulting from a need of luxury, from a pure desire to create: these undergo only a *partial* transformation.

Let us follow them in the accomplishment of their destinies.

a. The myths of the first class, answering the various needs of knowing in order afterwards to act, are much the more numerous. . . . Is primitive man by nature curious? The question has been variously answered; thus, Tylor says yes; Spencer, no.[1] The affirmative and negative answers are not, perhaps, irreconcilable, if we take account of the differences in races. Taking it generally, it is hard to believe that he is not curious—he holds his life at that price. He is in the presence of the universe just as we are when confronted with an unknown animal or fruit. Is it useful or hurtful? He has all the more need for a conception of the world since he feels himself dependent on everything. While our subordination as regards nature is limited by the knowledge of her laws, he is on

[1] On curiosity as the beginning of knowledge, compare the position held by Plato. (Tr.)

account of his animism in a position similar to ours before an assembly of persons whom we have to approach or avoid, conciliate or yield to. It is necessary that he be *practically* curious—that is indispensable for his preservation. There has been alleged the indifference of primitive man to the complicated engines of civilization (a steamboat, a watch, etc.). This shows, not lack of curiosity, but absence of intelligence or interest for what he does not consider immediately useful for his needs.

His conception of the world is a product of the imagination, because no other is possible for him. The problem is imperatively set, he solves it as best he can; the myth is a response to a host of theoretical and practical needs. For him, the imaginative explanation takes the place of the rational explanation which is yet unborn, and which for great reasons can not arise—first, because the poverty of his experience, limited to a small circle, engenders a multitude of erroneous associations, which remain unbroken in the absence of other experiences to contradict and shatter them; secondly, because of the extreme weakness of his logic and especially of his conception of causality, which most often reduces itself to a *post hoc, ergo propter hoc.* Whence we have the thorough subjectivity of his interpretation of the world.[1]   In short, primitive

[1] On this general subject consult the interesting though somewhat general article by Professor John Dewey, ''The Interpretation of the Savage Mind,'' in the *Psychological Review,* May, 1903. The author justly criticises the current description of

man makes without exception or reserve, and in terms of images, what science makes provisionally, with reserves, and by means of concepts—namely, hypotheses.

Thus, the explicative myths are as we see, an epitome of a practical philosophy, proportioned to the requirements of the man of the earliest, or slightly-cultured ages. Then comes the period of critical transformation: a slow, progressive substitution of a rational conception of the world for the imaginative conception. It results from a work of *depersonification* of the myth, which little by little loses its subjective, anthropomorphic character in order to become all the more objective, without ever succeeding therein completely.

This transformation occurs thanks to two principal supports: methodical and prolonged observation of phenomena, which suggests the objective notion of stability and law, opposed to the caprices of animism (example: the work of the ancient astronomers of the Orient); the growing power of reflection and of logical rigor, at least in well-endowed races.

It does not concern the subject in hand to trace here the fortunes of the old battle whereby the imagination, assailed by a rival power, loses little by little its position and preponderance in the interpretation of the world. A few remarks will suffice.

savages in negative terms, and contends that there is general misunderstanding of the true nature of the savage and of his activities. (Tr.)

To begin with, the myth is transformed into philosophic speculation, but without total disappearance, as is seen in the mystic speculations of the Pythagoreans, in the cosmology of Empedocles, ruled by two human-like antitheses, Love and Hate. Even to Thales, an observing, positive spirit that calculates eclipses, the world is full of *daemons,* remains of primitive animism.[1]   In Plato, even leaving out his theory of Ideas, the employment of myth is not merely a playful mannerism, but a real survival.

This work of elimination, begun by the philosophers, is more firmly established in the first attempts of pure science (the Alexandrian mathematicians; naturalists like Aristotle; certain Greek physicians). Nevertheless, we know how imaginary concepts remained alive in physics, chemistry, biology, down to the sixteenth century; we know the bitter struggle that the two following centuries witnessed against occult qualities and loose methods. Even in our day, Stallo has been able to propose to write a treatise "On Myth in Science." Without speaking at this time of the hypotheses admitted as such and on account of their usefulness, there yet remain in the sciences many latent signs of primitive anthropomorphism. At the beginning of the nineteenth

---

[1] It is now well accepted that Thales cannot be regarded as propounding a materialistic theory when he declares that everything is derived from water; for with him, "water" stands not merely for the substance that we call chemically "H_2O," but for the "spirit that is in water" as well—the water-spirit is the *Grundprincip.*   (Tr.)

century people believed in several "properties of matter" that we now regard as merely modes of energy. But this latter notion, an expression of permanence underneath the various manifestations of nature, is for science only an abstract, symbolical formula : if we attempt to embody it, to make it concrete and representable, then, whether we will or no, it resolves itself into the feeling of muscular effort, that is, takes on a human character. To produce no other examples, we see that so far as concerns the last term of this slow regression, the imagination is not yet completely annulled, although it may have had to recede incessantly before a more solid and better armed rival.

b. In addition to the explanatory myths, there are those having no claim to be in this class, although they have perhaps been originally suggested by some phenomenon of animate or inanimate nature. They are much less numerous than the others, since they do not answer multiple necessities of life. Such are the epic or heroic stories, popular tales, romances (which are found as early as ancient Egypt) : it is the first appearance of that form of esthetic activity destined later to become literature. Here, the mythic activity suffers only a superficial metamorphosis—the essence is not changed. Literature is mythology transformed and adapted to the variable conditions of civilization. If this statement appear doubtful or disrespectful, we should note the following.

Historically, from myths wherein there figure at

first only divine personages, there arise the epics of the Hindoos, Greeks, Scandinavians, etc., in which the gods and heroes are confounded, live in the same world, on a level. Little by little the divine character is rubbed out; the myth approaches the ordinary conditions of human life, until it becomes the romantic novel, and finally the realistic story.

Psychologically, the imaginative work that has at first created the gods and superior beings before whom man bows because he has unconsciously produced them, becomes more and more humanized as it becomes conscious; but it cannot cease being a projection of the feelings, ideas, and nature of man into the fictitious beings upon whom the belief of their creator and of his hearers confers an illusory and fleeting existence. The gods have become puppets whose master man feels himself, and whom he treats as he likes. Throughout the manifold techniques, esthetics, documentary collections, reproductions of the social life, the creative activity of the earliest time remains at bottom unchanged. Literature is a decadent and rationalized mythology.

III

Does the mythic activity of ancient times still exist among civilized peoples, unmodified as in literary creation, but in its pure form, as a non-individual, collective, anonymous, unconscious, work? Yes; as the popular imagination, when creating legends. In passing from natural phenomena to historic events and persons, the construc-

tive imagination takes a slightly different position
which we may characterize thus: legend is to myth
what illusion is to hallucination.

The psychological mechanism is the same in both
cases. Illusion and legend are partial imaginations,
hallucination and myth are total imaginations. Illusion may vary in all shades between exact perception and hallucination; legend can run all the way
from exact history to pure myth. The difference
between illusion and hallucination is sometimes
imperceptible; the same is sometimes true of legend
and myth. Sensory illusion is produced by an
addition of images changing perception; legend is
also produced by an addition of images changing
the historic personage or event. The only difference, then, is in the material used; in one case, a
datum of sense, a natural phenomenon; in the other,
a fact of history, a human event.

The psychological genesis of legends being thus
established in general, what, according to the facts,
are the unconscious processes that the imagination
employs for creating them? We may distinguish
two principal ones.

The first process is a fusion or combination. The
myth precedes the fact; the historical personage or
event enters into the mould of a pre-existing myth.
"It is necessary that the mythic form be fashioned
before one may pour into it, in a more or less fluid
state, the historic metal." Imagination had created
a solar mythology long before it could be incarnated
by the Greeks in Hercules and his exploits. "There

was historically a Roland, perhaps even an Arthur, but the greater part of the great deeds that the poetry of the Middle Ages attributes to them had been accomplished long before by mythological heroes whose very names had been forgotten."[1] At one time the man is completely hidden by the myth and becomes absolutely legendary; again, he assumes only an aureole that transfigures him. This is exactly what occurs in the simpler phenomenon of sensory illusion: now the real (the perception) is swamped by the images, is transformed, and the objective element reduced to almost nothing; at another time, the objective element remains master, but with numerous deformations.

The second process is idealization, which can act conjointly with the other. Popular imagination incarnates in a real man its ideal of heroism, of loyalty, of love, of piety, or of cowardice, cruelty, wickedness, and other abnormalities. The process is more complex. It presupposes in addition to mythic creation a labor of abstraction, through which a dominating characteristic of the historic personage is chosen and everything else is suppressed, cast into oblivion: the ideal becomes a center of attraction about which is formed the legend, the romantic tale. Compare the Alexander, the Charlemagne, the Cid of the Middle Age traditions to the character of history.

Even much nearer to us, this process of extreme simplification—which the law of mental inertia or

[1] Max Müller, op. cit., 39, 47-48, 59-60.

of least effort is sufficient to explain—always persists: Lucretia Borgia remains the type of debauch-
ery, Henry IV of good fellowship, etc. The pro-
tests of historians and the documentary evidence
that they produce avail nothing: the work of the
imagination resists everything.

To conclude: We have just passed over a period
of mental evolution wherein the creative imagination reigns exclusively, explains everything, is sufficient for everything. It has been said that the
imagination is "a temporary derangement." It
seems so to us, although it is often an effort toward
wisdom, i. e., toward the comprehension of things.
It would be more correct to say, with Tylor, that it
represents a state intermediate between that of a
man of our time, prosaic and well-to-do, and that
of a furious madman, or of a man in the delirium
of fever.

CHAPTER IV

THE HIGHER FORMS OF INVENTION

We now pass from primitive to civilized man, from collective to individual creation, the characters of which it remains for us to study as we find them in great inventors who exhibit them on a large scale. Fortunately, we may dismiss the treatment of the oft-discussed, never-solved problem of the psychological nature of genius. As we have already noted, there enter into its composition factors other than the creative imagination, although the latter is not the least among them. Besides, great men being exceptions, anomalies, or as the current expression has it, "spontaneous variations," we may ask *in limine* whether their psychology is explicable by means of simple formulæ, as with the average man, or whether even monographs teach us no more concerning their nature than general theories that are never applicable to all cases. Taking genius, then, as synonymous with great inventor, accepting it *de facto* historically and psychologically, our task is limited to the attempt to separate characters that seem, from observation and experiment, to belong to it as peculiarly its own.

Putting aside vague dissertations and dithyrambics in favor of theories with a scientific tendency as to the nature of genius, we meet first the one attributing to it a pathological origin. Hinted at in antiquity (Aristotle, Seneca, etc.), suggested in the oft-expressed comparison between inspiration and insanity, it has reached, as we know—through timid, reserved, and partial statements (Lélut)— its complete expression in the famous formula of Moreau de Tours, "Genius is a neurosis."

Neuropathy was for him the exaggeration of vital properties and consequently the most favorable condition for the hatching of works of genius. Later, Lombroso, in a book teeming with doubtful or manifestly false evidence, finding his predecessor's theory too vague, attempts to give it more precision by substituting for neurosis in general a specific neurosis—larvated epilepsy. Alienists, far from eagerly accepting this view, have set themselves to combat it and to maintain that Lombroso has compromised everything in wanting to make the term too precise. There are several possible hypotheses, they say: either the neuropathic state is the direct, immediate cause of which the higher faculties of genius are effects; or, the intellectual superiority, through the excessive labor and excitation it involves, causes neuropathic disturbances; or, there is no relation of cause and effect between genius and neurosis, but mere coexistence, since there are found very mediocre neuropaths, and men above the average without a neurotic blemish; or, the two states—

the one psychic, the other physiological—are both effects, resulting from organic conditions that produce according to circumstances genius, insanity, and divers nervous troubles. Every one of these hypotheses can allege facts in its favor. We must, however, recognize that in most men of genius are found so many peculiarities, physical eccentricities and disorders of all kinds that the pathologic theory retains much probability.

There remain for consideration the sane geniuses who, despite many efforts and subtleties, have not yet been successfully brought under the foregoing formula, and who have made possible the enunciation of another theory. Recently, Nordau, rejecting the theory of his master Lombroso, has maintained that it is just as reasonable to say that "genius is a neurosis" as that "athleticism is a cardiopathy" because many athletes are affected with heart disease. For him, "the essential elements of genius are judgment and will." Following this definition, he establishes the following hierarchy of men of genius: At the highest rung of the ladder are those in whom judgment and will are equally powerful; men of action who make world-history (Alexander, Cromwell, Napoleon)—these are masters of men. On the second level are found the geniuses of judgment, with no hyper-development of will—these are masters of matter (Pasteur, Helmholtz, Röntgen). On the third step are geniuses of judgment without energetic will—

thinkers and philosophers. What then shall we do with the emotional geniuses—the poets and artists? Theirs is not genius in the strict sense, "because it creates nothing new and exercises no influence on phenomena." Without discussing the value of this classification, without examining whether it is even possible,—since there is no common measure between Alexander, Pasteur, Shakespeare, and Spinoza,—and whether, on the other hand, common opinion is not right in putting on the same level the great creators, whoever they be, solely because they are far above the average, this remark is absolutely necessary: In the definition above cited the creative faculty *par excellence*—imagination—necessary to all inventors, is entirely left out.

We can, however, derive some benefit from this arbitrary division. Although it is impossible to admit that "emotional geniuses" create nothing new and have no influence on society, they do form a special group. Creative work requires of them a nervous excitability and a predominance of affective states that rapidly become morbid. In this way they have provided the pathological theory with most of its facts. It would perhaps be necessary to recognize distinctions between the various forms of invention. They require very different organic and psychic conditions in order that some may profit by morbid dispositions that are far from useful to others. This point should deserve a special study never made hitherto.

I

We shall reduce to three the characters ordinarily met in most great inventors. No one of them is without exception.

1. *Precocity,* which is reducible to innateness. The natural bent becomes manifest as soon as circumstances allow—it is the sign of the true vocation. The story is the same in all cases: at one moment the flash occurs; but this is not as frequent as is supposed. False vocations abound. If we deduct those attracted through imitation, environmental influence, exhortations and advice, chance, the attraction of immediate gain, aversion to a career imposed from without which they shun and adoption of an opposite one, will there remain many natural and irresistible vocations?

We have seen above that[1] the passage from reproductive to constructive imagination takes place toward the end of the third year. According to some authors, this initial period should be followed by a depression about the fifth year; thenceforward the upward progress is continuous. But the creative faculty, from its nature and content, develops in a very clear, chronological order. Music, plastic arts, poetry, mechanical invention, scientific imagination—such is the usual order of appearance.

In music, with the exception of a few child-prodigies, we hardly find personal creation before the age of twelve or thirteen. As examples of precocity

[1] See above, Chapter II.

may be cited: Mozart, at the age of three; Mendelssohn, five; Haydn, four; Handel, twelve; Weber, twelve; Schubert, eleven; Cherubini, thirteen; and many others. Those late in developing—Beethoven, Wagner, etc.—are fewer by far.[2]

In the plastic arts, vocation and creative aptitude are shown perceptibly later, on the average about the fourteenth year: Giotto, at ten; Van Dyck, ten; Raphael, eight; Guerchin, eight; Greuze, eight; Michaelangelo, thirteen; Albrecht Dürer, fifteen; Bernini, twelve; Rubens and Jordaens being also precocious.

In poetry we find no work having any individual character before sixteen. Chatterton died at that age, perhaps the only example of so young a poet leaving any reputation. Schiller and Byron also began at sixteen. Besides this, we know that the talent for versification, at least as imitation, is very early in developing.

In mechanical arts children have early a remarkable capacity for understanding and imitating. At nine, Poncelet bought a watch that was out of order in order to study it, then took it apart and put it together correctly. Arago tells that at the same age Fresnel was called by his comrades a "man of genius," because he had determined by correct experiments "the length and caliber of children's elder-wood toy cannon giving the longest range; also, which green or dry woods used in the

[2] Some of these and the following figures are borrowed from Oelzelt-Newin, *op. cit.*, pp. 70 ff.

manufacture of bows have most strength and lasting power." In general, the average of mechanical invention is later, and scarcely comes earlier than that of scientific discovery.

The form of abstract imagination requisite for invention in the sciences has no great personal value before the twentieth year: there are a goodly number, however, who have given proof of it before that age—Pascal, Newton, Leibniz, Gauss, Auguste Comte, etc. Almost all are mathematicians.

These chronological variations result not from chance, but from psychological conditions necessary for the development of each form of imagination. We know that the acquisition of musical sounds is prior to speech: many children can repeat a scale correctly before they are able to talk. On the other hand, as dissolution follows evolution in inverse order,[1] aphasic patients lacking the most common words, can nevertheless sing. Sound-images are thus organized before all others, and the creative power when acting in this direction finds very early material for its use. For the plastic arts a longer apprenticeship is necessary for the education of the senses and movements. To acquire manual dexterity one must become skilled in observing form, combinations of lines and colors, and apt at reproducing them. Poetry and first attempts at novel-writing presuppose some experience of the passions of human life and a certain reflection of which the

[1] Compare the well-known theory of Dr. Hughlings-Jackson. (Tr.)

child is incapable. Invention in the mechanic arts, as in the plastic arts, requires the education of the senses and movements; and, further, calculation, rational combination of means, rigorous adaptation to practical necessities. Lastly, scientific imagination is nothing without a high development of the capacity for abstraction, which is a matter of slow growth. Mathematicians are the most precocious because their material is the most simple; they have no need, as in the case of the experimental sciences, of an extended knowledge of facts, which is acquired only with time.

At this period of its development the imagination is in large part imitation. We must explain this paradox. The creator begins by imitating: this is such a well-known fact that it is needless to give proof of it, and it is subject to few exceptions. The most original mind is, at first, consciously or unconsciously somebody's disciple. It is necessarily so. Nature gives only one thing, "the creative instinct;" that is, the need of producing in a determined line. This internal factor alone is insufficient. Aside from the fact that the imagination at first has at its disposal only a very limited material, it lacks technique, the processes indispensable for realizing itself. As long as the creator has not found the suitable form into which to cast his creation he must indeed borrow it from another; his ideas must suffer the necessity of a provisional shelter. This explains how it is that later the inventor, reaching full consciousness of himself, in order to complete mastery of his methods, often breaks with his models, and burns what he at first adorned.

II

A second character consists of the necessity, the fatality of creation. Great inventors feel that they have a task to accomplish; they feel that they are charged with a mission. On this point we have a large number of testimonials and avowals. In the darkest days of his life Beethoven, haunted by the thought of suicide, wrote, "Art alone has kept me back. It seemed to me that I could not leave the world before producing all that I felt within me." Ordinarily, inventors are apt in only one line; even when they have a certain versatility, they remain bound to their own peculiar manner—they have their mark—like Michaelangelo; or, if they attempt to change it, if they try to be unfaithful as respects their vocation, they fall much below themselves.

This characteristic of irresistible impulsion which makes the genius create not because he wants to, but because he must do it, has often been likened to instinct. This very widespread view has been examined before (Part I, Chapter ii).

We have seen that there is no creative instinct in general, but *particular* tendencies, orientated in a definite direction, which in most respects resemble instinct. It is contrary to experience and logic to admit that the creative genius follows any path whatever at his choice—a proposition that Weis-

mann, in his horror of inheritance of acquired characters (which are a kind of innateness) is not afraid
to support. That is true only of the man of talent,
a matter of education and circumstances. The distinction between these two orders of creators—the
great and the ordinary—has been made too often
to need repetition, although it is proper to recognize
that it is not always easy in practice, that there are
names that cause us to hesitate, which we class
somewhat at hazard. Yet genius remains, as Schopenhauer used to say, *monstrum per excessum;* excessive development in one direction. Hypertrophy
of a special aptitude often makes genius fall, as far
as the others are concerned, below the average level.
Even those exceptional men who have given proof
of multiple aptitudes, such as Vinci, Michaelangelo,
Goethe, etc., always have a predominating tendency
which, in common opinion, sums them up.

III

A third characteristic is the clearly defined *individuality* of the great creator. He is the man of
his work; he has done this or that: that is his
mark. He is "representative." There is no other
opinion as to this; what is a subject of discussion
is the *origin,* not the nature of this individuality.
The Darwinian theory as to the all-powerful action
of environment has led to the question whether the
representative character of great inventors comes
from themselves, and from them alone, or must

not rather be sought in the unconscious influence of
the race and epoch of which they are at a given
instant only brighter sparks. This debate goes beyond the bounds of our subject. To decide whether
social changes are due mostly to the accumulated
influences of some individuals and their initiative,
or to the environment, to circumstances, to hereditary transmission, is not a problem for psychology
to solve. We can not, however, totally avoid this
discussion, for it touches the very springs of creation.

Is the inventive genius the highest degree of personality or a synthesis of masses?—the result of
himself or of others?—the expression of an individual activity or of a collective activity? In short,
should we look for his representative character
within him or without? Both these alternatives
have authoritative supporters.

For Schopenhauer, Carlyle (*Hero-worship*),
Nietzsche, *et al.*, the great man is an autonomous
product, a being without a peer, a demigod, *"Ueber-
mensch."* He can be explained neither by heredity,
nor by environment.

For others (Taine, Spencer, Grant, Allen, *et al.*),
the important factor is seen in the race and external
conditions. Goethe held that a whole family line is
summarized some day in a single one of its members, and a whole people in one or several men.
For him, Louis XIV and Voltaire are respectively
the French king and writer *par excellence.* "The

alleged great men," says Tolstoi, "are only the labels
of history, they give their names to events."[1]

Each party explains the same facts according to
its own principle and in its own peculiar way. The
great historic epochs are rich in great men (the
Greek republics of the fourth century B. C., the
Roman Republic, the Renaissance, French Revolution, etc.). Why? Because, say some, periods put
into ferment by the the deep working of the masses
make this blossoming possible. Because, say the
others, this flowering modifies profoundly the social
and intellectual condition of the masses and raises
their level. For the former the ferment is deep
down; for the latter it is on top.

Without presuming to solve this vexed question,
I lean toward the view of individualism pure and
simple. It seems to me very difficult to admit that
the great creator is only the result of his environment. Since this influence acts on many others,
it is very necessary that, in great men, there should
be in addition a personal factor. Besides, in opposition to the exclusively environmental theory we
may bring the well-known fact that most innovators and inventors at first arouse opposition. We
know the invariable sentence on everything novel—
it is "false" or "bad;" then it is adopted with the
statement that it had been known for a long time.

[1] For an elaborate and interesting discussion of this subject,
see Tolstoi's *Physiology of War*. As showing the later trend
of thought on this general theme, see the excellent summary by
Professor Seligman, *The Economic Interpretation of History*.
(Tr.)

In the hypothesis of collective invention, it seems that the mass of people should applaud inventors, recognizing itself in them, seeing its confused thought take form and body: but most often the contrary happens. The misoneism of crowds seems to me one of the strongest arguments in favor of the individual character of invention.

We can doubtless distinguish two cases—in the first, the creator sums up and clearly translates the aspirations of his *milieu;* in the second, he is in opposition to it because he goes beyond it. How many innovators have been disappointed because they came before their time! But this distinction does not reach to the bottom of the question, and is not at all sufficient as an answer.

Let us leave this problem, which, on account of its complexity, we can hardly solve through peremptory reasoning, and let us try to examine *objectively* the relation between creation and environment in order that we may see to what extent the creative imagination, without losing its individual character—which is impossible—depends on the intellectual and social surrounding.

If, with the American psychologists,[1] we term the disposition for innovating a "spontaneous variation"—a Darwinian term explaining nothing, but convenient—we may enunciate the following law:

[1] William James, *The Will to Believe and other Essays,* pp. 218 ff.; Jastrow, *Psych. Rev.,* May, 1898, p. 307; J. Royce, *ibid.,* March, 1898; Baldwin, *Social and Ethical Interpretations,* etc.

The tendency toward spontaneous variation (in-vention) is always in inverse ratio to the simplicity of the environment.

The savage environment is in its nature very simple, consequently homogeneous. The lower races show a much smaller degree of differentiation than the higher; in them, as Jastrow says, physical and psychic maturity is more precocious, and as the period just before the adult age is the plastic period *per se,* this diminishes the chances of a departure from the common type. Thus comparison between whites and blacks, between primitive and civilized peoples, shows that, for equal populations, there is an enormous disproportion as to the number of innovators.

The barbarian environment is much more complex and heterogeneous: it contains all the rudiments of civilized life. Consequently, it favors more individual variations and is richer in superior men. But these variations are rarely produced outside of a very restricted field—political, military, religious. So it seems impossible to agree with Joly[2] that neither primitive nor barbarian peoples produce superior minds, "unless," as he says, "by this name we mean those that simply surpass their congeners." But is there a criterion other than that? I see none. Greatness is altogether a relative idea; and would not our great creators seem, to beings better endowed than we, very small?

The civilized environment, requiring division of

[2] Joly, *Psychologie des grands hommes.*

labor and consequently a constantly growing complexity of heterogeneous elements, is an open door for all vocations. Doubtless, the social spirit always retains something of that tendency toward stagnation that is the rule in lower social orders; it is more favorable to tradition than to innovation. But the inevitable necessity of a warm competition between individuals and peoples is a natural antidote for that natural inertia; it favors useful variations. Moreover, civilization means evolution; consequently the conditions under which the imagination is active change with the times. Let us suppose, Weismann justly says, that in the Samoan Islands there were born a child having the singular and extraordinary genius of Mozart. What could he accomplish? At the most, extend the gamut of three or four tones to seven, and create a few more complex melodies; but he would be as unable to compose symphonies as Archimedes would have been to invent an electric dynamo. How many creators have been wrecked because the conditions necessary for their inventions were lacking? Roger Bacon foresaw several of our great discoveries; Cardan, the differential calculus; Van Helmont, chemistry; and it has been possible to write a book on the forerunners of Darwin.[1] We talk so much of the free flight of imagination, of the all-comprehensive power of the creator, that we forget the sociological conditions—not to mention others— on which they are every moment dependent. In

[1] Osborn, *From the Greeks to Darwin.*

this respect, no invention is personal in the strict sense; there always remains in it a little of that anonymous collaboration the highest expression of which, as we have seen, is the mythic activity.

By way of summary, and whatever be the causes, we may say that there is a universal tendency in all living matter toward variation, whether we consider vegetables, animals, or the physical and mental man. The need of innovating is only a special case, rare in the lower races, frequent in the higher. This tendency toward variation is fundamental or superficial: As fundamental, it corresponds to genius, and survives through processes analogous to natural selection, i. e., by its own power. As superficial, it corresponds to talent, survives and prospers chiefly through the help of circumstances and environment. Here, the orientation comes from without, not from within. According as the spirit of the time inclines rather to poetry or painting, or music, or scientific research, or industry, or military art, minds of the second order are dragged into the current—showing that a goodly part of their power is in the aptness, not for invention, but for *imitation*.

II

The determination of the characters belonging to the inventive genius has necessitated some seemingly irrelevant remarks on the action of the environment. Let us return to invention, strictly so-called.

For inventing there is always required a natural aptitude, sometimes, a happy chance.

The natural disposition should be accepted as a fact. Why does a man create? Because he is capable of forming new combinations of ideas. However naïve this answer may be, there is no other. The only thing possible, is the determination of the conditions necessary and sufficient for producing novel combinations: this has been done in the first part of this book, and there is no occasion for going over it again. But there is another aspect in creative work to be considered—its psychological *mechanism,* and the form of its development.

Every normal person creates little or much. He may, in his ignorance, invent what has been already done a thousand times. Even if this is not a creation as regards the species, it is none the less such for the individual. It is wrong to say, as has been said, that an invention "is a new and important idea." *Novelty* only is essential—that is the psychological mark: importance and utility are accessory, merely social marks. Invention is thus unduly limited when we attribute it to great inventors only. At this moment, however, we are concerned only with these, and in them the mechanism of invention is easier to study.

We have already seen how false is the theory that holds that there is always a sudden stroke of inspiration, followed by a period of rapid or slow execution. On the contrary, observation reveals many processes that apparently differ less in the *content* of invention than according to individual temperament. I distinguish two general processes of which the rest are variations. In all creation, great or small, there is a directing idea, an "ideal"— understanding the word not in its transcendental sense, but merely as synonymous with end or goal— or more simply, a problem to solve. The *locus* of the idea, of the given problem, is not the same in the two processes. In the one I term "complete" the ideal is at the beginning: in the "abridged" it is in the middle. There are also other differences which the following tables will make more clear:

First Process (*complete*).

1st phase	2nd phase	3d phase
IDEA (commencement	INVENTION, or	VERIFICATION, or
Special incubation of more or less duration	DISCOVERY (end)	APPLICATION

The idea excites attention and takes a fixed character. The period of brooding begins. For Newton it lasted seventeen years, and at the time of definitely establishing his discovery by calculation he was so overcome with emotion that he had to assign to another the task of completing it. The mathematician Hamilton tells us that his method of quaternians burst upon him one day, completely finished, while he was near a bridge in Dublin. "In that moment I had the result of fifteen years' labor." Darwin gathers material during his voyages, spends a long time observing plants and animals, then through the chance reading of Malthus' book, hits upon and formulates his theory. In literary and artistic creation similar examples are frequent.[1]

The second phase is only an instant, but essential—the moment of discovery, when the creator exclaims his "Eureka!"[2] With it, the work is virtually or really ended.

Second Process (abridged).

1st phase	2nd phase	3rd phase
General preparation (unconscious)	IDEA (commencement) INSPIRATION ERUPTION	CONSTRUCTIVE and DEVELOPING period.

This is the process in intuitive minds. Such seems to have been the case of Mozart, Poe, etc. Without attempting what would be a tedious enumeration of examples, we may say that this form of creation comprises two classes—those coming to maturity through an internal impulse, a sudden stroke of inspiration, and those who are suddenly illumined by chance. The two processes differ superficially rather than essentially. Let us briefly compare them.

With some, the first phase is long and fully con-

---

[1] Such, according to Binet and Passy, seem to be the cases of the Goncourts, Pailleron, etc. See "Psychologie des auteurs dramatiques," in L'année psychologique, I, 96.

[2] Compare the striking instance of this moment as given by Froebel, in his Autobiography, in connection with his idea of the Kindergarten. (Tr.)

scious; in others it seems negligible, equal to zero—
there is nothing of it because there exists a natural
or acquired tendency toward equilibrium. "For a
long time," says Schumann, "I had the habit of
racking my brain, and now I scarcely need to scratch
my forehead. Everything runs naturally."[1]

The second phase is almost the same in both
cases: it is only an instant, but it is essential—it
is the moment of imaginative synthesis.

Lastly, the third phase is very short for some,
because the main labor is already done, and there
remains only the finishing touch or the verification.
It is long for others, because they must pass from
the perceived idea to complete realization, and because the preparatory work is faulty; so that for
these the second creative process is shortened in
appearance only.

Such seem to me the two principal forms of the
mechanism of creation. These are genera; they
include species and varieties that a patient and
minute study of the processes peculiar to various
inventors would reveal to us. We must bear in
mind that this work makes no claim of being a
monograph on invention, but merely a sketch.[2]

The two processes above described seem to corre-

---

[1] Quoted by Arréat, *Mémoire et Imagination*, p. 118. (Paris,
F. Alcan.)

[2] Paulhan ("De l'invention," *Rev. Philos.*, December, 1898,
pp. 590 ff.) distinguishes three kinds of development in invention: (1) Spontaneous or reasoned—the directing idea persists to the end; (2) transformation, which comprises several
contradictory evolutions succeeding and replacing one another

spond on the whole to the oft-made distinction between the intuitive or spontaneous, and the combining or reflective imagination.

The intuitive, essentially synthetic form, is found principally in the purely imaginative types, children and savages. The mind proceeds from the whole to details. The generative idea resembles those concepts which, in the sciences, are of wide range because they condense a generalization rich in consequences. The subject is at first comprehended as a whole; development is organic, and we may compare it to the embryological process that causes a living being to arise from the fertilized ovum, analogous to an immanent logic. As a type of this creative form there has often been given a letter wherein Mozart explains his mode of conception. Recently (and that is why I do not reprint it here) it has been suspected of being apocryphal. I regret this—it was worthy of being authentic. According to Goethe, Shakespeare's *Hamlet* could have been created only through an intuitive process, etc.

The combining, discursive imagination proceeds from details to the vaguely-perceived unity. It starts from a fragment that serves as a matrix, and becomes completed little by little. An adventure, an anecdote, a scene, a rapid glance, a detail, suggests a literary or artistic creation; but the organic form does not appear in a trice. In science, Kepler furnishes a good example of this combining imagina-

in consequence of impressions and feelings; (3) deviation, which is a composite of the two preceding forms.

tion. It is known that he devoted a part of his life trying strange hypotheses, until the day when, having discovered the elliptical orbit of Mars, all his former work took shape and became an organized system. Did we want to make use once more of an embryological comparison, it would be necessary to look for it in the strange conceptions of ancient cosmogonies: they believed that from an earthly slime arose parts of bodies and separate organs which through a mysterious attraction and happy chance ended by sticking together, and forming living bodies.[1]

It is an accepted view that of these two modes, one, the abridged or intuitive process, is superior to the other. I confess to having held this prejudice. On examination, I find it doubtful, even false. There is a *difference*, not any "higher" and "lower."

First of all, both these forms of creation are necessary. The intuitive process can suffice for an invention of short duration: a rhyme, a story, a profile, a *motif*, an ornamental stroke, a little mechanical contrivance, etc. But as soon as the work requires time and development the discursive process becomes absolutely necessary: with many inventors one easily perceives the change from one form to the other. We have seen that in the case of Chopin, "creation was spontaneous, miraculous," coming complete and sudden. But George Sand adds: "The crisis over, then commenced the most heartrending labor at which I have ever been pres-

[1] Cf. the well-known doctrine of Empedocles. (Tr.)

ent," and she pictures him to us agonized, for days and weeks, running after the bits of lost inspiration. Goethe, likewise, in a letter to Humboldt regarding his Faust, which occupied him for sixty years, full of interruptions and gaps: "The difficulty has been to get through strength of will what is really to be gotten only by a spontaneous act of nature." Zola, according to his biographer, Toulouse, "imagines a novel, always starting out with a general idea that dominates the work; then, from induction to induction, he draws out of it the characters and all the story."

To sum up: Pure intuition and pure combination are exceptional; ordinarily, it is a mixed process in which one of the two elements prevails and permits its qualification. If we note, in addition, that it would be easy to group under these two headings names of the first rank, we shall conclude that the difference is altogether in the *mechanism,* not in the *nature* of creation, and is consequently accessory; and that this difference is reducible to natural dispositions, which we may contrast as follows:

Ready-witted minds, excelling in conception, making the whole almost out of one piece.	Logically - developing minds, excelling in elaboration.
Work primarily unconscious.	Patience the preponderating rôle.
	Work primarily conscious.
Actions quick.	Actions slow.

III

"Were we to raise monuments to inventors in the arts and sciences, there would be fewer statues to men than to children, animals, and especially *fortune*." In this wise expressed himself one of the sage thinkers of the eighteenth century, Turgot. The importance of the last factor has been much exaggerated. Chance may be taken in two senses— one general, the other narrow.

(1) In its broad meaning, chance depends on entirely internal, purely psychic circumstances. We know that one of the best conditions for inventing is abundance of material, accumulated experience, knowledge—which augment the chances of original association of ideas. It has even been possible to maintain that the nature of memory implies the capacity of creating in a special direction. The revelations of inventors or of their biographers leave no doubt as to the necessity of a large number of sketches, trials, preliminary drawings, no matter whether it is a matter of industry, commerce, a machine, a poem, an opera, a picture, a building, a plan of campaign, etc. "Genius for discovery," says Jevons, depends on the number of notions and chance thoughts coming to the inventor's mind. To be fertile in hypotheses—that is the first requirement for finding something new. The inventor's brain must be full of forms, of melodies, of mechanical agents, of commercial combinations, of figures, etc., according to the nature of his work. "But it is

very rare that the ideas we find are exactly those we were seeking. In order to find, *we must think along other lines.*"[1]   Nothing is more true.

So much for chance within: it is indisputable, whatever may have been said of it, but it depends finally on individuality—from it arises the non-anticipated synthesis of ideas. The abundance of memory-ideas, we know, is not a sufficient condition for creation; it is not even a necessary condition. It has been remarked that a relative ignorance is sometimes useful for invention: it favors assurance. There are inventions, especially scientific and industrial, that could not have been made had the inventors been arrested by the ruling and presumably invincible dogmas. The inventor was all the more free the more he was unaware of them. Then, as it was quite necessary to bow before the accomplished fact, theory was broadened to include the new discovery and explain it.

(2)   Chance, in the narrow sense, is a fortunate occurrence stimulating invention: but to attribute to it the greater part, is a partial, erroneous view. Here, what we call chance, is the meeting and convergence of *two* factors—one internal (individual genius), the other, external (the fortuitous occurrence).

It is impossible to determine all that invention owes to chance in this sense. In primitive humanity its influence must have been enormous: the use of fire, the manufacture of weapons, of utensils, the

[1] P. Souriau, *Théorie de l'invention*, pp. 6-7.

casting of metals: all that came about through accidents as simple as, for example, a tree falling across
a stream suggesting the first idea of a bridge.

In historic times—and to keep merely to the
modern period—the collection of authentic facts
would fill a large volume. Who does not know of
Newton's apple, Galileo's lamp, Galvani's frog?
Huyghens declared that, were it not for an unforeseen combination of circumstances, the invention of
the telescope would require "a superhuman genius;"
it is known that we owe it to children who were
playing with pieces of glass in an optician's shop.
Schönbein discovered ozone, thanks to the phos-
phorous odor of air traversed by electric sparks.
The discoveries of Grimaldi and of Fresnel in regard to interferences, those of Faraday, of Arago,
of Foucault, of Fraunhofer, of Kirchoff, and of
hundreds of others owed something to "fortune."
It is said that the sight of a crab suggested to Watt
the idea of an ingenious machine. To chance, also,
many poets, novelists, dramatists, and artists have
owed the best part of their inspirations: literature
and the arts abound in fictitious characters whose
real originals are known.

So much for the external, fortuitous factor; its
rôle is clear. That of the internal factor is less so.
It is not at all apparent to the ordinary mind, escaping the unreflecting. Yet it is extremely important.
The same fortuitous event passes by millions of
men without exciting anything. How many of
Pisa's inhabitants had seen the lamp of their cathe-

dral before Galileo! He does not necessarily find who wants to find. The happy chance comes only to those worthy of it. In order to profit thereby, one must first possess the spirit of observation, wide-awake attention, that isolates and fixates the accident; then, if it is a matter of scientific or practical inventions, the penetration that seizes upon relations and finds unforeseen resemblances; if it concerns esthetic productions, the imagination that constructs, organizes, gives life.

Without repeating an evident truism, although it is often misunderstood, we ought to end by remarking that *chance is an occasion for, not an agent of, creation.*

CHAPTER V

LAW OF THE DEVELOPMENT OF THE IMAGINATION

Is imagination, so often called "a capricious faculty," subject to some law? The question thus asked is too simple, and we must make it more precise.

As the direct cause of invention, great or small, the imagination acts without assignable determinatoin; in this sense it is what is known as "spontaneity"—a vague term, which we have attempted to make clear. Its appearance is irreducible to any law; it results from the often fortuitous convergence of various factors previously studied.

Leaving aside the moment of origin, does the inventive power, considered in its individual and specific development, seem to follow any law, or, if this term appear too ambitious, does it present, in the course of its evolution, any perceptible regularity? Observation separates out an empirical law; that is, extracts directly an abridged formula that is only a condensation of facts. We may enunciate it thus: The creative imagination in its complete development passes through two periods separated

by a critical phase: a period of autonomy or efflorescence, a critical moment, a period of definitive constitution presenting several aspects.

This formula, being only a summary of experience, should be justified and explained by the latter.
For this purpose we can borrow facts from two distinct sources: (a) individual development, which is
the safest, clearest, and easiest to observe; (b) the
development of the species, or historical development, according to the accepted principle that phylo-
genesis and ontogenesis follow the same general
line.

I

First Period.   We are already acquainted with
it: it is the imaginative age.   In normal man, it
begins at about the age of three, and embraces infancy, adolescence, youth: sometimes a longer,
sometimes a shorter period.   Play, romantic invention, mythic and fantastic conceptions of the world
sum it up first; after that, in most, imagination is
dependent on the influence of the passions, and
especially sexual love.   For a long time it remains
without any rational element.

Nevertheless, little by little, the latter wins a
place.   Reflection—including under the term the
working of the intelligence—begins very late, grows
slowly, and the proportion as it asserts itself, gains
an influence over the imaginative activity and tends
to reduce it.   This growing antagonism is represented in the following figure.

The curve IM is that of the imagination during this first period. It rises at first very slowly, then attains a rapid ascent and keeps at a height that marks its greatest attainment in this earliest form. The dotted line RX represents the rational develop-

ment that begins later, advances much more slowly, but progressively, and reaches at X the level of the imaginative curve. The two intellectual forms are present like two rivals. The position MX on the ordinate marks the beginning of the second period.

Second Period. This is a critical period of indeterminate length, in any case, always much briefer than the other two. This critical moment can be characterized only by its causes and results. Its causes are, in the physiological sphere, the formation of an organism and a fully developed brain; in the psychologic order, the antagonism between the pure subjectivity of the imagination and the objectivity of ratiocinative processes; in other words, between mental instability and stability. As for the results, they appear only in the third period, the resultant of this obscure, metamorphic stage.

Third Period. It is definite: in some way or another and in some degree the imagination has become rationalized, but this change is not reducible to a single formula.

(1) The creative imgination falls, as is indicated in the figure, where the imagination curve MN′ descends rapidly toward the line of abcissas without ever reaching it. This is the most general case; only truly imaginative minds are exceptions. One falls little by little into the prose of practical life—such is the downfall of love which is treated as a phantom, the burial of the dreams of youth, etc. This is a regression, not an end; for the creative imagination disappears completely in no man; it only becomes accessory.

(2) It keeps up but becomes transformed; it adapts itself to the conditions of rational thought; it is no longer pure imagination, but becomes a mixed form—the fact is indicated in the diagram by the union of the two lines, MN, the imagination, and XO, the rational. This is the case with truly imaginative beings, in whom inventive power long remains young and fresh.

This period of preservation, of definitive constitution with rational transformation, presents several varieties. First, and simplest, *transformation into logical form.* The creative power manifested in the first stage remains true to itself, and always follows the same trend. Such are the precocious inventors, those whose vocation appeared early and never changed direction. Invention loses its childish

or juvenile character in becoming virile; there are
no other changes. Compare Schiller's *Robbers,*
written in his teens, with his *Wallenstein,* dating
from his fortieth year; or the vague sketches of
the adolescent James Watt with his inventions as a
man.

Another case is the *metamorphosis* or *deviation*
of creative power. We know what numbers of men
who have left a great name in science, politics, mechanical or industrial invention started out with
mediocre efforts in music, painting, and especially
poetry, the drama, and fiction. The imaginative
impulse did not discover its true direction at the outset; it imitated while trying to invent. What has
been said above concerning the chronological development of the imagination would be tiresome repetition. The need of creating followed from the first
the line of least resistance, where it found certain
materials ready to hand. But in order to arrive
to full consciousness of itself it needed more time,
more knowledge, more accumulated experience.

We might here ask whether the contrary case is
also met with; i. e., where the imagination, in this
third period, would return to the inclinations of the
first period. This regressive metamorphosis—for I
cannot style it otherwise—is rare but not without
examples. Ordinarily the creative imagination,
when it has passed its adult stage, becomes atten-
uated by slow atrophy without undergoing serious
change of form. Nevertheless, I am able to cite the
case of a well-known scholar who began with a

taste for art, especially plastic art, went over rapidly to literature, devoted his life to biologic studies,
in which he gained a very deserved reputation; then,
in turn, became totally disgusted with scientific research, came back to literature and finally to the
arts, which have entirely monopolized him.

Finally—for there are very many forms—in some
the imagination, though strong, scarcely passes beyond the first stage, always retains its youthful, almost childish form, hardly modified by a minimum
of rationality. Let us note that it is not a question
here of the characteristic ingenuousness of some inventors, which has caused them to be called "grown-
up children," but of the candor and inherent simplicity of the imagination itself. This exceptional
form is hardly reconcilable except with esthetic creation. Let us add the mystic imagination. It could
furnish examples, less in its religious conceptions,
which are without control, than in its reveries of a
scientific turn. Contemporary mystics have invented
adaptations of the world that take us back to the
mythology of early times. This prolonged childhood of the imagination, which is, in a word, an
anomaly, produces curiosities rather than lasting
works.

At this third period in the development of the
imagination appears a second, subsidiary law, that of
increasing complexity; it follows a progressive line
from the simple to the complex. Indeed, it is not,
strictly speaking, a law of the imagination but of
the rational development exerting an influence on

it by a counter-action. It is a law of the mind that *knows,* not of one that *imagines.*

It is needless to show that theoretical and practical intelligence develops as an increasing complex. But from the time that the mind distinguishes clearly between the possible and the impossible, between the fancied and the real—which is a capacity wanting in primitive man—as soon as man has formed ratoinal habits and has undergone experience the impress of which is ineffaceable, the creative imagination is subject, *nolens volens,* to new conditions; it is no longer absolute mistress of itself, it has lost the assurance of its infancy, and is under the rules of logical thought, which draws it along in its train. Aside from the exceptions given above—and even they are partial exceptions only—creative power depends on the ability to understand, which imposes upon it its form and developmental law. In literature and in the arts comparison between the simplicity of primitive creations and the complexity of advanced civilizations has become commonplace. In the practical, technical, scientific and social worlds the higher up we go the more we have to know in order to create, and in default of this condition we merely repeat when we think we are inventing.

II

Historically considered, in the species, the development of the imagination follows the same line of progress as in the individual. We will not repeat it; it would be mere reiteration in a vaguer form of what we have just said.   A few brief notes will suffice.

Vico—whose name deserves to be mentioned here because he was the first to see the good that we can get from myths for the study of the imagination— divided the course of humanity into three successive ages: divine or theocratic, heroic or fabulous, human or historic, after which the cycle begins over again.   Although this too hypothetic conception is now forgotten, it is sufficient for our purposes. What, indeed, are those first two stages that have everywhere and always been the harbingers and pre- parers of civilization, if not the triumphant period of the imagination?   It has produced myths, re- ligions, legends, epics and martial narratives, and imposing monuments erected in honor of gods and heroes.   Many nations whose evolution has been in- complete have not gone beyond this stage.

Let us now consider this question under a more definite, more limited, better known form—the his- tory of intellectual development in Europe since the fall of the Roman Empire.   It shows very distinctly our three periods.

No one will question the preponderance of the imagination during the middle Ages: intensity of religious feeling, ceaselessly repeated epidemics of superstition; the institution of chivalry, with all its accessories; heroic poetry, chivalric romances; courts of love, efflorescence of Gothic art, the beginning of modern music, etc.   On the other hand, the *quan- tity* of imagination applied during this epoch to practical, industrial, commercial invention is very small. Their scientific culture, buried in Latin jargon, is made up partly of antique traditions, partly of fancies; what the ten centuries added to positive science is almost *nil*. Our figure, with its two curves, one imaginative, the other rational, thus applies just as well to historical development as to individual development during this first period.

No more will anyone question that the Renaissance is a critical moment, a transition period, and a transformation analogous to that which we have noted in the individual, when there rises, opposed to imagination, a rival power.

Finally, it will be admitted without dissent that during the modern period social imagination has become partly decayed, partly rationalized, under the influence of two principal factors—one scientific, the other economic. On the one hand the development of science, on the other hand the great maritime discoveries, by stimulating industrial and commercial inventions, have given the imagination a new field of activity. There have arisen points of attraction that have drawn it into other paths, have imposed upon it other forms of creation that have often been neglected or misunderstood and that we shall study in the Third Part.

THIRD PART

THE PRINCIPAL TYPES OF IMAGINATION

PRELIMINARY

After having studied the creative imagination in its constitutive elements and in its development we purpose, in this last part, describing its principal forms. This will be neither analytic nor genetic but concrete. The reader need not fear wearisome repetition; our subject is sufficiently complex to permit a third treatment without reiteration.

The expression "creative imagination," like all general terms, is an abbreviation and an abstraction. There is no "imagination in general," but only *men who imagine*, and who do so in different ways; the reality is in them. The diversities in creation, however numerous, should be reducible to types that are *varieties* of imagination, and the determination of these varieties is analogous to that of character as related to will. Indeed, when we have settled upon the physiological and psychological conditions of voluntary activity we have only done a work in *general* psychology. Men being variously constituted, their modes of action bear the stamp of their individuality; in each one there is a personal factor that, whatever its ultimate nature, puts its mark on the will and makes it energetic or weak, rapid or slow, stable or unstable, continuous or intermittent. The same is true of the creative imagination. We cannot know it completely without a study of its varieties, without a special psychology, toward which the following chapters are an attempt.

How are we to determine these varieties? Many will be inclined to think that the method is indicated in advance. Have not psychologists distinguished, according as one or another of image-groups preponderates, visual, auditory, motor and mixed types? Is not the way clear and is it not well enough to go in this direction? However natural this solution may appear, it is illusory and can lead to naught. It rests on the equivocal use of the word "imagination," which at one time means mere reproduction of images, and at another time creative activity, and which, consequently, keeps up the erroneous notion that in the creative imagination images, the raw materials, are the essential part. The materials, no doubt, are not a negligible element, but by themselves they cannot reveal to us the species and varieties that have their origin in an anterior and superior tendency of mind. We shall see in the sequel that the very nature of constructive imagination may express itself indifferently in sounds, words, colors, lines, and even numbers. The method that should allege to settle the various orientations of creative activity according to the nature of images would no more go to the bottom of the matter than would a classification of architecture according to the materials employed (as rock, brick, iron, wood, etc.) with no regard for differences of style.

This method aside, since the determination must be made according to the individuality of the architect, what method shall we follow? The matter is even more perplexing than the study of character. Although various authors have treated the latter subject (we have attempted it elsewhere), no one of the proposed classifications has been universally accepted. Nevertheless, despite their differences, they coincide in several points, because these have the advantage of resting on a common basis—the large manifestations of human nature, feeling, doing, thinking. In our subject I find nothing like this and I seek in vain for a point of support. Classifications are made according to the essential dominating attributes; but, as regards the varieties of the creative imagination, what are they?

We may, indeed, as was said above, distinguish two great classes—the intuitive and the combining. From another point of view we may distinguish invention of free range (esthetic, religious, mystic) from invention more or less restricted (mechanical, scientific, commercial, military, political, social). But these two divisions are too general, leading to nothing. A true classification should be in touch with facts, and this one soars too high.

Leaving, then, to others, more skilled or more fortunate, the task of a rational and systematic determination, if it be possible, we shall try merely to distinguish and describe the principal forms, such as experience gives them to us, emphasizing those that have been neglected or misinterpreted. What follows is thus neither a classification nor even a complete enumeration.

We shall study at first two general forms of the creative imagination—the plastic and the diffluent—and later, special forms, determined by their content and subject.

Wundt, in a little-noticed passage of his *Physiological Psychology,* has undertaken to determine the composition of the "principal forms of talent," which he reduces to four:

The first element is imagination. It may be intuitive, "that is, conferring on representations a clearness of sense-perception," or combining; "then it operates on multiple combinations of images." A very marked development in both directions at the same time is uncommon; the author assigns reasons for this.

The second element is understanding (*Verstand*). It may be inductive—i. e., inclining toward the collection of facts in order to draw generalizations from them—or deductive, taking general concepts and laws to trace their consequences.

If the intuitive imagination is joined to the inductive spirit we have the talent for observation of the naturalist, the psychologist, the pedagogue, the man of affairs.

If the intuitive imagination is combined with the deductive spirit we have the analytical talent of the systematic naturalist, of the geometrician. In Linnaeus and Cuvier the intuitive element predominates; in Gauss, the analytical element.

The combining imagination joined to the inductive spirit constitutes "the talent for invention strictly so-called," in industry, in the technique of science; it gives the artist and the poet the power of composing their works.

The combining imagination plus the deductive spirit gives the speculative talent of the mathematician and philosopher; deduction predominates in the former, imagination in the latter.[1]

[1] Wundt, *Physiologische Psychologie*, 4th German edition, Vol. II, pp. 490-95.

CHAPTER I

THE PLASTIC IMAGINATION

I

By "plastic imagination" I understand that which
has for its special characters clearness and precision
of form; more explicitly those forms whose materials are clear images (whatever be their nature),
approaching perception, giving the impression of
reality; in which, too, there predominate *associations
with objective relations,* determinable with precision.
The plastic mark, therefore, is in the images, and in
the modes of association of images. In somewhat
rough terms, requiring modifications which the
reader himself can make, it is the imagination that
materializes.

Between perception—a very complex synthesis of
qualities, attributes and relations—and conception—
which is only the consciousness of a quality, quantity, or relation, often of only a single word accompanied by vague outlines and a latent, potential
knowledge; between concrete and abstract, the
image occupies an intermediate position and can run
from one pole to another, now full of reality, now

almost as poor and pale as a concept. The representation here styled plastic descends towards its point of origin; it is an external imagination, arising from sensation rather than from feeling and needing to become objective.

Thus its general characters are easy of determination. First and foremost, it makes use of visual images; then of motor images; lastly, in practical invention, of tactile images. In a word, the three groups of images present to a great extent the character of externality and objectivity. The clearness of form of these three groups proceeds from their origin, because they arise from sensation well determined in space—sight, movement, touch. Plastic imagination depends most on spatial conditions. We shall see that its opposite, diffluent imagination, is that which depends least upon that factor, or is most free from it. Among these naturally objective elements the plastic imagination chooses the most objective, which fact gives its creations an air of reality and life.

The second characteristic is inferiority of the affective element; it appears only intermittently and is entirely blotted out before sensory impression. This form of the creative imagination, coming especially from sensation, aims especially at sensation. Thus it is rather superficial, greatly devoid of that internal mark that comes from feeling.

But if it chance that both sensory and affective elements are equal in power; if there is at the same time intense vision adequate to reality, and profound emotion, violent shock, then there arise extraordinary imaginative personages, like Shakespeare, Carlyle, Michelet. It is needless to describe this form of imagination, excellent pen-pictures of which have been given by the critics;[1] let us merely note that its psychology reduces itself to an alternately ascending and descending movement between the two limiting points of perception and idea. The ascending process assigns to inanimate objects life, desires and feelings. Thus Michelet: "The great streams of the Netherlands, *tired* with their very long course, *perish* as though from *weariness* in the *unfeeling* ocean."[2] Elsewhere, the great folio begets the octavo, "which becomes the parent of the small volume, of booklets, of ephemeral pamphlets, invisible spirits flying in the night, creating under the very eyes of tyrants the circulation of liberty." The descending process materializes abstractions, gives them body, makes them flesh and bone; the Middle

[1] Thus Taine says of Carlyle: "He cannot stick to simple expression; at every step he drops into figures, gives body to every idea, must touch forms. We see that he is possessed and haunted by glittering or saddening visions; in him every thought is an explosion; a flood of seething passion reaches the boiling-point in his brain, which overflows, and the torrent of images runs over the banks and rushes with all its mud and all its splendor. He cannot reason, he must paint." Despite the vigor of this sketch, the perusal of ten pages of *Sartor Resartus* or of the *French Revolution* teaches more in regard to the nature of this imagination than all the commentaries.

[2] For a point of view in criticism that has seemed correct to many on this matter, compare the well-known chapter on the "Pathetic Fallacy" by Ruskin, in his *Modern Painters*. (Tr.)

Ages become "a poor child, torn from the bowels
of Christianity, born amidst tears, grown up in
prayer and revery, in anguish of heart, dying without achieving anything." In this dazzle of images
there is a momentary return to primitive animism.

II

In order to more fully understand the plastic imagination, let us take up its principal manifestations.

1. First, the arts dealing with form, where its
necessity is evident. The sculptor, painter, architect, must have visual and tactile-motor images; it
is the material in which their creations are wrapped
up. Even leaving out the striking acts requiring
such a sure and tenacious external vision (portraits
executed from memory, exact remembrance of faces
at the end of twenty years, as in the case of Ga-
varni, etc.[1]), and limiting ourselves merely to the
usual, the plastic arts demand an observant imagination. For the majority of men the concrete image
of a face, a form, a color, usually remains vague and
fleeting; "red, blue, black, white, tree, animal, head,
mouth, arm, etc., are scarcely more than words, symbols expressing a rough synthesis. For the painter,
on the other hand, images have a very high precision
of details, and what he sees beneath the words or
in real objects are analyzed facts, positive elements
of perception and movement."[2]

[1] Arréat (Psychologie du peintre, pp. 62 ff.) gives a large
number of examples of this.

[2] Ibid., p. 115.

The rôle of tactile-motor images is not insignificant. There has often been cited the instance of sculptors who, becoming blind, have nevertheless been able to fashion busts of close resemblance to the original. This is memory of touch and of the muscular sense, entirely equivalent to the visual memory of the portrait painters mentioned above. Practical knowledge of design and modeling—i. e., of contour and relief—though resulting from natural or acquired disposition, depends on cerebral conditions, the development of definite sensory-motor regions and their connections; and on psychological conditions—the acquisition and organization of appropriate images. "We learn to paint and carve," wrote a contemporary painter, "as we do sewing, embroidery, sawing, filing and turning." In short, like all manual labor requiring associated and combined acts.

2. Another form of plastic imagination uses words as means for evoking vivid and clear impressions of sight, touch, movement; it is the poetic or literary form. Of it we find in Victor Hugo a finished type. As all know, we need only open his works at hazard to find a stream of glittering images. But what is their nature? His recent biographers, guided by contemporary psychology, have well shown that they always paint scenes or movements. It is unnecessary to give proofs. Some facts have a broader range and throw light upon his psychology. Thus we are told that "he never dictates or rhymes from memory and composes only in writ-

ing, for he believes that writing has its own features, and he wants to *see the words*. Théophile Gautier, who knows and understands him so well, says: 'I also believe that in the sentence we need most of all an *ocular* rhythm. A book is made to be read, not to be spoken aloud.' " It is added that "Victor Hugo never spoke his verses but wrote them out and would often illustrate them on the margin, as if he needed to fixate the image in order to find the appropriate word."[1]

After visual representations come those of movement: the steeple *pierces* the horizon, the mountain *rends* the cloud, the mountain *raises himself* and looks about, "the cold caverns open their mouths *drowsily*," the wind lashes the rock into tears with the waterfall, the thorn is an enraged plant, and so on indefinitely.

A more curious fact is the transposition of sonorous sensations or images of sound, and like them without form or figure, into visual and motor images: "The *ruffles* of sound that the fifer cuts out; the flute *goes up* to alto like a frail capital on a column." This thoroughly plastic imagination remains identical with itself while reducing everything spontaneously, unconsciously, to spatial terms.

In literature this altogether foreign mode of cre-

---

[1] For further details on this point, consult Mabilleau, *Victor Hugo*, 2nd part, chaps. II, III, IV.—Renouvier, in the book devoted to the poet, asserts that "on account of his aptitude for representing to himself the details of a figure, order and position in space, beyond any present sensation," Victor Hugo could have become a mathematician of the highest order.

ative activity has found its most complete expression among the *Parnassiens* and their congeners, whose creed is summed up in the formula, faultless form and impassiveness. Théophile Gautier claims that "a poet, no matter what may be said of him, is a *workman;* it is not necessary that he have more intelligence than a laborer and have knowledge of a state other than his own, without which he does badly. I regard as perfectly absurd the mania that people have of hoisting them (the poets) up onto an ideal pedestal; *nothing is less ideal than a poet.* For him words have in themselves and outside the meaning they express, their own beauty and value, just like precious stones not yet cut and mounted in bracelets, necklaces and rings; they charm the understanding that looks at them and takes them from the finger to the little pile where they are put aside for future use." If this statement, whether sincere or not, is taken literally, I see no longer any difference, save as regards the materials employed, between the imagination of poets and the imagination active in the mechanical arts. For the usefulness of the one and the "uselessness" of the other is a characteristic foreign to invention itself.

3. In the teeming mass of myths and religious conceptions that the nineteenth century has gathered with so much care we could establish various classifications—according to race, content, intellectual level; and, in a more artificial manner but one suitable for our subject, according to the degree of precision or fluidity.

Neglecting intermediate forms, we may, indeed, divide them into two groups; some are clear in outline, are consistent, relatively logical, resembling a definite historical relation; others are vague, multiform, incoherent, contradictory; their characters change into one another, the tales are mixed and are imperceptible in the whole.

The former types are the work of the plastic imagination. Such are, if we eliminate oriental influences, most of the myths belonging to Greece when, on emerging from the earilest period, they attained their definite constitution. It has been held that the plastic character of these religious conceptions is an effect of esthetic development: statues, bas-reliefs, poetry, and even painting, have made definite the attributes of the gods and their history. Without denying this influence we must nevertheless understand that it is only auxiliary. To those who would challenge this opinion let us recall that the Hindoos have had gigantic poems, have covered their temples with numberless sculptures, and yet their fluid mythology is the opposite of the Greek. Among the peoples who have incarnated their divinities in no statue, in no human or animal form, we find the Germans and the Celts. But the mythology of the former is clear, well kept within large lines; that of the latter is fleeting and inconsistent—the despair of scholars.[1]

[1] As bearing out the position of the author, we may also call attention to the fact that while the Hebrew race has had very slight development in the plastic arts, yet its mythology has

It is, then, certain that myths of the plastic kind are the fruits of an innate quality of mind, of a mode of feeling and of translating, at a given moment in its history, the preponderating characters of a race; in short, of a form of imagination and ultimately of a special cerebral structure.

4. The most complete manifestation of the plastic imagination is met with in mechanical invention and what is allied thereto, in consequence of the need of very exact representations of qualities and relations. But this is a specialized form, and, as its importance has been too often misunderstood, it deserves a separate study. (See Chapter V, *infra.*)

III

Such are the principal traits of this type of imagination: clearness of outline, both of the whole and of the details. It is not identical with the form called realistic—it is more comprehensive; it is a genus of which "realism" is a species. Moreover, the latter expression being reserved by custom for esthetic creation, I purposely digress in order to dwell on this point: that the esthetic imagination has no essential character belonging exclusively to it, and that it differs from other forms (scientific, mechanical, etc.) only in its materials and in its end, not in its primary nature.

On the whole, the plastic imagination could be summed up in the expression, *clearness in complex-*

always taken a very definite form, even when dealing with the vaguest and most abstract subjects. (Tr.)

ity. It always preserves the mark of its original source—i. e., in the creator and those disposed to enjoy and understand him it tends to approach the clearness of perception.

Would it be improper to consider as a variety of the genus a mode of representation that could be expressed as *clearness in simplicity?* It is the dry and rational imagination. Without depreciating it we may say that it is rather a condition of imaginative poverty. We hold with Fouillée that the average Frenchman furnishes a good example of it. "The Frenchman," says he, "does not usually have a very strong imagination. His internal vision has neither the hallucinative intensity nor the exuberant fancy of the German and Anglo-Saxin mind; it is an intellectual and distant view rather than a sensitive resurrection or an immediate contact with, and possession of, the things themselves. Inclined to deduce and construct, our intellect excels less in representing to itself real things than in discovering relations between possible or necessary things. In other words, it is a logical and combining imagination that takes pleasure in what has been termed the abstract view of life. The Chateaubriands, Hugos, Flauberts, Zolas, are exceptional with us. We reason more than we imagine."[1]

Its psychological constitution is reducible to two elements: slightly concrete images, *schemas* approaching general ideas; for their association, relations predominantly rational, more the products of

[1] Fouillée, *Psychologie du peuple français*, p. 185.

the logic of the intellect than of the logic of the feelings. It lacks the sudden, violent shock of emotion that gives brilliancy to images, making them arise and grouping them in unforeseen combinations. It is a form of invention and construction that is more the work of reason than of imagination proper.

Consequently, is it not paradoxical to relate it to plastic imagination, as species to genus? It would be idle to enter upon a discussion of the subject here without attempting a classification; let us merely note the likenesses and differences. Both are above all objective—the first, because it is sensory; the other, because it is rational. Both make use of analogous modes of association, dependent more on the nature of things than on the personal impression of the subject. Opposition exists only on one point: the former is made up of vivid images that approach perception; the latter is made up of internal images bordering upon concepts. Rational imagination is plastic imagination desiccated and simplified.

CHAPTER II

THE DIFFLUENT IMAGINATION

I

The diffluent imagination is another general form, but one that is completely opposed to the foregoing. It consists of vaguely-outlined, indistinct images that are evoked and joined according to the least rigorous modes of association. It presents, then, two things for our consideration—the nature of the images and of their associations.

(1) It employs neither the clear-cut, concrete, reality-penetrated images of the plastic imagination, nor the semi-schematic representations of the rational imagination, but those midway in that ascending and descending scale extending from perception to conception. This determination, however, is insufficient, and we can make it more precise. Analysis, indeed, discovers a certain class of ill-understood images, which I call emotional abstractions, and which are the proper material for the diffluent imagination. These images are reduced to certain qualities or attributes of things, taking the place of the whole, and chosen from

among the others for various reasons, the origin of which is affective. We shall comprehend their nature better through the following comparison:

Intellectual or rational abstraction results from the choice of a fundamental, or at least principal, character, which becomes the substitute for all the rest that is omitted. Thus, extension, resistance, or impenetrability, come to represent, through simplification and abbreviation, what we call "matter."

Emotional abstraction, on the other hand, results from the permanent or temporary predominance of an emotional state. Some aspect of a thing, essential or not, comes into relief, solely because it is in direct relation to the disposition of our sensibility, with no other preoccupation; a quality, an attribute is spontaneously, arbitrarily selected because it impresses us at the given instant—in the final analysis, because it somehow pleases or displeases us. The images of this class have an "impressionist" mark. They are abstractions in the strict sense—i. e., extracts from and simplifications of the sensory data. They act less through a direct influence than by evoking, suggesting, whispering; they permit a glance, a passing glimpse: we may justly call them crepuscular or twilight ideas.

(2) As for the forms of association, the relations linking these images, they do not depend so much on the order and connections of things as on the changing dispositions of the mind. They have a very marked subjective character. Some depend on the intellectual factor; the most usual are based on

chance, on distant and vacillating analogies—further down, even on assonance and alliteration. Others depend on the affective factor and are ruled by the disposition of the moment: association by contrast, especially those alike in emotional basis, which have been previously studied. (First Part, Chapter II.)

Thus the diffluent imagination is, trait for trait, the opposite of the plastic imagination. It has a general character of inwardness because it arises less from sensation than from feeling, often from a simple and fugitive impression. Its creations have not the organic character of the other, lacking a stable center of attraction; but they act by diffusion and inclusion.

II

By its very nature it is *de jure,* if not *de facto,* excluded from certain territories—if it ventures therein it produces only abortions. This is true of the practical sphere, which permits neither vague images nor approximate constructions; and of the scientific world, where the imagination may be used only to create a theory or invent processes of discovery (experiments, schemes of reasoning). Even with these exceptions there is still left for it a very wide range.

Let us rapidly pass over some very frequent, very well-known manifestations of the diffluent imagination—those obliterated forms in which it does not reach complete development and cannot give the full measure of its power.

(1) Revery and related states. This is perhaps the purest specimen of the kind, but it remains embryonic.

(2) The romantic turn of mind. This is seen in those who, confronted by any event whatever or an unknown person, make up, spontaneously, involuntarily, in spite of themselves, a story out of whole cloth. I shall later give examples of it according to the written testimony of several people.[1]   In whatever concerns themselves or others they create an imagined world, which they substitute for the real.

(3) The fantastic mind. Here we come away from the vague forms; the diffluent imagination becomes substantial and asserts itself through its permanence. At bottom this fantastic form is the romantic spirit tending toward objectification. The invention, which was at first only a thoroughly internal construction and recognized as such, aspires to become external, to become realized, and when it ventures into a world other than its own, one requiring the rigorous conditions of the practical imagination, it is wrecked, or succeeds only through chance, and that very rarely. To this class belong those inventors, known to everyone, who are fertile in methods of enriching themselves or their country by means of agricultural, mining, industrial or commercial enterprises; the makers of the utopias of

[1] See Appendix E.

finance, politics, society, etc. It is a form of imagination unnaturally oriented toward the practical.[2]

(4) The list increases with myths and religious conceptions; the imagination in its diffuse form here finds itself on its own ground.

Depending on linguistics, it has recently been maintained that, among the Aryans at least, the imagination created at first only momentary gods (*Augenblicksgötter*).[1] Every time that primitive man, in the presence of a phenomenon, experienced a perceptible emotion, he translated it by a name, the manifestation of what was imagined the divine part in the emotion felt. "Every religious emotion gives rise to a new name—i. e., a new divinity. But the religious imagination is never identical with itself; though produced by the same phenomenon, it translates itself, at two different moments, by two different words." As a consequence, "during the early periods of the human race, religious names must have been applied not to *classes* of beings or events but to *individual* beings or events. Before

[2] Let us cite merely the case of Balzac who, says one of his biographers, "was always odd." He buys a property, in order to start a dairy there with "the best cows in the world," from which he expects to receive a net income of 3,000 francs. In addition, high-grade vegetable gardens, same income; vineyard, with Malaga plants, which should bring about 2,000 fr. He has the commune of Sèvres deed over to him a walnut tree, worth annually 2,000 francs to him, because all the townspeople dump their rubbish there. And so on, until at the end of four years he sees himself obliged to sell his domain for 3,000 francs, after spending on it thrice that sum.

[1] Usener, *Götternamen*, 1896.

worshipping the comet or the fig-tree, men must have worshiped each one of the comets they beheld crossing the sky, everyone of the fig-trees that their eyes saw." Later, with advancing capacity for generalization, these "instantaneous" divinities would be condensed into more consistent gods. If this hypothesis, which has aroused many criticisms, be sound—if this state were met with—it would be the ideal type of imaginative instability in the religious order.

Nearer to us, authentic evidence shows that certain peoples, at given stages of their history, have created such vague, fluid myths, that we cannot succeed in delimiting them. Every god can change himself into another, different, or even opposite, one. The Semitic religions might furnish examples of this. There has been established the identity of Istar, Astarte, Tanit, Baalath, Derketo, Mylitta, Aschera, and still others. But it is in the early religion of the Hindoos that we perceive best this kaleidoscopic process applied to divine beings. In the vedic hymns not only are the clouds now serpents, now cows and later fortresses (the retreats of dark Asuras), but we see Agni (fire) becoming Kama (desire or love), and Indra becoming Varuna, and so on. "We cannot imagine," says Taine, "such a great clearness. The myth here is not a disguise, but an expression; no language is more true and more supple. It permits a glimpse of, or rather, it causes us to discern the forms of clouds, movements of the air, changes of seasons,

all the happenings of sky, fire, storm: external
nature has never met a mind so impressionable and
pliant in which to mirror itself in all the inexhaustible variety of its appearances.   However changeable nature may be, this imagination corresponds to
it.   It has no fixed gods; they are changeable like
the things themselves; they blend one into another.
Everyone of them is in turn the supreme deity; no
one of them is a distinct personality; everyone is
only a moment of nature, able, according to the
apperception of the moment, to include its neighbor
or be included by it.   In this fashion they swarm
and teem.   Every moment of nature and every
apperceptive moment may furnish one of them."[1]
Let us, indeed, note that, for the worshiper, the
god to whom he addresses himself and while he is
praying, is always the greatest and most powerful.
The assignment of attributes passes suddenly from
one to the other, regardless of contradiction.   In
this versatility some writers believe they have discovered a vague pantheistic conception.   Nothing is
more questionable, fundamentally, than this interpretation.   It is more in harmony with the psychology of these naïve minds to assume simply an
extreme state of "impressionism," explicable by the
logic of feeling.

Thus, there is a complete antithesis between the
imagination that has created the clear-cut and
definite polytheism of the Greeks and that whence
have issued those fluctuating divinities that allow

[1] *Nouveaux Essais de critique,* p. 320.

the presentation of the future doctrine of *Mâya*, of universal illusion—another more refined form of the diffluent imagination. Finally, let us note that the Hellenic imagination realized its gods through anthropomorphism—they are the ideal forms of human attributes[1]—majesty, beauty, power, wisdom, etc. The Hindoo imagination proceeds through symbolism: its divinities have several heads, several arms, several legs, to symbolize limitless intelligence, power, etc.; or better still, animal forms, as e. g., Ganesa, the god of wisdom, with the head of the elephant, reputed the wisest of animals.

(5) It would be easy to show by the history of literature and the fine arts that the vague forms have been preferred according to peoples, times, and places. Let us limit ourselves to a single contemporary example that is complete and systematically created—the art of the "symbolists." It is not here a question of criticism, of praise, or even of appreciation, but merely of a consideration of it as a psychological fact likely to instruct us in regard to the nature of the diffluent imagination.

This form of art despises the clear and exact representation of the outer world: it replaces it by a sort of music that aspires to express the changing and fleeting inwardness of the human soul. It is the school of the subject "who wants to know only mental states." To that end, it makes use of a

[1] Or, as it has been expressed, "human qualities raised to their highest power." (Tr.)

natural or artificial lack of precision: everything floats in a dream, men as well as things, often without mark in time and space. Something happens, one knows not where or when; it belongs to no country, is of no period in time: it is *the* forest, *the* traveler, *the* city, *the* knight, *the* wood; less frequently, even *He, She, It*. In short, all the vague and unstable characters of the pure, contentless affective state. This process of "suggestion" sometimes succeeds, sometimes fails.

The word is the sign *par excellence*. As, according to the symbolists, it should give us emotions rather than representations, it is necessary that it lose, partially, its intellectual function and undergo a new adaptation.

A principal process consists of employing usual words and changing their ordinary acceptation, or rather, associating them in such a way that they lose their precise meaning, and appear vague and mysterious: these are the words "written in the depths." The writers do not name—they leave it for us to infer. "They banish commonplaces through lack of precision, and leave to things only the power of moving." A rose is not described by the particular sensations that it causes, but by the general condition that it excites.

Another method is the employment of new words or words that have fallen into disuse. Ordinary words retain, in spite of everything, somewhat of their customary meaning, associations and thoughts codnensed in them through long habit; words forgotten during four or five centuries escape this condition—they are coins without fixed value.

Lastly, a still more radical method is the attempt to give to words an exclusively emotional valuation. Unconsciously or as the result of reflection some symbolists have come to this extreme trial, which the logic of events imposed upon them. Ordinarily, thought expresses itself in words; feeling, in gestures, cries, interjections, change of tone: it finds its complete and classic expression in music. The symbolists want to transfer the rôle of sound to words, to make of them the instrument for translating and suggesting emotion through sound alone: words have to act not as signs but as sounds: they are "musical notes in the service of an impassioned psychology."

All this, indeed, concerns only imagination expressing itself in words; but we know that the symbolic school has applied itself to the plastic arts, to treat them in its own way. The difference, however, is in the vesture that the esthetic ideal assumes. The pre-Raphaelites have attempted, by effacing forms, outlines, semblances, colors, "to cause things to appear as mere sources of emotion," in a word, to *paint* emotions.

To sum up—In this form of the diffluent imagination the emotional factor exercises supreme authority.

May the type of imagination, the chief manifestations of which we have just enumerated, be considered as identical with the idealistic imagination?

This question is similar to that asked in the preceding chapter, and permits the same answer. In idealistic art, doubtless, the material element furnished in perception (form, color, touch, effort) is minimized, subtilized, sublimated, refined, so as to approach as nearly as possible to a purely internal state. By the nature of its favorite images, by its preference for vague associations and uncertain relations, it presents all the characteristics of diffluent imagination; but the latter covers a much broader field: it is the genus of which the other is a species. Thus, it would be erroneous to regard the fantastic imagination as idealistic; it has no claim to the term: on the contrary, it believes itself adapted for practical work and acts in that direction.

In addition, it must be recognized that were we to make a complete review of all the forms of esthetic creation, we should frequently be embarrassed to classify them, because there are among them, as in the case of characters, mixed or composite forms. Here, for example, are two kinds seemingly belonging to the diffluent imagination which, however, do not permit it to completely include them.

(a) The "wonder" class (fairy-tales, the Thousand and One Nights, romances of chivalry, Ariosto's poem, etc.) is a survival of the mythic epoch, when the imagination is given free play without control or check; whereas, in the course of centuries, art—and especially literary creation—

becomes, as we have already said, a decadent and rationalized mythology. This form of invention consists neither of idealizing the external world, nor reproducing it with the minuteness of realism, but *remaking* the universe to suit oneself, without taking into account natural laws, and despising the impossible: it is a liberated realism. Often, in an environment of pure fancy, where only caprice reigns, the characters appear clear, well-fashioned, living. The "wonder" class belongs, then, to the vague as well as to the plastic imagination; more or less to one or to the other, according to the temperament of the creator.

(b) The fantastic class develops under the same conditions. Its chiefs (Hoffmann, Poe, *et al.*) are classed by critics as realists. They are such by virtue of their vision, intensified to hallucination, the precision in details, the rigorous logic of characters and events: they rationalize the improbable.[1] On the other hand, the environment is strange, shrouded in mystery: men and things move in an unreal atmosphere, where one feels rather than perceives. It is thus proper to remark that this class easily glides into the deeply sad, the horrible, terrifying, nightmare-producing, "satanic literature;" Goya's paintings of robbers and thieves being garroted; Wiertz, a genius bizarre to the point of

[1] The same statement holds good as regards the "Temptations of Saint Anthony" and other analogous subjects that have often attracted painters.

extravagance, who paints only suicides or the heads of guillotined criminals.

Religious conceptions could also furnish a fine lot of examples: Dante's *Inferno,* the twenty-eight hells of Buddhism, which are perhaps the master-pieces of this class, etc. But all this belongs to another division of our subject, one that I have expressly eliminated from this essay—the pathology of the creative imagination.

III

There yet remains for us to study two important varieties that I connect with the diffluent imagination.

NUMERICAL IMAGINATION

Under this head I designate the imagination that takes pleasure in the unlimited—in infinity of time and space—under the form of number. It seems at first that these two terms—imagination and number—must be mutually exclusive. Every num-ber is precise, rigorously determined, since we can always reduce it to a relation with unity; it owes nothing to fancy. But the *series* of numbers is unlimited in two directions: starting from any term in the series, we may go on ever increasingly or ever decreasingly. The working of the mind gives rise to a possible infinity that is limitless: it thus traces a route for the movement of the imagination. The number, or rather the series of numbers, is less an object than a vehicle.

This form of imagination is produced in two principal ways—in religious conceptions and cosmogonies, and in science.

(1) Numerical imagination has nowhere been more exuberant than among the peoples of the Orient. They have played with number with magnificent audacity and prodigality. Chaldean cosmogony relates that *Oannes,* the Fish-god, devoted 259,200 years to the education of mankind, then came a period of 432,000 years taken up with the reigns of mythical personages, and at the end of these 691,000 years, the deluge renewed the face of the earth. The Egyptians, also, were liberal with millions of years, and in the face of the brief and limited chronology of the Greeks (another kind of imagination) were wont to exclaim, "You, O Greeks, you are only children!" But the Hindoos have done better than all that. They have invented enormous units to serve as basis and content for their numerical fancies: the *Koti,* equivalent to ten millions; the *Kalpa* (or the age of the world between two destructions), 4,328,000,000 years. Each *Kalpa* is merely one of 365 days of divine life: I leave to the reader, if he is so inclined, the work of calculating this apalling number. The Djanas divide time into two periods, one ascending, the other descending: each is of fabulous duration, 2,000,000,000,000,000 oceans of years; each ocean being itself equivalent to 1,000,000,000,000,000 years. "If there were a lofty rock, sixteen miles in each dimension, and one touched it once in a hun-

dred years with a bit of the finest Benares linen, it would be reduced to the size of a wango-stone before a fourth of one of these *Kalpas* had rolled by." In the sacred books of Buddhism, poor, dry, colorless, as they ordinarily are, imagination in its numerical forms is triumphant. The *Lalitavistara* is full of nomenclatures and enumerations of fatiguing monotony: Buddha is seated on a rock shaded by 100,000 parasols, surrounded by minor gods forming an assemblage of 68,000 *Kotis* (i. e., 680,000,000 persons), and—this surpasses all the rest —"he had experienced many vicissitudes during 10,100,000,000 *Kalpas.*" This makes one dizzy.

(2) Numerical imagination in the sciences does not take on these delirious forms; it has the advantage of resting on an objective basis: it is the substitute of an unrepresentable reality. Scientific culture, which people often accuse of stifling imagination, on the contrary opens to it a field much vaster than esthetics. Astronomy delights in infinitudes of time and space: it sees worlds arise, burn at first with the feeble light of a nebular mass, glow like suns, become chilled, covered with spots, and then become condensed. Geology follows the development of our earth through upheavals and cataclysms: it foresees a distant future when our globe, deprived of the atmospheric vapors that protect it, will perish of cold. The hypotheses of physics and chemistry in regard to atoms and molecules are not less reckless than the speculations of the Hindoo imagination. "Physicists have determined the vol-

ume of a molecule, and referring to the numbers that they give, we find that a cube, a millimeter each way (scarcely the volume of a silkworm's egg), would contain a number of molecules at least equal to the cube of 10,000,000—i. e., unity followed by twenty-one zeros. One scientist has calculated that if one had to count them and could separate in thought a million per second, it would take more than 250,000,000 years: the being who commenced the task at the time that our solar system could have been no more than a formless nebula, would not yet have reached the end."[1] Biology, with its protoplasmic elements, its plastids, gemmules, hypotheses on hereditary transmission by means of infinitesimal subdivisions; the theory of evolution, which speaks off-hand of periods of a hundred thousand years; and many other scientific theses that I omit, offer fine material for the numerical imagination.

More than one scientist has even made use of this form of imagination for the pleasure of developing a purely fanciful notion. Thus Von Baer, supposing that we might perceive the portions of duration in another way, imagines the changes that would result therefrom in our outlook on nature: "Suppose we were able, within the length of a second, to note 10,000 events distinctly, instead of barely 10, as now; if our life were then destined to hold the same number of impressions, it might be 1,000 times

[1] R. Dubois, *Leçons de physiologie générale et comparée,* p. 286.

as short. We should live less than a month, and personally know nothing of the change of seasons. If born in winter, we should believe in summer as we now believe in the heats of the Carboniferous era. The motions of organic beings would be so slow to our senses as to be inferred, not seen. The sun would stand still in the sky, the moon be almost free from change, and so on. But now reverse the hypothesis and suppose a being to get only one 1,000th part of the sensations that we get in a given time, and consequently to live 1,000 times as long. Winters and summers will be to him like quarters of an hour. Mushrooms and the swifter-growing plants will shoot into being so rapidly as to appear instantaneous creations; annual shrubs will rise and fall from the earth like restlessly boiling water springs; the motions of animals will be as invisible as are to us the movements of bullets and cannon-balls; the sun will scour through the sky like a meteor, leaving a fiery trail behind him, etc."[1]

The psychologic conditions of this variety of the creative imagination are, then, these: Absence of limitation in time and space, whence the possibility of an endless movement in all directions, and the possibility of filling either with a myriad of dimly-perceived events. These events not being susceptible of clear representation as to their nature and quantity, escaping even a schematic representation, the imagination makes its constructions with substitutes that are, in this case, numbers.

[1] Von Baer, in James, *Psychology*, I, 639.

IV

Musical Imagination

Musical imagination deserves a separate mono-graph. As the task requires, in addition to psychological capacity, a profound knowledge of musical history and technique, it cannot be undertaken here. I purpose only one thing, namely, to show that it has its own individual mark—that it is the type of affective imagination.

I have elsewhere[2] attempted to prove that, contrary to the general opinion of psychologists, there exists, in many men at least, an affective memory; that is, a memory of emotions strictly so called, and not merely of the intellectual conditions that caused and accompanied them. I hold that there exists also a form of the creative imagination that is purely emotional—the contents of which are wholly made up of states of mind, dispositions, wants, aspirations, feelings, and emotions of all kinds, and that it is the characteristic of the composer of genius, of the born musician.

The musician sees in the world what concerns him. "He carries in his head a coherent system of tone-images, in which every element has its place and value; he perceives delicate differences of sound, of *timbre;* he succeeds, through exercise, in penetrating into their most varied combinations, and the knowledge of harmonious relations is for him what design and the knowledge of color are for the

[2] *Psychology of the Emotions,* Part I, Chapter IX.

painter: intervals and harmony, rhythm and tone-qualities are, as it were, standards to which he relates his present perceptions and which he causes to enter into the marvelous constructions of his fancy."[1]

These sound-elements and their combinations are the words of a special language that is very clear for some, impenetrable for others. People have spoken to a tiresome extent of the vagueness of musical expression; some have been pleased to hold that every one may interpret it in his own way. We must surely recognize that emotional language does not possess the precision of intellectual language; but in music it is the same as in any other idiom: there are those who do not understand at all; those who half understand and consequently always give wrong renderings; and those who understand well— and in this last category there are grades as varying as the aptitude for perceiving the delicate and subtle shades of speech.

[1] Arréat, *Mémoire et Imagination,* p. 118.

[2] Mendelssohn wrote to an author who composed verses for his *Lieder:* "Music is more definite than speech, and to want to explain it by means of words is to make the meaning obscure. I do not think that words suffice for that end, and were I persuaded to the contrary, I would not compose music. There are people who accuse music of being ambiguous, who allege that words are always understood: for me it is just the other way; words seem to me vague, ambiguous, unintelligible, if we compare them to the true music that fills the soul with a thousand things better than words. What the music that I like expresses to me seems to me *too definite,* rather than too indefinite, for anyone to be able to match words to it."

The materials necessary for this form of imaginative construction are gathered slowly. Many centuries passed between the early ages when man's voice and the simple instruments imitating it translated simple emotions, to the period when the efforts of antiquity and of the middle ages finally furnished the musical imagination with the means of expressing itself completely, and allowed complex and difficult constructions in sound. The development of music—slow and belated as compared to the other arts—has perhaps been due, in part at least, to the fact that the affective imagination, its chief province (imitative, descriptive, picturesque music being only an episode and accessory), being made up, contrary to sensorial imagination, of tenuous, subtle, fugitive states, has been long in seeking its methods of analysis and of expression. However it be, Bach and the contrapuntists, by their treatment in an independent manner of the different voices constituting harmony, have opened a new path. Henceforth melody will be able to develop and give rise to the richest combinations. We shall be able to associate various melodies, sing them at the same time, or in alternation, assign them to various instruments, vary indefinitely the pitch of singing and concerted voices. The boundless realm of musical combinations is open; it has been worth while to take the trouble to invent. Modern polyphony with its power of expressing at the same time different, even opposing, feelings is a marvelous instrument

for a form of imagination which, alien to the forms
clear-cut in space, moves only in time.

What furnishes us the best entrance into the
psychology of this form of imagination is the natural transposition operative in musicians. It consists in this: An external or internal impression,
any occurrence whatever, even a metaphysical idea,
undergoes change of a certain kind, which the following examples will make better understood than
any amount of commentary.

Beethoven said of Klopstock's *Messiah,* "always
maestoso, written in *D flat major."* In his fourth
symphony he expressed musically the destiny of
Napoleon; in the ninth symphony he tries to give
a proof of the existence of God. By the side of a
dead friend, in a room draped in black, he impro-
vises the *adagio* of the sonata in *C sharp minor.*
The biographers of Mendelssohn relate analogous
instances of transposition under musical form.
During a storm that almost engulfed George Sand,
Chopin, alone in the house, under the influence of
his agony, and half unconsciously, composed one of
his *Préludes.* The case of Schumann is perhaps
the most curious of all: "From the age of eight,
he would amuse himself with sketching what might
be called musical portraits, drawing by means of
various turns of song and varied rhythms the shades
of character, and even the physical peculiarities, of
his young comrades. He sometimes succeeded in
making such striking resemblances that all would

recognize, with no further designation, the figure indicated by the skillful fingers that genius was already guiding." He said later: "I feel myself affected by all that goes on in the world—men, politics, literature; I reflect on all that in my own way and it issues outwards in the form of music. That is why many of my compositions are so hard to understand: they relate to events of distant interest, though important; but everything remarkable that is furnished me by the period I must express musically." Let us recall again that Weber interpreted in one of the finest scenes of his *Freyschütz* (the bullet-casting scene) "a landscape that he had seen near the falls of Geroldsau, at the hour when the moon's rays cause the basin in which the water rushes and boils to glisten like silver."[1] In short, the events go into the composer's brain, mix there, and come out changed into a musical structure.

The plastic imagination furnishes us a counterproof: it transposes inversely. The musical impression traverses the brain, sets it in turmoil, but comes out transformed into visual images. We have already cited examples from Victor Hugo (ch. I); Goethe, we know, had poor musical gifts. After having the young Mendelssohn render an overture from Bach, he exclaimed, "How pompous and grand that is! It seems to me like a procession of grand

---

[1] Oelzelt-Newin, *op. cit.*, pp. 22-23. For analogous facts from contemporary musicians, see Paulhan, *Rev. Phil.*, 1898, pp. 234-35.

personages, in gala attire, descending the steps of a gigantic staircase."

We might generalize the question and ask whether or no there exists a natural antagonism between true musical imagination and plastic imagination. An answer in the affirmative seems scarcely liable to be challenged. I had undertaken an investigation which, at the outset, made for a different goal. It happens that it answered clearly enough the question propounded above: the conclusion has arisen of itself, unsought; which fact saves me from any charge of a preconceived opinion.

The question asked orally of a large number of people was this: "Does hearing or even remembering a bit of *symphonic* music excite visual images in you and of what kind are they?" For self evident reasons dramatic music was expressly excluded: the appearance of the theater, stage, and scenery impose on the observer visual perceptions that have a tendency to be repeated later in the form of memories.

The result of observation and of the collected answers are summed up as follows:

Those who possess great musical culture and—this is by far more important—taste or passion for music, generally have no visual images. If these arise, it is only momentarily, and by chance. I give a few of the answers: "I see absolutely nothing; I am occupied altogether with the pleasure of the music: I live entirely in a world of sound. In accordance with my knowledge of harmony, I analyze the harmonies but not for long. I follow the development of the phrasing." "I see nothing: I am given up wholly to my impressions. I believe that the chief effect of music is to heighten in everyone the predominating feelings."

Those who possess little musical culture, and especially those having little taste for music, have very clear visual representations. It must nevertheless be admitted that it is very hard to investigate these people. Because of their anti-musical natures, they avoid concerts, or at the most, resign themselves to sit through an opera. However, since the nature and quality of the music does not matter here, we may quote: "Hearing a Barbary organ in the street, I picture the instrument to myself. I see the man turning the crank. If military music sounds from afar, I *see* a regiment marching." An excellent pianist plays for a friend Beethoven's sonata in C sharp minor, putting into its execution all the pathos of which he is capable. The other sees in it "the tumult and excitement of a fair." Here the musical rendering is misinterpreted through misapprehension. I have several times noted this—in people familiar with design or painting, music calls up pictures and various scenes; one of these persons says that he is "besieged by visual images." Here the hearing of music evidently acts as excitant.[1]

[1] For the sake of brevity and clearness I do not give here the observations and evidence. They will be found at the end of this work, as Appendix D.

Under the title "An experimental test of musical expressive-

In a word, insofar as it is permissible in psychology to make use of general formulas—and with the proviso that they apply to most, not to all cases—we may say that during the working of the musical imagination the appearance of visual images is the exception; that when this form of imagination is weak, the appearance of images is the rule.

Furthermore, this result of observation is altogether in accord with logic. There is an irreducible antithesis between affective imagination, the characteristic of which is interiority, and visual imagination, basically objective. Intellectual language—

ness," Gilman, in *American Journal of Psychology*, vol. IV, No. 4, and vol. V, No. 1 (1892-3), has studied from another point of view the effect of music on various listeners. Eleven selections were given; I note that three or four at the most excited visual images—ten (perhaps eleven), emotional states. More recently, the *Psychological Review* (September, 1898, pp. 463 ff.) has published a personal observation of Macdougal in which sight-images accompany the hearing of music only exceptionally and under special conditions. The author characterizes himself as a "poor visualizer;" he declares that music arouses in him only very rarely visual representations; "even then they are fragmentary, consisting of simple forms without bond between them, appearing on a dark background, remaining visible for a moment or two, and soon disappearing." But, having gone to the concert fatigued and jaded, he sees nothing during the first number: the visions begin during the *andante* of the second, and accompany "in profusion" the rendering of the third. (See Appendix D.) May we not assume that the state of fatigue, by lowering the vital tone, which is the basis of the emotional life, likewise diminishes the tendency of affective dispositions to arise again under the form of memory On the other hand, sensory images remain without opposition and come to the front; at least, unless they are reënforced by a state of semi-morbid excitation.

speech—is an arrangement of words that stand for objects, qualities, relations, extracts of things: in order to be understood they must call up in consciousness the corresponding images. Emotional language—music—is an appropriate ordering of successive or simultaneous sounds, of melodies and harmonies that are signs of affective states: in order to be understood, they must call up in consciousness the corresponding affective modifications. But, in the non-musically inclined, the evocative power is small—sonorous combinations excite only superficial and unstable internal states. The exterior excitation, that of the sounds, follows the line of least resistance, and acting according to the psychic nature of the individual, tends to arouse objective images, pictures, visual representations, well or ill adapted.

To sum up: In contrast to sensorial imagination, which has its origin without, affective imagination begins within. The *stuff* of its creation is found in the mental states enumerated above, and in their innumerable combinations, which it expresses and fixes in language peculiar to itself, of which it has been able to make wonderful use. Taking it altogether, the only great division possible between the different types of imagination is perhaps reducible to this: To speak more exactly, there are exterior and interior imaginations. These two chapters have given a sketch of them. There now remains for us to study the less general forms of the creative power.

CHAPTER III

THE MYSTIC IMAGINATION

Mystic imagination deserves a place of honor, as it is the most complete and most daring of purely theoretic invention. Related to diffluent imagination, especially in the latter's affective form, it has its own special characters, which we shall try to separate out.

Mysticism rests essentially on two modes of mental life—feeling, which we need not study; and imagination, which, in the present instance, represents the intellectual factor. Whether the part of consciousness that this state of mind requires and permits be imaginative in nature and nothing else it is easy to find out. Indeed, the mystic considers the data of sense as vain appearances, or at the most as signs revealing and frequently laying bare the world of reality. He therefore finds no solid support in perception. On the other hand, he scorns reasoned thought, looking upon it as a cripple, halting half-way. He makes neither deductions nor inductions, and does not draw conclusions after the method of scientific hypotheses. The conclusion, then, is that he imagines, i. e., that he realizes a construction in images that is for him knowledge of the world; and he never proceeds, and does not proceed here, save *ex analogia hominis.*

I

The root of the mystic imagination consists of a tendency to incarnate the ideal in the sensible, to discover a hidden "idea" in every material phenomenon or occurrence, to suppose in things a supranatural principle that reveals itself to whoever may penetrate to it. Its fundamental character, from which the others are derived, is thus a way of thinking *symbolically;* but the algebraist also thinks by means of symbols, yet is not on that account a mystic. The nature of this symbolism must, then, be determined.

In doing so, let us note first of all that our images —understanding the word "image" in its broadest sense—may be divided into two distinct groups:

(1) *Concrete* images, earliest to be received, being representations of greatest power, residues of our perceptions, with which they have a direct and immediate relation.

(2) *Symbolic* images, or signs, of secondary acquirement, being representations of lesser power, having only indirect and mediate relations with things.

Let us make the differences between the two clear by a few simple examples.

Concrete images are: In the visual sphere, the

recollection of faces, monuments, landscapes, etc.; in the auditory sphere, the remembrance of the sounds of the sea, wind, the human voice, a melody, etc.; in the motor sphere, the tossings one feels when resting after having been at sea, the illusions of those who have had limbs amputated, etc.

Symbolic images are: In the visual order, written words, ideographic signs, etc.; in the auditory order, spoken words or verbal images; in the motor order, significant gestures, and even better, the finger-language of deaf-mutes.

Psychologically, these two groups are not identical in nature. Concrete images result from a persistence of perceptions and draw from the latter all their validity; symbolic images result from a mental synthesis, from an association of perception and image, or of image and image. If they have not the same origin, no more do they disappear in the same way, as is proven by very numerous examples of aphasia.

The originality of mystic imagination is found in this fact: It transforms concrete images into symbolic images, and uses them as such. It extends this process even to perceptions, so that all manifestations of nature or of human art take on a value as signs or symbols. We shall later find numerous examples of this. Its mode of expression is necessarily synthetic. In itself, and because of the materials that it makes use of, it differs from the affective imagination previously described; it also differs from sensuous imagination, which makes use of forms, movements, colors, as having a value of their own; and from the imagination developing in the functions of words, through an analytic process. It has thus a rather special mark.

Other characters are related to this one of symbolism, or else are derived from it, viz.:

(1) An external character: the manner of writing and of speaking, the mode of expression, whatever it is. "The dominant style among mystics," says von Hartmann, "is metaphorical in the extreme— now flat and ordinary, more often turgid and emphatic. Excess of imagination betrays itself there, ordinarily, in the thought and in the form in which that is rendered. . . . A sign of mysticism which it has been believed may often be taken as an essential sign, is obscurity and unintelligibility of language. We find it in almost all those who have written."[1] We might add that even in the plastic arts, symbolists and *"décadents"* have attempted, as far as possible, methods that merely indicate and suggest or hint instead of giving real, definite objects: which fact makes them inaccessible to the greater number of people.

This characteristic of obscurity is due to two causes. First, mystical imagination is guided by the logic of feeling, which is purely subjective, full of leaps, jerks, and gaps. Again, it makes use of the language of images, especially visual images— a language whose ideal is vagueness, just as the

[1] *Philosophy of the Unconscious,* I, part 2, ch. IX.

ideal of verbal language is precision. All this can be summed up in a phrase—the subjective character inherent in the symbol. While seeming to speak like everyone else, the mystic uses a personal idiom: things becoming symbols at the pleasure of his fancy, he does not use signs that have a fixed and universally admitted value. It is not surprising if we do not understand him.

(2) An extraordinary abuse of analogy and comparison in their various forms (allegory, parable, etc.)—a natural consequence of a mode of thinking that proceeds by means of symbols, not concepts. It has been said, and rightly, that "the only force that makes the vast field of mysticism fruitful is analogy."[1] Bossuet, a great opponent of mystics, had already remarked: "One of the characteristics of these authors is the pushing of allegories to the extreme limit." With warm imagination, having at their disposal overexcited senses, they are lavish of changes of expressions and figures, hoping thereby to explain the world's mysteries. We know to what inventive labors the Vedas, the Bible, the Koran, and other sacred books have given rise. The distinction between literal and figurative sense, which is boundlessly arbitrary, has given commentators a freedom to imagine equal to that of the myth-creators.

All this is yet very reasonable; but the imagination left to itself stops at no extravagance. After

---

[1] J. Darmesteter, in Récéjac, *Essai sur les fondements de la connaissance mystique*, p. 124.

having strained the meaning of expressions, the imaginative mind exercises itself on words and letters. Thus, the caballists would take the first or the last letters of the words composing a verse, and would form with them a new word which was to reveal the hidden meaning. Again, they would substitute for the letters composing words the numbers that these letters represent in the Hebrew numerical system and form the strangest combinations with them. In the *Zohar,* all the letters of the alphabet come before God, each one begging to be chosen as the creative element of the universe.

Let us also bring to mind numerical mysticism, different from numerical imagination heretofore studied. Here, number is no longer the means that mind employs in order to soar in time and space; it becomes a symbol and material for fanciful construction. Hence arise those "sacred numbers" teeming in the old oriental religions:—3, symbol of the trinity; 4, symbol of the cosmic elements; 7, representing the moon and the planets, etc.[1] Besides these fantastic meanings, there are more complicated inventions—calculating, from the letters of one's name, the years of life of a sick person, the auspices of a marriage, etc. The Pythagorean philosophy, as Zeller has shown, is the systematic form of this mathematical mysticism, for which

[1] In such notions may perhaps be best found the genesis of the present superstitions in regard to "lucky" and "unlucky" numbers, like the number 13, which have such persistence. (Tr.)

numbers are not symbols of quantitative relations, but the very essence of things.

This exaggerated symbolism, which makes the works of mystics so fragile, and which permits the mind to feed only on glimpses, has nevertheless an undeniable source of energy in its enchanting capacity to suggest. Without doubt suggestion exists also in art, but much more weakly, for reasons that we shall indicate.

(3) Another characteristic of mystic imagination is the nature and the great degree of belief accompanying it. We already know[1] that when an image enters consciousness, even in the form of a recollection, of a purely passive reproduction, it appears at first, and for a moment, just as real as a percept. Much more so, in the case of imaginative constructions. But this illusion has degrees, and with mystics it attains its maximum.

In the scientific and practical world, the work of the imagination is accompanied by only a conditional and provisional belief. The construction in images must justify its existence, in the case of the scientist, by explaining; and in the case of the man of affairs, by being embodied in an invention that is useful and answers its purpose.

In the esthetic field, creation is accompanied by a momentary belief. Fancy, remarks Groos, is necessarily joined to appearance. Its special character does not consist merely in freedom in images; what distinguishes it from association and from

[1] See Part Two, chapter II.

memory is this—that what is merely representative is taken for the reality. The creative artist has a conscious illusion *(bewusste Selbsttäuschung): the esthetic pleasure is an oscillation between the appearance and the reality.*[1]

Mystic imagination presupposes an unconditioned and permanent belief. Mystics are believers in the true sense—they have faith. This character is peculiar to them, and has its origin in the intensity of the affective state that excites and supports this form of invention. Intuition becomes an object of knowledge only when clothed in images. There has been much dispute as to the objective value of those symbolic forms that are the working material of the mystic imagination. This contest does not concern us here; but we may make the positive statement that the constructive imagination has never obtained such a frequently hallucinatory form as in the mystics. Visions, touch-illusions, external voices, inner and "wordless" voices, which we now regard as psycho-motor hallucinations—all that we meet every moment in their works, until they become commonplace. But as to the nature of these psychic states there are only two solutions possible—one, naturalistic, that we shall indicate; the other, supernatural, which most theologians hold, and which regards these phenomena as valid and true revelation. In either case, the mystic imagination seems to us naturally tending toward objectification. It tends outwardly, by a spontaneous movement that

[1] Groos, *Die Spiele der Thiere,* pp. 308-312.

places it on the same level as reality. Whichever conclusion we adopt, no imaginative type has the same great gift of energy and permanence in belief.

II

Mystic imagination, working along the lines peculiar to it, produces cosmological, religious, and metaphysical constructions, a summary exposition of which will help us understand its true nature.

(1) The all-embracing cosmological form is the conception of the world by a purely imaginative being. It is rare, abnormal, and is nowadays met with only in a few artists, dreamers, or morbidly esthetic persons, as a kind of survival and temporary form. Thus, Victor Hugo sees in each letter of the alphabet the pictured imitation of one of the objects essential to human knowledge: "*A* is the head, the gable, the cross-beam, the arch, *arx;* D is the back, *dos;* E is the basement, the console, etc., so that man's house and its architecture, man's body and its structure, and then justice, music, the church, war, harvesting, geometry, mountains, etc. —all that is comprised in the alphabet through the mystic virtue of form."[1] Even more radical is Gérard de Nerval (who, moreover, was frequently subject to hallucinations) : "At certain times everything takes on for me a new aspect—secret voices come out of plant, tree, animals, from the humblest insects, to caution and encourage me. Formless and lifeless objects have mysterious turns the meaning

[1] Mabilleau, *op. cit.,* p. 132.

of which I understand." To others, contemporaries, "the real world is a fairy land."

The middle ages—a period of lively imagination and slight rational culture—overflowed in this direction. "Many thought that on this earth everything is a sign, a figure, and that the visible is worth nothing except insofar as it covers up the invisible." Plants, animals—there is nothing that does not become subject for interpretation; all the members of the body are emblems; the head is Christ, the hairs are the saints, the legs are the apostles, the eye is contemplation, etc. There are extant special books in which all that is seriously explained. Who does not know the symbolism of the cathedrals, and the vagaries to which it has given rise? The towers are prayer, the columns the apostles, the stones and the mortar the assembly of the faithful; the windows are the organs of sense, the buttresses and abutments are the divine assistance; and so on to the minutest detail.

In our day of intense intellectual development, it is not given to many to return sincerely to a mental condition that recalls that of the earliest times. Even if we come near it, we still find a difference. Primitive man puts life, consciousness, activity, into everything; symbolism does likewise, but it does not believe in an autonomous, distinct, particular soul inherent in each thing. The absence of abstraction and generalization, characteristic of humanity in its early beginnings, when it peoples the world with myriads of animate beings, has disappeared. Every source of activity revealed by symbols appears as a fragmentary manifestation; it descends from a single primary, personal or impersonal, spring. At the root of this imaginative construction there is always either theism or pantheism.

(2) Mystical imagination has often and erroneously been identified with religious imagination. Although it may be held that every religion, no matter how dull and poor, presupposes a latent mysticism, because it supposes an Unknown beyond the reach of sense, there are religions very slightly mystical in fact—those of savages, strictly utilitarian; among barbarians, the martial cults of the Germans and the Aztecs; among civilized races, Rome and Greece.[1] However, even though the mystic imagination is not confined to the bounds of religious thought, history shows us that there it attains its completest expansion.

To be brief, and to keep strictly within our subject, let us note that in the completely developed great religions there has arisen opposition between the rationalists and the imaginative expounders, between the dogmatists and the mystics. The former, rational architects, build by means of abstract ideas, logical relations and methods, by deduction and induction; the others, imaginative builders, care

---

[1] If we leave out oriental influences and the Mysteries, which, according to Aristotle, were not dogmatic teaching, but a show, an assemblage of symbols, acting by evocation, or suggestion, following the special mode of mystic imagination that we already know.

little for this learned magnificence—they excel in vivid creations because the moving energy with them is in their feelings, "in their hearts;" because they speak a language made up of concrete images, and consequently their wholly symbolic speech is at the same time an original construction. The mystic imagination is a transformation of the mythic imagination, the myth changing into symbols. It cannot escape the necessity of this. On the other hand, the affective states cannot longer remain vague, diffuse, purely internal; they must become fixed in time and space, and condensed into images forming a personality, legend, event, or rite. Thus, Buddha represents the tendencies towards pity and resignation, summing up the aspirations for final rest. On the other hand, abstract ideas, pure concepts, being repugnant to the mystic's nature, it is also necessary that they take on images through which they may be seen—e. g., the relations between God and man, in the various forms of communion; the idea of divine protection in incarnations, mediators, etc. But the images made use of are not dry and colorless like words that by long use have lost all direct representative value and are merely marks or tags. Being symbolic, i. e., concrete, they are, as we have seen, direct substitutes for reality, and they differ as much from words as sketching and drawing differ from our alphabetical signs, which are, however, their derivatives or abbreviations.

It must, however, be noted that if "the mystic fact is a naïve effort to apprehend the absolute, a mode of symbolic, not dialectic, thinking, that lives on symbols and finds in them the only fitting expression,"[1] it seems that this imaginative phase has been to some minds only an internal form, for they have attempted to go beyond it through ecstacy, aspiring to grasp the ultimate principle as a pure unity, without image and without form,[2] which metaphysical realism hopes to attain by other methods and by a different route. However interesting they may be for psychology, these attempts, luring one on further and further, by their seeming or real elimination of every symbolic element, become foreign to our subject, and we cannot consider them at greater length here.

(3) "History shows that philosophy has done nothing but transform ideas of mystic production, substituting for the form of images and undemonstrated statements the form of assertions of a rational system."[3] This declaration of a metaphysician saves us from dwelling on the subject long.

When we seek the difference between religious and metaphysical or philosophical symbolism, we find it in the nature of the constitutive elements. Turned in the direction of religion, mystic symbolism presupposes two principal elements—imagination and feeling; turned in a metaphysical direction, it

[1] Récéjac, *op cit.*, pp. 139 ff.

[2] One at once calls to mind Plotinus, whose highest philosophy is a kind of indescribable ecstacy. (Tr.)

[3] Hartmann, *op. cit.*, vol. I, part 2, chapter IX.

presupposes imagination and a very small rational element. This substitution involves appreciable deviation from the primitive type. The construction is of greater logical regularity. Besides, and this is the important characteristic, the subject-matter— though still resembling symbolic images—tends to become concepts: such are vivified abstractions, allegorical beings, hereditary entities of spirits and of gods. In short, metaphysical mysticism is a transition-form towards metaphysical rationalism, although these two tendencies have always been inimical in the history of philosophy, just as in the history of religion.

In this imaginative plan of the world we may recognize stages according to the increasing weakness of the systems, depending on the number and quality of the hypotheses. For example, the progression is apparent between Plotinus and the frenzied creations of the Gnostics and the Cabalists. With the latter, we come into a world of unbridled fancy which, in place of human romances, invents cosmic romances. Here appear the allegorical beings mentioned above, half concept, half symbol; the ten Sephiros of the Cabala, immutable forms of being; the *syzygies* or couples of Gnosticism—soul and reflection, depth and silence, reason and life, inspiration and truth, etc.; the absolute manifesting itself by the unfolding of fifty-two attributes, each unfolding comprising seven *eons,* corresponding to the 364 days of the year, etc. It would be wearisome to follow these extravagant thoughts, which, though the learned may treat them with some respect, have for the psychologist only the interest of pathologic evidence. Moreover, this form of mystic imagination presents too little that is new for us to speak of it without repeating ourselves.

To conclude: The mystic imagination, in its alluring freedom, its variety, and its richness, is sceond to no form, not even to esthetic invention, which, according to common prejudice, is the type *par excellence*. Following the most venturesome methods of analogy, it has constructed conceptions of the world made up almost wholly of feelings and images—symbolic architectures.

CHAPTER IV

THE SCIENTIFIC IMAGINATION

It is quite generally recognized that imagination is indispensable in all sciences; that without it we could only copy, repeat, imitate; that it is a stimulus driving us onward and launching us into the unknown. If there does exist a very widespread prejudice to the contrary—if many hold that scientific culture throttles imagination—we must look for the explanation of this view first, in the equivocation, pointed out several times, that makes the essence of the creative imagination consist of images, which are here most often replaced by abstractions or extracts of things—whence it results that the created work does not have the living forms of religion, of art, or even of mechanical invention; and then, in the rational requirements regulating the development of the creative faculty—it may not wander at will. In either case its end is determined, and in order to exist, i. e., in order to be accepted, the invention must become subject to preëstablished rules.

This variety of imagination being, after the

esthetic form, the one that psychologists have best described, we may therefore be brief. A complete study of the subject, however, remains yet to be made. Indeed, we may remark that there is no "scientific imagination" in general, that its form must vary according to the nature of the science, and that, consequently, it really resolves itself into a certain number of genera and even of species. Whence arises the need of monographs, each one of which should be the work of a competent man.

No one will question that mathematicians have a way of thinking all their own; but even this is too general. The arithmetician, the algebraist, and more generally the analyst, in whom invention obtains in the most abstract form of discontinuous functions—symbols and their relations—cannot imagine like the geometrician. One may well speak of the ideal figures of geometry—the empirical origin of which is no longer anywhere contested—but we cannot escape from representing them as somehow in space. Does anyone think that Monge, the creator of descriptive geometry, who by his work has aided builders, architects, mechanics, stone cutters in their labors, could have the same type of imagination as the mathematician who has been given up all his life to the theory of number? Here, then, are at least two well-marked varieties, to say nothing of mixed forms. The physicist's imagination is necessarily more concrete; since he is incessantly obliged to refer to the data of sense or to that totality of visual, tactile, motor, acoustic, thermic, etc., representations that we term the "properties of matter." Our eye, says Tyndall, cannot see sound waves contract and dilate, but we construct them in thought—i. e., by means of visual images. The same remarks are true of chemists. The founders of the atomic theory certainly *saw* atoms, and pictured them in the mind's eye, and their arrangement in compound bodies. The complexity of the imagination increases still more in the geologist, the botanist, the zoologist; it approaches more and more, with its increasing details, to the level of perception. The physician, in whom science becomes also an art, has need of visual representations of the exterior and interior, microscopic and macroscopic, of the various forms of diseased conditions; auditory representations (auscultation); tactile representations (touch, reverberation, etc.); and let us also add that we are not speaking merely of diagnosis of diseases, which is a matter of reproductive imagination, but of the discovery of a new pathologic "entity," proven and made certain from the symptoms. Lastly, if we do not hesitate to give a very broad extension to the term "scientific," and apply it also to invention in social matters, we shall see that the latter is still more exacting, for one must represent to oneself not only the elements of the past and of the present, but in addition construct a picture of the future according to probable inductions and deductions.

It might be objected that the foregoing enumeration proves a great variety in the *content* of creative imagination but not in the imagination itself, and that nothing has proven that, under all these various aspects, there does not exist a so-called scientific imagination, that always remains identical. This position is untenable. For we have seen above[1] that there exists no creative instinct in general, no one mere indeterminate "creative power," but only wants that, in certain cases, excite novel combinations of images. The nature of the separable materials, then, is a factor of the first importance; it is determining, and indicates to the mind the direction in which it is turned, and all treason in this regard is paid for by aborted construction, by painful labor for some petty result. Invention, separated from what gives it body and soul, is nothing but a pure abstraction.

The monographs called for above would, then, be a not unneeded work. It is only from them collectively that the rôle of the imagination in the sciences could be completely shown, and we might by abstraction separate out the characters common to all varieties—the essential marks of this imaginative type.

Mathematics aside, all the sciences dealing with facts—from astronomy to sociology—suppose three moments, namely, observation, conjecture, verification. The first depends on external and internal sense, the second on the creative imagination, the third on rational operations, although the imagination is not entirely barred from it. In order to study its influence on scientific development, we

[1] See Part I, chapter II.

shall study it (a) in the sciences in process of formation; (b) in the established sciences; (c) in the processes of verification.

II

It has often been said that the perfection of a science is measured by the amount of mathematics it requires; we might say, conversely, that its lack of completeness is measured by the amount of imagination that it includes. It is a psychological necessity. Where the human mind cannot explain or prove, there it invents; preferring a semblance of knowledge to its total absence.[1] Imagination fulfills the function of a substitute; it furnishes a subjective, conjectural solution in place of an objective, rational explanation. This substitution has degrees:

(1) The sway of the imagination is almost complete in the pseudo-sciences (alchemy, astrology, magic, occultism, etc.), which it would be more proper to call embryonic sciences, for they were the beginnings of more exact disciplines and their fancies have not been without use. In the history of science, this is the golden age of the creative imagination, corresponding to the myth-making period already studied.

(2) The semi-sciences, incompletely proved (cer-

[1] Cf. the Preface to Kant's *Critique of Pure Reason.* ''Our reason . . . is always troubled with questions which cannot be ignored, because they spring from the very nature of reason, and which cannot be answered, because they transcend the powers of human reason. (Tr.)

tain portions of biology, psychology, sociology, etc.), although they show a regression of imaginative explanation repulsed by the hitherto absent or insufficient experimentation, nevertheless abound in hypotheses, that succeed, contradict, destroy one another. It is a commonplace truism that does not need to be dwelt on—they furnish *ad libitum* examples of what has been rightly termed scientific mythology.

Aside from the quantity of imagination expended, often without great profit, there is another character to be noted—the nature of the belief that accompanies imaginative creation. We have already seen repeatedly that the intensity of the imaginary conception is in direct ratio to the accompanying belief, or rather, that the two phenomena are really one—merely the two aspects of one and the same state of consciousness. But faith—i. e., the adherence of the mind to an undemonstrated assertion—is here at its maximum.

There are in the sciences hypotheses that are not believed in, that are preserved for their didactic usefulness, because they furnish a simple and convenient method of explanation. Thus the "properties of matter" (heat, electricity, magnetism, etc.), regarded by physicists as distinct qualities even in the first half of the last century; the "two electric fluids;" cohesion, affinity, etc., in chemistry—these are some of the convenient and admitted expressions to which, however, we attach no explanatory value.

There is also to be mentioned the hypothesis held

as an approximation of reality—this is the truly scientific position. It is accompanied by a provisional and ever-revocable belief. This is admitted, in principle at least, by all scientists, and has been put into practice by many of them.

Lastly, there is the hypothesis regarded as the truth itself—one that is accompanied by a complete, absolute, belief. But daily observation and history show us that in the realm of embryonic and ill-proven sciences this disposition is more flourishing than anywhere else. *The less proof there is, the more we believe.* This attitude, however wrong from the standpoint of the logician, seems to the psychologist natural. The mind clings tenaciously to the hypothesis because the latter is its own creation, or, because in adopting it, it seems to the mind that it should have itself discovered the hypothesis, so much does the latter harmonize with its inner states. Let us take the hypothesis of evolution, for example: we need not mention its high philosophical bearing, and the immense influence that it exerts on almost all forms of human thought. Nevertheless, it still remains an hypothesis; but for many it is an indisputable and inviolable dogma, raised far above all controversy. They accept it with the uncompromising fervor of believers: a new proof of the underlying connection between imagination and belief—they increase and decrease *pari passu.*

III

Should we assign as belonging solely to the

imagination every invention or discovery—in a word, whatever is new—in the well-organized sciences that form a body of solid, constantly-broadening doctrine? It is a hard question. That which raises scientific knowledge above popular knowledge is the use of an experimental method and rigorous reasoning processes; but, is not induction and deduction going from the known to the unknown? Without desiring to depreciate the method and its value, it must nevertheless be admitted that it is preventive, not inventive. It resembles, says Condillac, the parapets of a bridge, which do not help the traveler to walk, but keep him from falling over. It is of value especially as a habit of mind. People have wisely discoursed on the "methods" of invention. There are none; but for which fact we could manufacture inventors just as we make mechanics and watchmakers. It is the imagination that invents, that provides the rational faculties with their materials, with the position, and even the solution of their problems. Reasoning is only a means for control and proof; it transforms the work of the imagination into acceptable, logical results. If one has not imagined beforehand, the logical method is aimless and useless, for we cannot reason concerning the completely unknown. Even when a problem seems to advance towards solution wholly through the reason, the imagination ceaselessly intervenes in the form of a succession of groupings, trials, guesses, and possibilities that it proposes. The function of method is to determine its value, to accept or reject it.[1]

Let us show by a few examples that conjecture, the work of the combining imagination, is at the root of the most diverse scientific inventions.[2]

Every mathematical invention is at first only an hypothesis that must be demonstrated, i. e., must be brought under previously established general principles: prior to the decisive moment of rational verification it is only a thing imagined. "In a conversation concerning the place of imagination in scientific work," says Liebig, "a great French mathematician expressed the opinion to me that the greater part of mathematical truth is acquired not through deduction, but through the imagination. He might have said 'all the mathematical truths,' without being wrong." We know that Pascal discovered the thirty-second proposition of Euclid all by himself. It is true that it has been concluded,

[1] In the rare *Notes* that he has left, James Watt writes that one afternoon he had gone out for a stroll on the Green at Glasgow, and his thoughts were absorbed with the experiments in which he was busied, trying to prevent the cooling of the cylinder. The thought then came to him that steam, being an elastic fluid, should expand and be precipitated in a space formerly void; and having made a vacuum in a separate vessel and opened communication between the steam of the cylinder and the vacant space, we see what should follow. Thus, having imagined the masterpiece of his discovery, he enumerates the processes that, employed in turn, allowed him to perfect it.

[2] For further information we refer to the *Logique de l'hypothèse*, by E. Naville, from which are borrowed most of the facts here given.

wrongly perhaps, that he had also discovered all the earlier ones, the order followed by the Greek geometrician not being necessary, and not excluding other arrangements. However it be, reasoning alone was not enough for that discovery. "Many people," says Naville, "of whom I am one, might have thought hard all their lives without finding out the thirty-two propositions of Euclid." This fact alone shows clearly the difference between invention and demonstration, imagination and reason.

In the sciences dealing with facts, all the best-established experimental truths have passed through a conjectural stage. History permits no doubt on this point. What makes it appear otherwise is the fact that for centuries there has gradually come to be formed a body of solid belief, making a whole, stored away in classic treatises from which we learn from childhood, and in which they seem to be arranged of themselves. We are not told of the series of checks and failures through which[1] they have passed. Innumerable are the inventions that remained for a long time in a state of conjecture, matters of pure imagination, because various circumstances did not permit them to take shape, to be demonstrated and verified. Thus, in the thirteenth century, Roger Bacon had a very clear idea

---

[1] This much-criticised defect has been only partially overcome in our methods of education through "object" lessons, and, if we may call them so, evolutionary methods, showing to the child "wie es eigentlich gewesen." Cf. J. Dewey, "*The School and Society.*" (Tr.)

of a construction on rails similar to our railroads; of optical instruments that would permit, as does the telescope, to see very far, and to discover the invisible. It is even claimed that he must have foreseen the phenomena of interferences, the demonstration of which had to be awaited ten centuries.

On the other hand, there are guesses that have met success without much delay, but in which the imaginative phase—that of the invention preceding all demonstration—is easy to locate. We know that Tycho-Brahé, lacking inventive genius but rich in capacity for exact observation, met Kepler, an adventurous spirit: together, the two made a complete scientist. We have seen how Kepler, guided by a preconceived notion of the "harmony of the spheres," after many trials and corrections, ended by discovering his laws. Copernicus recognized expressly that his theory was suggested to him by an hypothesis of Pythagoras—that of a revolution of the earth about a central fire, assumed to be in a fixed position. Newton imagined his hypothesis of gravitation from the year 1666 on, then abandoned it, the result of his calculations disagreeing with observation; finally he took it up again after a lapse of a few years, having obtained from Paris the new measure of the terrestrial meridian that permitted him to prove his guess. In relating his discoveries, Lavoisier is lavish in expressions that leave no doubt as to their originally conjectural character. "He *suspects* that the air of the atmosphere is not a simple thing, but is composed of two very different substances." He *presumes* that the permanent alkalies (potash, soda) and the earths (lime, magnesia) should not be considered simple substances." And he adds: "What I present here is at the most no more than a mere *conjecture.*" We have mentioned above the case of Darwin. Besides, the history of scientific discoveries is full of facts of this sort.

The passage from the imaginative to the rational phase may be slow or sudden. "For eight months," says Kepler, "I have seen a first glimmer; for three months, daylight; for the last week I see the sunlight of the most wonderful contemplation." On the other hand, Haüy drops a bit of crystallized calcium spar, and, looking at one of the broken prisms, cries out, "All is found!" and immediately verifies his quick intuition in regard to the true nature of crystallization. We have already indicated[1] the psychological reasons for these differences.

Underneath all the reasoning, inductions, deductions, calculations, demonstrations, methods, and logical apparatus of every sort, there is something animating them that is not understood, that is the work of that complex operation—the constructive imagination.

To conclude: The hypothesis is a creation of the mind, invested with a provisional reality that may, after verification, become permanent. False hypotheses are characterized as imaginary, by which designation is meant that they have not become freed

[1] See above, Part Two, chapter IV.

from the first state.   But for psychology they are
different neither in their origin nor in their nature
from those scientific hypotheses that, subjected to
the power of reason or of experiment, have come out
victorious.   Besides,   in   addition   to   abortive
hypotheses, there are dethroned ones.   What theory
was more clinging, more fascinating in its applications, than that of phlogiston?   Kant[1] praised it as
one of the greatest discoveries of the eighteenth century.   The development of the sciences is replete
with these downfalls.   They are psychological re-
gressions: the invention, considered for a time as
adequate to reality, decays, returns to the imaginative phase whence it seems to have emerged, and
remains pure imagination.

IV

Imagination is not absent from the third stage of
scientific research, in demonstration and experimentation, but here we must be brief, (1) because it
passes to a minor place, yielding its rank to other
modes of investigation, and (2) because this study
would have to become doubly employed with the
practical and mechanical imagination, which will
occupy our attention later.   The imagination is here
only an auxiliary, a useful instrument, serving:

(1) In the sciences of reasoning, to discover ingenious methods of demonstration, stratagems for
avoiding or overcoming difficulties.

[1] Preface to the *Critique of Pure Reason.*

(2) In the experimental sciences for inventing methods of research or of control—whence its analogy, above mentioned, to the practical imagination. Furthermore, the reciprocal influence of these two forms of imagination is a matter of common observation: a scientific discovery permits the invention of new instruments; the invention of new instruments makes possible experiments that are increasingly more complicated and delicate.

One remark further: This constructive imagination at the third stage is the only one met with in many scientists. They lack genius for invention, but discover details, additions, corrections, improvements. A recent author distinguishes (a) those who have created the hypothesis, prepared the experiments, and imagined the appropriate apparatus; (b) those who have imagined the hypothesis and the experiment, but use means already invented; and (c) those who, having found the hypothesis made and demonstrated, have thought out a new method of verification.[1] The scientific imagination becomes poorer as we follow it down this scale, which, however, bears no relation to exactness of reasoning and firmness of method.

Neglecting species and varieties, we may reduce the fundamental characters of the scientific imagination to the following:

[1] Colozza, *L'immaginazione nella Scienza* (Paravia, 1900), pp. 89 ff. In this author will be found abundant details respecting famous discoveries or experiments—those of Galileo, Franklin, Grimaldi, etc.

For its material, it has concepts, the degree of abstraction of which varies with the nature of the science.

It employs only those associational forms that have an objective basis, although its mission is to form new combinations, "the discoveries consisting of the relation of ideas, capable of being united, which hitherto have been isolated."[1]   (Laplace.) All association with an affective basis is strictly excluded.

It aims toward objectivity: in its conjectural construction it attempts to reproduce the order and connection of things.   Whence its natural affinity for realistic art, which is midway between fiction and reality.

It is unifying, and so just the opposite of the esthetic imagination, which is rather developmental. It puts forward the master idea (Claude Bernard's *idée directrice*), a center of attraction and impulse that enlivens the entire work.   The principle of unity, without which no creation succeeds, is nowhere more visible than in the scientific imagination.

[1] Here is an example in confirmation, taken from Duclaux's book on Pasteur: Herschel established a relation between the crystalline structure of quartz and the rotatory power of the substance; later on, Biot established it for sugar, tartaric acid, etc.—i. e., for substances in solution, whence he concluded that the rotatory power is due to the form of the molecule itself, not to the arrangement of the molecules in relation to one another. Pasteur discovered a relation between molecular dyssymetry and hemiedry, and the study of hemiedry in crystals led him logically to that of fermentation and spontaneous generation.

Even when illusory, it is useful. Pasteur, scrupulous scientist that he was, did not hesitate to say: "The experimenter's illusions are a part of his power: they are the preconceived ideas serving as guides for him."

V

It does not seem to me wrong to regard the imagination of the metaphysician as a variety of the scientific imagination. Both arise from one and the same requirement. Several times before this we have emphasized this point—that the various forms of imagination are not the work of an alleged "creative instinct," but that each particular one has arisen from a special need. The scientific imagination has for its prime motive the need of *partial* knowledge or explanation; the metaphysical imagination has for its prime motive the need of a *total* or complete explanation. The latter is no longer an endeavor on a restricted group of phenomena, but a conjecture as to the totality of things, as aspiration toward completely unified knowledge, a need of final explanation that, for certain minds, is just as imperious as any other need.

This necessity is expressed by the creation of a cosmic or human hypothesis constructed after the type and methods of scientific hypotheses, but radically subjective in its origin—only apparently objective. *It is a rationalized myth.*

The three moments requisite for the constitution of a science are found here, but in a modified form:

reflection replaces observation, the choice of the hypothesis becomes all-important, and its application to everything corresponds to scientific proof.

(1) The first moment or preparatory stage, does not belong to our subject. It requires, however, a word in passing. In all science, whether well or ill established, firm or weak, we start from facts derived from observation or experiment. Here, facts are replaced by general ideas. The terminus of every science is, then, the starting-point of philosophical speculation:—metaphysics begins where each separate science ends; and the limits of the latter are theories, hypotheses. These hypotheses become working material for metaphysics which, consequently, is an hypothesis built on hypotheses, a conjecture grafted on conjecture, a work of imagination superimposed on works of imagination. Its principal source, then, is imagination, to which reflection applies itself.

Metaphysicians, indeed, hold that the object of their researches, far from being symbolic and abstract, as in science, or fictitious and imaginary, as in art, is the very essence of things,—absolute reality. Unfortunately, they have never proven that it suffices to seek in order to find, and to wish in order to get.

(2) The second stage is critical. It is concerned with finding the principle that rules and explains everything. In the invention of his theory the metaphysician gives his measure, and permits us to value his imaginative power. But the hypothesis, which

in science is always provisional and revocable, is here the supreme reality, the fixed position, the *inconcussum quid.*

The choice of the principle depends on several causes: The chief of these is the creator's individuality. Every metaphysician has a point of view, a personal way of contemplating and interpreting the totality of things, a belief that tends to recruit adherents.

Secondary causes are: the influence of earlier systems, the sum of acquired knowledge, the social *milieu,* the variable predominance of religions, sciences, morality, esthetic culture.

Without troubling ourselves with classifications, otherwise very numerous, into which we may group systems (idealism, materialism, monism, etc.) we shall, for our purpose, divide metaphysicians into the imaginative and rational, according as the imagination is superior to the reason or the reason rules the imagination. The differences between these two types of mind, already clearly shown in the choice of the hypothesis, are proven in its development.

(3) The fundamental principle, indeed, must come out of its state of involution and justify its universal validity by explaining everything. This is the third moment, when the scientific process of verification is replaced by a process of construction.

All imaginative metaphysics have a dynamic basis, e. g., the Platonic *Ideas,* Leibniz' *Monadology,* the *Nature-philosophy* of Schelling, Schopenhauer's

Will, and Hartmann's *Unconscious,* the mystics, the systems that assume a world-soul, etc. Semi-abstract, semi-poetic constructions, they are permeated with imagination not only in the general conception, but also in the numberless details of its application. Such are the "fulgurations" of Leibniz, those very rich digressions of Schopenhauer, etc. They have the fascination of a work of art as much as that of science, and this is no longer questioned by metaphysicians themselves;[1] they are living things.

Rational metaphysics, on the other hand, have a chilly aspect, which brings them nearer the abstract sciences. Such are most of the mechanical conceptions, the Hegelian *Dialectic,* Spinoza's construction *more geometrico,* the *Summa* of the Middle Ages. These are buildings of concepts solidly cemented together with logical relations. But art is not wholly absent; it is seen in the systematic concatenation, in the beautiful ordering, in the symmetry of division, in the skill with which the generative principle is constantly brought in, in showing it ever-present, explaining everything. It has been possible to compare these systems with the architecture of the Gothic cathedrals, in which the dominant idea is incessantly repeated in the numberless details of the construction, and in the branching multiplicity of ornamentation.

Further, whatever view we adopt as to its ultimate value, it must be recognized that the imagina-

[1] On this point cf. Fouillee, *L'Avenir de la Metaphysique,* pp. 79 ff.

tion of the great metaphysicians, by the originality and fearlessness of its conceptions, by its skill in perfecting all parts of its work, is inferior to no other form. It is equal to the highest, if it does not indeed surpass them.

CHAPTER V

THE PRACTICAL AND MECHANICAL IMAGINATION

The study of the practical imagination is not without difficulties. First of all, it has not hitherto attracted psychologists, so that we enter the field at random, and wander unguided in an unexplored region. But the principal obstacle is in the lack of determination of this form of imagination, and in the absence of boundary lines. Where does it begin, and where does it end? Penetrating all our life even in its least details, it is likely to lead us astray through the diversity, often insignificant, of its manifestations. To convince ourselves of this fact, let us take a man regarded as least imaginative:—subtract the moments when his consciousness is busied with perceptions, memories, emotions, logical thought and action—all the rest of his mental life must be put down to the credit of the imagination. Even thus limited, this function is not a negligible quantity:—it includes the plans and constructions for the future, and all the dreams of escaping from the present; and there is no man but makes such. This had to be mentioned on account of its very triteness, because it is often forgotten, and consequently the field of the creative imagination is unduly restricted, being limited little by little to exceptional cases.

It must, however, be recognized that these small facts teach us little. Consequently, following our adopted procedure, dwelling longest on the clearer and more evident cases in which the work of creating appears distinctly, we shall rapidly pass over the lower forms of the practical imagination, in order to dwell on the higher form—technical or mechanical imagination.

I

If we take an ordinary imaginative person,—understanding by this expression, one whom his nature singles out for no special invention—we see that he excels in the small inventions, adapted for a moment, for a detail, for the petty needs constantly arising in human life. It is a fruitful, ingenious, industrious mind, one that knows how to "take hold of things." The active, enterprising American, capable of passing from one occupation to another according to circumstances, opportunity, or imagined profits, furnishes a good example.

If we descend from this form of sane imagination toward the morbid forms, we meet first the unstable—knights of industry, hunters of adventure, inventors frequently of questionable means, people hungry for change, always imagining what they haven't, trying in turn all professions, becoming workmen, soldiers, sailors, merchants, etc., not from expediency, but from natural instability.

Further down are found the acknowledged "freaks" at the brink of insanity, who are but the extreme form of the unstable, and who, after having wasted haphazard much useless imagination, end in an insane asylum or worse still.

Let us consider these three groups together. Let us eliminate the intellectual and moral qualities characteristic of each group, which establish notable differences between them, and let us consider only their inventive capacity as applied to practical life. One character common to all is mobility—the tendency to change. It is a matter of current observation that men of lively imagination are changeable. Common opinion, which is also the opinion of moralists and of most psychologists, attributes this mobility, this instability, to the imagination. This, in my opinion, is just upside down. *It is not because they have an active imagination that they are changeable, but it is because they are changeable that their imagination is active.* We thus return to the *motor* basis of all creative work. Each new or merely modified disposition becomes a center of attraction and pull. Doubtless the inner push is a necessary condition, but it is not sufficient. If there were not within them a sufficient number of concrete, abstract, or semi-abstract representations, susceptible of various combinations, nothing would happen; but the origin of invention and of its frequent or constant changes of direction lies in the emotional and motor constitution, not in the quantity or quality of representations. I shall not dwell longer on a subject already treated,[1] but it was proper to show, in passing, that common opinion starts from an erroneous conception of the primary conditions of invention—whether great or small, speculative or practical.

In the immense empire of the practical imagination, superstitious beliefs form a goodly province.

What is superstition? By what positive signs do we recognize it? An exact definition and a sure criterion are impossible. It is a flitting notion that depends on the times, places, and nature of minds. Has it not often been said that the religion of one is superstition to another, and *vice versâ?* This, too, is only a single instance from among many others; for the common opinion that restricts superstition within the bounds of religious faith is an incomplete view. There are peculiar beliefs, foreign to every dogma and every religious feeling, from which the most radical freethinker is not exempt; for example, the superstitions of gamblers. Indeed, at the bottom of all such beliefs, we always find the vague, semi-conscious notion of a mysterious power —destiny, fate, chance.

Without taking the trouble to set arbitrary limits, let us take the facts as they are, without possible question, i. e., imaginary creations, subjective fancies, having reality only for those admitting them. Even a summary collection of past and present su-

[1] See above, Part One, chapter II.

perstitions would fill a library. Aside from those having a frankly religious mark, others almost as numerous surround civil life, birth, marriage, death, appearance and healing of diseases, *dies fasti atque nefasti,* propitious or fateful words, auguries drawn from the meeting or acts of certain animals. The list would be endless.[1]

All that can be attempted here is a determination of the principal condition of that state of mind, the psychology of which is in the last analysis very simple. We shall thus answer in an indirect and incomplete manner the question of criterion.

First, since we hold that the origin of all imaginative creation is a need, a desire, a tendency, where then is the origin of that inexhaustible fount of fancies? *In the instinct for individual preservation,* orientated in the direction of the future. Man seeks to divine future events, and by various means to act on the order of things to modify it for his own advantage or to appease his evil fate.

As for the mental mechanism that, set in motion by this desire, produces the vain images of the superstitious, it implies:

(1) A deep idea of causality, reduced to a *post hoc, ergo propter hoc.* Herodotus says of the Egyptian priests: "They have discovered more prodigies and presages than any other people, because, when some extraordinary thing appears, they note it as

---

[1] For a complete and recent study of the question, see A. Lehmann, *Aberglaube und Zauberei von den ältesten Zeiten bis in die Gegenwart,* 1898.

well as all the events following it, so that if a similar prodigy appears anew, they expect to see the
same events reproduced." It is the hypothesis of an
indissoluble association between two or more events,
assumed without verification, without criticism. This
manner of thinking depends on the weakness of the
logical faculties or on the excessive influence of the
feelings.

(2) The abuse of reasoning by analogy. This
great artisan of the imagination is satisfied with
likenesses so vague and agreements so strange, that
it dares everything. Resemblance is no longer a
quality of things imposed on the mind, but an hypothesis of the mind imposed on things. Astrology
groups into "constellations" stars that are billions of
miles apart, believes that it discovers there an animal shape, human or any other, and deduces therefrom alleged "influences." This star is reddish
(Mars), sign of blood; this other is of a pure, brilliant silvery light (Venus) or livid (Saturn), and
acts in a different way. We know what clever
structures of conjectures and prognoses have been
built on these foundations. Need we mention the
Middle Age practice of charms, which even in our
day still has adherents among cultured people?
The physicians of the time of Charles II, says Lang,
gave their patients "mummy powder" (pulverized
mummies) because the mummies, having lasted a
long time, must prolong life.[1] Gold in solution has

[1] Lang, *op cit.*, I, 96. There will be found many other facts
of this kind.

been esteemed as a medicine—gold, being a perfect substance, should produce perfect health. In order to get rid of a disease nothing is more frequent among primitive men than to picture the sick person on wood or on the ground, and to strike the injured part with an arrow or knife, in order to annihilate the sickening principle.

(3) Finally, there is the magic influence ascribed to certain words. It is the triumph of the theory of *nomina numina;* we need not return to it. But the working of the mind on words, erecting them into entities, conferring life and power on them— in a word, the activity that creates myths and is the final basis of all constructive imagination—appears also here.[2]

II

Up to this point we have considered the practical imagination only in its somewhat petty aspect in small inventions or as semi-morbid in superstitious

[2] If this book were not merely an essay, we should have had to study language as an instrument of the practical life in its relations to the creative imagination, especially the function of analogy, in the extension and transformation of the meanings of words. Works on linguistics are full of evidence on this point. One could do better still by attending exclusively to the vernacular, to slang, which shows us creative force in action. "Slang," says one philologist, "has the property of figuring, expressing, and picturing language. . . . With it, however low its origin, one could reconstruct a people or a society." Its principal, not only, means, are metaphor and allegory. It lends itself equally to methods that degrade or ennoble existing words, but with a very marked preference for the worse or degrading meanings.

fancies. We now come to its higher form, mechanical invention.

This subject has not been studied by psychologists. Not that they have misunderstood its rôle, which is, after all, very evident; but they limit themselves to speak of it cursorily, without emphasizing it.

In order to appreciate its importance, I see no other way than to put ourselves face to face with the works that it has produced, to question the history of discovery and useful arts, to profit by the disclosures of inventors and their biographers.

Of a work of this kind, which would be very long because the materials are scattered, we can give here only a rough sketch, merely to take therefrom what is of interest for psychology and what teaches us in regard to the characters peculiar to this type of imagination.

The erroneous view that opposes imagination to the useful, and claims that they are mutually exclusive, is so widespread and so persistent, that we shall seem to many to be expressing a paradox when we say that if we could strike the balance of the imagination that man has spent and made permanent in esthetic life on the one hand, and in technical and mechanical invention on the other, the balance would be in favor of the latter. This assertion, however, will not seem paradoxical to those who have considered the question. Why, then, the view above mentioned? Why are people inclined to believe that our present subject, if not entirely foreign to the imagination, is only an impoverished form of it? I account for it by the following reasons:

Esthetic imagination, when fully complete, is simply *fixed,* i. e., remains a fictitious matter recognized as such. It has a frankly subjective, personal character, arbitrary in its choice of means. A work of art—a poem, a novel, a drama, an opera, a picture, a statue—might have been otherwise than it is. It is possible to modify the general plan, to add or reduce an episode, to change an ending. The novelist who in the course of his work changes his characters; the dramatic author who, in deference to public sentiment, substitutes a happy *denoûement* in place of a catastrophe, furnish naïve testimony of this freedom of imagination. Moreover, artistic creation, expressing itself in words, sounds, lines, forms, colors, is cast in a mould that allows it only a feeble "material" reality.

The mechanical imagination is objective—it must be embodied, take on a form that gives it a place side by side with products of nature. It is arbitrary neither in its choice nor in its means; it is not a free creature having its end in itself. In order to succeed, it is subjected to rigorous physical conditions, to a determinism. It is at this cost that it becomes a reality, and as we instinctively establish an antithesis between the imaginary and the real, it seems that mechanical invention is outside the realm of the imagination. Moreover, it requires the constant intervention of calculation, of reasoning, and lastly, of a manual operation of supreme importance. We may say without exaggerating that the success of many mechanical creations depends on the skillful manipulation of materials. But this last moment, because it is decisive, should not make us forget its antecedents, especially the initial moment, which is, for psychology, similar to all other instances of invention, when the idea arises, tending to become objective.

Otherwise, the differences here pointed out between the two forms of imagination—esthetic and mechanical—are but relative. The former is not independent of technical apprenticeship, often of long duration (e. g., in music, sculpture, painting). As for the latter, we should not exaggerate its determinism. Often the same end can be reached by different inventions—by means differently imagined, through different mental constructions; and it follows that, after all allowances are made, these differently realized imaginations are equally useful.

The difference between the two types is found in the nature of the need or desire stimulating the invention, and secondly in the nature of the materials employed. Others have confounded two distinct things—liberty of imagination, which belongs rather to esthetic creation, and quality and power of imagination, which may be identical in both cases.

I have questioned certain inventors very skillful in mechanics, addressing myself to those, preferably, whom I knew to be strangers to any preconceived psychological theory. Their replies agree, and prove that the birth and development of mechanical invention are very strictly like those found in other forms of constructive imagination. As an example, I cite the following statement of an engineer, which I render literally:

"The so-called creative imagination surely proceeds in very different ways, according to temperament, aptitudes, and, in the same individual, following the mental disposition, the *milieu*.

"We may, however, as far as regards mechanical inventions, distinguish four sufficiently clear phases—the germ, incubation, flowering, and completion.

"By germ I mean the first idea coming to the mind to furnish a solution for a problem that the whole of one's observations, studies, and researches has put before one, or that, put by another, has struck one.

"Then comes incubation, often very long and painful, or, again, even unconscious. Instinctively as well as voluntarily one brings to the solution of the problem all the materials that the eyes and ears can gather.

"When this latent work is sufficiently complete, the idea suddenly bursts forth, it may be at the end of a voluntary tension of mind, or on the occasion of a chance remark, tearing the veil that hides the surmised image.

"But this image always appears simple and clear. In order to get the ideal solution into practice, there is required a struggle against matter, and the bringing to an issue is the most thankless part of the inventor's work.

"In order to give consistence and body to the idea caught sight of enthusiastically in an aureole, one must have patience, a perseverance through all trials. One must view on all sides the mechanical agencies that should serve to set the image together, until the latter has attained the simplicity that alone makes invention viable. In this work of bringing to a head, the same spirit of invention and imagination must be constantly drawn upon for the solution of all the details, and it is against this arduous requirement that the great majority of inventors rebel again and again.

"This is then, I believe, how one may in a general way understand the genesis of an invention. It follows from this that here, as almost everywhere, the imagination acts through association of ideas.

"Thanks to a profound acquaintance with known mechanical methods, the inventor succeeds, through association of ideas, in getting novel combinations producing new effects, towards the realization of which his mind has in advance been bent."

But for a slightly explored subject, the foregoing remarks are not enough. It is necessary to determine more precisely the general and special characters of this form of imagination.

1. General Characters

I term general characters those that the mechanical imagination possesses in common with the best known, least questioned forms of the constructive imagination. In order to be convinced that, so far as concerns these characters it does not differ from the rest, let us take, for the sake of comparison, esthetic imagination, since it is agreed, rightly or wrongly, that this is the model *par excellence*. We shall see that the essential psychological conditions coincide in the two instances.

The mechanical imagination thus has like the other its ideal, i. e., a perfection conceived and put forward as capable, little by little, of being realized. The idea is at first hidden; it is, to use our correspondent's phrase, "the germ," the principle of unity, center of attraction, that suggests, excites, and groups appropriate associations of images, in which it is enwrapped and organized into a structure, an *ensemble* of means converging toward a common end. It thus presupposes a dissociation of experience. The inventor undoes, decomposes, breaks up in thought, or makes of experience a tool, an instrument, a machine, an agency for building anew with the débris.

The practical imagination is no more foreign to inspiration than the esthetic imagination. The history of useful inventions is full of men who suffered privations, persecution, ruin; who fought to the bitter end against relatives and friends—drawn by the need of creating, fascinated not by the hope of future gain but by the idea of an imposed mission, of a destiny they had to fulfill. What more have poets and artists done? The fixed and irresistible idea has led more than one to a foreseen death, as in the discovery of explosives, the first attempts at lightning conductors, aeronautics, and many others. Thus, from a true intuition, primitive civilizations have put on a level great poets and great inventors, erected into divinities or demigods historical or legendary personages in whom the genius of discovery is personified:—among the Hindoos, Vicavakarma; among the Greeks, Hephaestos, Prometheus, Triptolemus, Daedalus and Icarus. The Chinese, despite their dry imagination, have done the same; and we find the same condition in Egypt, Assyria, and everywhere. Moreover, the practical and mechanical arts have passed through a first period of no-change, during which the artisan, subjected to fixed rules and an undisputed tradition, considers himself an instrument of divine revelation.[1] Little by little he has emerged from that theological age, to enter the humanistic age, when, being fully conscious of being the author of his work, he labors freely, changes and modifies according to his own inspiration.

Mechanical and industrial imagination, like esthetic imagination, has its preparatory period, its zenith and decline: the periods of the precursors, of the great inventors, and of mere perfectors. At first a venture is made, effort is wasted with small result,—the man has come too early or lacks clear vision; then a great imaginative mind arises, blossoms; after him the work passes into the hands of *dii minores,* pupils or imitators, who add, abridge,

[1] Ample information on this point will be found in the work of Espinas, *Les Origines de la Technologie.*

modify: such is the order.   The many-times written history of the application of steam, from the
time of the eolipile of Hero of Alexandria to the
heroic period of Newcomen and Watt, and the improvements made since their time, is one proof of
the statement.   Another example:—the machine for
measuring duration is at first a simple clepsydra;
then there are added marks indicating the subdivisions of time, then a water gauge causes a hand to
move around a dial, then two hands for the hours
and minutes; then comes a great moment—by the
use of weights the clepsydra becomes a clock, at
first massive and cumbersome, later lightened, becoming capable, with Tycho-Brahé, of marking sec-
onds; and then another moment—Huyghens invents
the spiral spring to replace the weights, and the
clock, simplified and lightened, becomes the watch.

2. Special Characters

The special characteristics of the mechanical
imagination being the marks belonging to this type,
we shall study them at greater length.

(I) There is first of all, at least in great inventors, an inborn quality,—that is, a natural disposition,—that does not originate in experience and
owes the latter only its development.   This quality
is a bent in a practical, useful direction; a tendency
to act, not in the realm of dreams or human feeling,
not on individuals or social groups, not toward the
attainment of theoretical knowledge of nature, but

to become master over natural forces, to transform them and adapt them toward an end.

Every mechanical invention arises from a need: from the strict necessity for individual preservation in the case of primitive man who wages war against the powers of nature; from the desire for well-being and the necessity for luxury in growing civilization; from the need of creating little engines, imitating instruments and machines, in the child. In a word, *every particular invention, great or small, arises from a particular need;* for, we repeat again, there is no creative instinct in general. A man distinguished for various inventions along practical lines, writes: "As far as my memory allows, I can state that in my case conception always results from a material or mental need.[1] It springs up suddenly. Thus, in 1887, a speech of Bismarck made me so angry that I immediately thought of arming my

[1] The same correspondent, without my having asked him in regard to this, gives me the following details: "When about seven years old I saw a locomotive, its fire and smoke. My father's stove also made fire and smoke, but lacked wheels. If, then, I told my father, we put wheels under the stove, it would move like a locomotive. Later, when about thirteen, the sight of a steam threshing-machine suggested to me the idea of making a horseless wagon. I began a childish construction of one, which my father made me give up," etc. The tendency toward mechanical invention shows itself very early in some children— we gave examples of it before. Our inventor adds: "My imagination was strongest at about the age of 25 to 35 (I am now 45 years old). After that time it seems to me that the remainder of life is good only for producing less important conceptions, forming a natural consequence of the principal conceptions born of the period of youth."

country with a repeating rifle. I had already made various applications to the ministry of war, when I learned that the Lebel system had just been adopted. My patriotism was fully satisfied, but I still have the design of the gun that I invented." This communication mentions two or three other inventions that arose under analogous circumstances, but have had a chance of being adopted.

Among the requisite qualities I mention the natural and necessary preëminence of certain groups of sensations or images (visual, tactile, motor) that may be decisive in determining the direction of the inventor.

(II) Mechanical invention grows by successive stratifications and additions, as in the sciences, but more completely. It is a fine verification of the "subsidiary law of growing complexity" previously discussed.[1] If we measure the distance traversed since the distant ages when man was naked and unarmed before nature to the present time of the reign of machinery, we are astonished at the amount of imagination produced and expended, often uselessly lavished, and we ask ourselves how such a work could have been misunderstood or so lightly appreciated. It does not pertain to our subject to make even a summary table of this long development. The reader can consult the special works which, unfortunately, are most often fragmentary and lack a general view. So we should feel grateful to a historian of the useful arts, L. Bourdeau, for

[1] See above, Part Two, chapter V.

having attempted to separate out the philosophy of the subject, and for having fastened it down in the following formulas:[1]

(a) The exploitation of the powers of nature is made according to their degree of power.

(b) The extension of working instruments has followed a logical evolution in the direction of growing complexity and perfection.

Man, according to the observations of M. Bourdeau, has applied his creative activity to natural forces and has set them to work according to a regular order, viz.:

(1) Human forces, the only ones available during the "state of nature" and the savage state. Before all else, man created weapons: the most circumscribed primitive races have invented engines for attack and defense—of wood, bone, stone, as they were able. Then the weapon became a tool by special adaptation:—the battle-club serves as a lever, the tomahawk as a hammer, the flint ax as a hatchet, etc. In this manner there is gradually formed an arsenal of instruments. "Inferior to most animals as regards certain work that would have to be done with the aid of our organic resources alone, we are superior to all as soon as we set our tools at work. If the rodents with their sharp teeth cut wood better than we can, we do it still better with the ax, the chisel, the saw. Some birds, with

[1] L. Bourdeau, *Les Forces de l'Industrie*, Paris, 1884. This very substantial work, abounding in facts, conceived after a systematic plan, has aided us much in this study.

the help of a strong beak, by repeated blows, penetrate the trunk of a tree: but the auger, the gimlet, the wimble do the same work better and more quickly. The knife is superior to the carnivore's teeth for tearing meat; the hoe better than the mole's paw for digging earth, the trowel than the beaver's tail for beating and spreading mortar. The oar permits us to rival the fish's fin; the sail, the wing of the bird. The distaff and spindle allow our imitating the industry of insect spinners; etc. Man thus reproduces and sums up in his technical contrivances the scattered perfections of the animal world. He even succeeds in surpassing them, because, in the form of tools, he uses substances and combinations of effects that cannot figure as part of an organism."[1] It is scarcely likely that most of these inventions arose from a voluntary imitation of animals: but even supposing such an origin, there would still remain a fine place for personal creative work. Man has produced by conscious effort what life realizes by methods that escape us; so that the creative imagination in man is a *succedaneum* of the generative powers of nature.

(2) During the pastoral stage man brought animals under subjection and discipline. An animal is a machine, ready-made, that needs only to be trained to obedience; but this training has required and stimulated all sorts of inventions, from the harness with which to equip it, to the chariots, wagons, and roads with which and on which it moves.

[1] *Op. cit.,* pp. 45-46.

(3) Later, the natural motors—air and water—have furnished new material for human ingenuity, e. g., in navigation; wind- and water-mills, used at first to grind grain, then for a multitude of uses—sawing, milling, lifting hammers; etc.

(4) Lastly, much later, come products of an already mature civilization, artificial motors, explosives,—powder and all its derivatives and substitutes—steam, which has made such great progress.

If the reader please to represent to himself well the immense number of facts that we have just indicated in a few lines; if he please to note that every invention, great or small, before becoming a fixed and realized thing, was at first an imagination, a mere contrivance of the brain, an assembly of new combinations or new relations, he will be forced to admit that nowhere—not excepting even esthetic production—has man imagined to such a great extent.

One of the reasons—though not the only one—that supports the contrary opinion is, that by the very law of their growing complexity, inventions are grafted one on another. In all the useful arts improvements have been so slow, and so gradually wrought, that each one of them passed unperceived, without leaving its author the credit for its discovery. The immense majority of inventions are anonymous—some great names alone survive. But, whether individual or collective, imagination remains imagination. In order that the plow, at first a simple piece of wood hardened by the fire and pushed along with the human hand, should become what it is to-day, through a long series of modifications described in the special works, who knows how many imaginations have labored! In the same way, the uncertain flame of a resinous branch guiding vaguely in the night leads us, through a long series of inventions, to gas and electric lighting. All objects, even the most ordinary and most common that now serve us in our everyday-life, are *condensed imagination*.

(III) More than any other form, mechanical imagination depends strictly on physical conditions. It cannot rest content with combining images, it postulates material factors that impose themselves unyieldingly. Compared to it, the scientific imagination has much more freedom in the building of its hypotheses. In general, every great invention has been preceded by a period of abortive attempts. History shows that the so-called "initial moment" of a mechanical discovery, followed by its improvements, is the moment ending a series of unsuccessful trials: we thus skip a phase of pure imagination, of imaginative construction that has not been able to enter into the mold of an appropriate determinism. There must have existed innumerable inventions that we might term mechanical romances, which, however, we cannot refer to because they have left us no trace, not being born viable. Others are known as curiosities because they have blazed the path. We know that Otto de Guericke made four fruitless attempts before discovering his air-pump. The brothers Montgolfier were possessed with the desire to make "imitation clouds," like those they saw moving over the Alps. "In order to imitate nature," they at first enclosed water-vapor in a light, stout case, which fell on cooling. Then they tried hydrogen; then the production of a gas with electrical properties; and so on. Thus, after a succession of hypotheses and failures, they finally succeeded. From the end of the sixteenth century there was offered the possibility of communicating at a distance by means of electricity. "In a work published in 1624 the Jesuit, Father Leurechon, described an imaginary apparatus (by means of which, he said, people could converse at a distance) for the aid of lovers who, by the connection of their movements, would cause a needle to move about a dial on which would be written the letters of the alphabet; and the drawing accompanying the text is almost a picture of Breguet's telegraph." But the author considered it impossible "in the absence of lovers having such ability."[1]

Mechanical inventions that fail correspond to erroneous or unverified scientific hypotheses. They do not emerge from the stage of pure imagination,

[1] Quoted by L. Bourdeau (*op. cit.*, p 354), who also mentions many other attempts: an anonymous Scot in 1753, Lesage of Geneva, 1780, Lhomond (France, 1787), Battencourt (Spain, 1787), Reiser, a German (1794), Salva (Madrid, 1796). The insufficient study of dynamic electricity did not permit them to succeed.

but they are instructive to the psychologist because they give in bare form the initial work of the constructive imagination in the technical field.

There still remain the requirements of reasoning, of calculation, of adaptation to the properties of matter. But, we repeat, this determinism has several possible forms—one can reach the same goal through different means. Besides, these determining conditions are not lacking in any type of imagination; there is only a difference as between lesser and greater. Every imaginative construction from the moment that it is little more than a group of fancies, a spectral image haunting a dreamer's brain, must take on a body, submit to external conditions on which it depends, and which materialize it somewhat. In this respect, architecture is an excellent example. It is classed among the fine arts; but it is subject to so many limitations that its process of invention strongly resembles technical and mechanical creations. Thus it has been possible to say that "Architecture is the least personal of all the arts." "Before being an art it is an industry in the sense that it has nearly always a useful end that is imposed on it and rules its manifestations. Whatever it builds—a temple, a theater, a palace—it must before all else subordinate its work to the end assigned to it in advance. This is not all:—it must take account of materials, climate, soil, location, habits—of all things that may require much skill, tact, calculation, which, however, do not interest

art as such, and do not permit architecture to manifest its purely esthetic qualities."[1]

Thus, at bottom, there is an identity of nature
between the constructive imagination of the mechanic and that of the artist: the difference is only
in the end, the means, and the conditions. The
formula, *Ars homo additus naturae,* has been too
often restricted to esthetics—it should comprehend
everything artificial. Esthetes, doubtless, hold that
their imagination has for them a loftier quality—
a disputed question that psychology need not discuss; for it, the essential mechanism is the same in
the two cases: a great mechanic is a poet in his own
way, because he makes instruments imitating life.
"Those constructions that at other times are the
marvel of the ignorant crowd deserve the admiration of the reflecting:—Something of the power that
has organized matter seems to have passed into combinations in which nature is imitated or surpassed.
Our machines, so varied in form and in function,
are the representatives of a new kingdom intermediate between senseless and animate forms, having the passivity of the former and the activity of the
latter, and exploiting everything for our sake. They
are counterfeits of animate beings, capable of giving inert substances a regular functioning. Their
skeleton of iron, organs of steel, muscles of leather,
soul of fire, panting or smoking breath, rhythm of
movement—sometimes even the shrill or plaintive

[1] E. Veron, *L'Esthétique,* p. 315.

cries expressing effort or simulating pain:—all that contributes to give them a fantastic likeness to life—a specter and dream of inorganic life."

[1] L. Bourdeau, *op. cit.*, p. 233.

CHAPTER VI

THE COMMERCIAL IMAGINATION

Taking the word "commercial" in its broadest signification, I understand by this expression all those forms of the constructive imagination that have for their chief aim the production and distribution of wealth, all inventions making for individual or collective enrichment. Even less studied than the form preceding, this imaginative manifestation reveals as much ingenuity as any other. The human mind is largely busied in that way. There are inventors of all kinds—the great among these equal those whom general opinion ranks as highest. Here, as elsewhere, the great body invent nothing, live according to tradition, in routine and imitation.

Invention in the commercial or financial field is subject to various conditions with which we are not concerned:

(1) External conditions:—Geographical, political, economic, social, etc., varying according to time, place, and people. Such is its external determinism—human and social here in place of cosmic, physical, as in mechanical invention.

(2) Internal, psychological conditions, most of which are foreign to the primary and essential inventive act:—on one hand, foresight, calculation, strength of reasoning;—in a word, capacity for reflection; on the other hand, assurance, recklessness, soaring into the unknown—in a word, strong capacity for action. Whence arise, if we leave out the mixed forms, two principal types—the calculating, the venturesome. In the former the rational element is first. They are cautious, calculating, selfish exploiters, with no great moral or social preoccupations. In the latter, the active and emotional element predominates. They have a broader sweep. Of this sort were the merchant-sailors of Tyre, Carthage, and Greece; the merchant-travelers of the Middle Ages, the mercantile and gain-hungry explorers of the fifteenth, sixteenth, and seventeenth centuries; later, in a changed form, the organizers of great companies, the inventors of monopolies, American "trusts," etc. These are the great imaginative minds.

Eliminating, then, from our subject, what is not the purely imaginative element in order to study it alone, I see only two points for us to treat, if we would avoid repetition—at the initial moment of invention, the intuitive act that is its germ; during the period of development and organization, the necessary and exclusive rôle of schematic images.

I

By "intuition" we generally understand a practical, immediate judgment that goes straight to the goal. Tact, wisdom, scent, divination, are synonymous or equivalent expressions. First let us note that intuition does not belong exclusively to this part of our subject, for it is found *in parvo* throughout; but in commercial invention it is preponderating on account of the necessity of perceiving quickly and surely, and of grasping chances. "Genius for business," someone has said, "consists in making exact hypotheses regarding the fluctuations of values." To characterize the mental state is easy, if it is a matter merely of giving examples; very difficult, if one attempts to discover its mechanism.

The physician who in a trice diagnoses a disease, who, on a higher level, groups symptoms in order to deduce a new disease from them, like Duchenne de Boulogne; the politician who knows human nature, the merchant who scents a good venture, etc., furnish examples of intuition. It does not depend on the degree of culture;—not to mention women, whose insight into practical matters is well known, there are ignorant people—peasants, even savages—who, in their limited sphere, are the equals of fine diplomats.

But all these facts teach us nothing concerning its psychological nature. Intuition presupposes acquired experience of a special nature that gives the judgment its validity and turns it in a particular direction. Nevertheless, this accumulated knowledge of itself gives no evidence as to the future. Now, every intuition is an anticipation of the future, resulting from only two processes:—inductive or deductive reasoning, e. g., the chemist foreseeing a reaction; imagination, i. e., a representative construction. Which is the chief process here? Evidently the former, because it is not a matter of fancied hypothesis, but of adaptation of former experience to a new case. Intuition resembles logical operations much more than it does imaginative combinations. We may liken it to unconscious reasoning, if we are not afraid of the seeming contradiction of this expression which supposes a logical operation without consciousness of the middle term. Although questionable, it is perhaps to be preferred to other proposed explanations—such as automatism, habit, "instinct," "nervous connections." Carpenter, who as promoter of "unconscious cerebration," deserves to be consulted, likens this state to reflection. In ending, he reprints a letter that John Stuart Mill wrote to him on the subject, in which he says in substance that this capacity is found in persons who have experience and lean toward practical things, but attach little importance to theory.[1]

Every intuition, then, becomes concrete as a judgment, equivalent to a conclusion. But what seems obscure and even mysterious in it is the fact that, from among many possible solutions, it finds at the first shot the proper one. In my opinion this difficulty arises largely from a partial comprehension of the problem. By "intuition" people mean only

[1] Carpenter, *Mental Physiology*, chapter XI (end).

cases in which the divination is correct; they forget
the other, far more numerous, cases that are failures.
The act by which one reaches a conclusion is a special case of it.   What constitutes the originality of
the operation is not its accuracy, but its *rapidity*—
the latter is the essential character, the former accessory.

Further, it must be acknowledged that the gift of
seeing correctly is an inborn quality, vouchsafed to
one, denied to another:—people are born with it,
just as they are born right- or left-handed: experience does not give it—only permits it to be put to
use.   As for knowing why the intuitive act now succeeds and at another time fails, that is a question
that comes down to the natural distinction between
accurate and erroneous minds, which we do not need
to examine here.

Without dwelling longer on this initial stage, let
us return to the commercial imagination, and follow
it in its development.

II

The human race passed through a pre-commercial
age.   The Australians, Fuegians, and their class
seem to have had no idea whatever of exchange.
This primitive period, which was long, corresponds
to the age of the horde or large clan.   Commercial
invention, arising like the other forms from needs,—
simple and indispensable at first, artificial and superfluous later,—could not arise in that dim period
when the groups had almost their sole relations with

one another as war. Nothing called it to arise. But at a higher stage the rudimentary form of commerce, exchange in kind or truck, appeared early and almost everywhere. Then this long, cumbersome, inconvenient method gave place to a more ingenious invention—the employment of "standard values," beings or material objects serving as a common measure for all the rest:—their choice varied with the time, place, and people—e. g., certain shells, salt, cocoa-seeds, cloth, straw-matting, cattle, slaves, etc.; but this innovation held all the remainder in the germ, for it was the first attempt at substitution. But during the earliest period of commercial evolution the chief effort at invention consisted of finding increasingly more simple methods in the mechanism of exchange. Thus, there succeeded to these disparate values, the precious metals, in the form of powder and ingots, subject to theft and the inconveniences of weighing. Then, money of fixed denomination, struck under the authority of a chief or of a social group. Finally, gold and silver are replaced by the letter of credit, the bank check, and the numerous forms of fiduciary money.[1]

[1] Historically, the evolution has not always proceeded strictly in this order, which, however, seems the most logical one. Negotiable drafts were known to the Assyrians and Carthaginians. For thousands of years Egypt used ingots, not real money, but it was acquainted with fiduciary money. In the new world, the Peruvians made use of the scale, the Aztecs were ignorant of its use, etc. For details, see Letourneau, *L'Evolution du commerce dans les diverses races humaines*, Paris, 1897, especially pp. 264, 330, 354, 384, etc.

Every one of these forward steps is due to inventors. I say inventors, in the plural, because it
is proven that every change in the means of exchange has been imagined several times, in several
ages—though in the same way—on the surface of
our earth.

Summing up—the inventive labor of this period
is reduced to creating increasingly more simple and
more rapid methods of *substitution* in the commercial mechanism.

The appearance of commerce on a large scale has
depended on the state of agriculture, industry, ways
of communication, social and economic conditions
and political extension. It came into being toward
the end of the Roman Republic. After the interrup-
tion of the Middle Ages the activity is taken up
again by the Italian cities, the Hanseatic League,
etc.; in the fifteenth century with the great maritime
discoveries; in the sixteenth century by the *Con-
quistadores,* hungering for adventure and wealth;
later on, by the mixed expeditions, whose expenses
are defrayed by merchants in common, and which
are often accompanied by armed bands that fight
for them; lastly comes the incorporation of great
companies that have been wittily dubbed *"Conquista-
dores* of the counting-house."

We now come to the moment when commercial
invention attains its complex form and must move
great masses. Taken as a whole, its psychological
mechanism is the same as that of any other creative
work. In the first instance, the idea arises, from

inspiration, from reflection, or by chance.   Then comes a period of fermenting during which the inventor sketches his construction in images, represents to himself the material to be worked upon, the grouping of stockholders, the making up of a capital, the mechanism of buying and selling, etc.   All this differs from the genesis of an esthetic or mechanical work only in the end, or in the nature of the images.   In the second phase it is necessary to proceed to execution—a castle in the air must be made a solid structure.   Then appear a thousand obstructions in the details that must be overcome.   As everywhere else, minor inventions become grafted on the principal invention; the author lets us see the poverty or richness in resource of his mind. Finally, the work is triumphant, fails, or is only half-successful.

Did it keep only to these general traits, commercial imagination would be merely the reiteration, with slight changes, of forms already studied; but it has characteristics all its own that must be distinguished.

(1) It is a combining or tactical imagination. Heretofore, we have met nothing like it. This special mark is derived from the very nature of its determinism, which is very different from that limiting the scientific or mechanical imagination. Every commercial project, in order to emerge from the internal, purely imaginative phase, and become a reality, requires "coming to a head," very exact calculation of frequently numerous, divergent, even

contrary elements. The American dealer speculating in grain is under the absolute necessity of being quickly and surely informed regarding the agricultural situation in all countries of the world that are rich in grain, that export or import; in regard to the probable chances of rain or drouth; the tariff duties of the various countries, etc. Lacking that, he buys and sells haphazard. Moreover, as he deals in enormous quantities, the least error means great losses, the smallest profit on a unit is of account, and is multiplied and increased into a noticeable gain.

Besides that initial intuition that shows opportune business and moments, commercial imagination presupposes a well-studied, detailed campaign for attack and defense, a rapid and reliable glance at every moment of execution in order to incessantly modify this plan—it is a kind of war. All this totality of special conditions results from a general condition,—namely, competition, strife. We shall come back to this point at the end of the chapter.

Let us follow to the end the working of this creative imagination. Like the other forms, this kind of invention arises from a need, a desire—that of the spreading of "self-feeling," of the expansion of the individual under the form of enrichment. But this tendency, and with it the resulting imaginative creation, can undergo changes.

It is a well-known law of the emotional life that what is at first sought as a means may become an end and be desired for itself. A very sensual passion may at length undergo a sort of idealization; people study a science at first because it is useful, and later because of its fascination; and we may desire money in order to spend it, and later in order to hoard it.   Here it is the same: the financial inventor is often possessed with a kind of intoxication—he no longer labors for lucre, but for art; he becomes, in his own way, an author of romance.   His imagination, set at the beginning toward gain, now seeks only its complete expansion, the assertion and eruption of its creative power, the pleasure of inventing for invention's sake,[1] daring the extraordinary, the unheard-of—it is the victory of pure construction.   The natural equilibrium between the three necessary elements of creation—mobility, combination of images, calculation—is destroyed.   The rational element gives way, is obliterated, and the speculator is launched into adventure with the possibility of a dazzling success or astounding catastrophe.   But let us note well that the primary and sole cause of this change is in the affective and motor element, in an hypertrophy of the lust for power, in an unmeasured and morbid want of expansion of self.   Here, as everywhere, the source of invention is the emotional nature of the inventor.

(2) A second special character of commercial imagination is the exclusive employment of schematic representations.   Although this process is also met with in the sciences and especially in social

[1] This condition has been well-described by various novelists, among them Zola, in *Money*.

inventions, the imaginative type that we are now considering has the privilege of using them without exception. This, then, is the proper moment for a description.

By "schematic images" I mean those that are, by their very nature, intermediate between the concrete image and the pure concept, but approach more nearly the concept. We have already pointed out very different kinds of representations—concrete images, material pertaining to plastic and mechanical imagination; the emotional abstractions of the diffluent imagination; affective images, the type of which is found in musicians; symbolic images, familiar in mystics. It may seem improper to add another class to this list, but it is not a meaningless subtlety. Indeed, there are no images in general that, according to the ordinary conception, would be copies of reality. Even their separation into visual, auditory, motor, etc., is not sufficient, because it distinguishes them only with regard to their *origin*. There are other differences. We have seen that the image, like everything living, undergoes corrosions, damages, twisting, and transformation: whence it comes about that this remainder of former impressions varies according to its composition, i. e., in simplicity, complexity, grouping of its constitutive elements, etc., and takes on many aspects. On the other hand, as the difference between the chief types of creative imagination depends in part on the materials employed—on the nature of the images that serve in mental building—a precise determination of the nature of the images belonging to each type is not an idle operation.

In order to clearly explain what we mean by schematic images, let us represent by a line, *PC,* the scale of images acording to the degree of complexity, from the percept, *P,* to the concept, *C.*

P————————————X——G——S——C

As far as I am aware, this determination of all the degrees has never been made.   The work would be delicate; I do not regard it as impossible.   I have no intention to undertake it, even as I do not pretend that I have given above the complete list of the various forms of images.

If, then, we consider the foregoing figure merely as a means of representing the gradation to the eye, the image in moving, by hypothesis, from the moment of perception, *P,* is less and less in contact with reality, becomes simplified, impoverished, and loses some of its constitutive elements.   At *X* it crosses the middle threshold to approach nearer and nearer to the concept.   At *G* let us locate generic images, primitive forms of generalization, whose nature and process of becoming are well-known;[1] we should place farther along, at *S,* schematic images, which require a higher function of mind. Indeed, the generic image results from a spontaneous fusion of like or very analogous images—such as the vague representation of the oak, the horse,

---

[1] For further details on this point, we refer the reader to our *Evolution of General Ideas* (chapter I).

the negro, etc.; it belongs to only one class of objects. The schematic image results from a voluntary act; it is not limited to exact resemblances—it rises into abstraction; so it is scarcely accompanied by a fleeting representation of concrete objects—it is almost reduced to the word. At a higher level, it is freed from all sensuous elements or pictures, and is reduced, in the present instance, to the mere notion of value—it is not different from a pure concept. While the artist and the mechanic build with concrete images, the commercial imagination can act directly neither on things nor on their immediate representations, because from the time that it goes beyond the primitive age it requires a substitution of increasing generality; materials become values that are in turn reducible to symbols. Consequently, it proceeds as in the stating and solving of abstract problems in which, after having substituted for things and their relations figures and letters, calculation works with signs, and indirectly with things.

Aside from the first moment of invention, the finding of the idea—an invariable psychological state—it must be recognized that in its development and detailed construction the commercial imagination is made up chiefly of calculations and combinations that hardly permit concrete images. If we admit, then,—and this is unquestionable—that these are the materials *par excellence* of the creative imagination, we shall be disposed to hold that the imaginative type we are now studying is a kind of involution, a case of impoverishment—an unacceptable thesis as regards the invention itself, but strictly acceptable as regards the conditions that necessity imposes upon it.

In closing, let us note that financial imagination does not always have as its goal the enriching of an individual or of a closely limited group of associates: it can aim higher, act on greater masses, address itself strenuously to a problem as complex as the reformation of the finances of a powerful state. All the civilized nations count in their history men who imagined a financial system and succeeded, with various fortunes, in making it prevail. The word "system," consecrated by usage, makes unnecessary any comment, and relates this form of imagination to that of scientists and philosophers. Every system rests on a master-conception, on an ideal, a center about which there is assembled the mental construction made up of imagination and calculation which, if circumstances permit, must take shape, must show that it can live.

Let us call to mind the author of the first, or at least, of the most notorious of these "systems." Law claimed that he was applying "the methods of philosophy, the principles of Descartes, to social economy, abandoned hitherto to chance and empiricism." His ideal was the institution of *credit* by the state. Commerce, said he, was during its first stage the exchange of merchandise in kind; in a second stage, exchange by means of another, more managable, commodity or universal value, security equivalent to the object it represented; it must enter a third stage when exchange will be made by a purely conventional sign having no value of its own. Paper represents money, just as the latter represents goods, "with the difference that the paper is not security, but a simple promise, constituting credit." The state must do systematically what individuals have done instinctively; but it must also do what individuals cannot do—create currency by printing on the paper of exchange the seal of public authority. We know the history of the downfall of this system, the eulogies and criticisms it has received:—but because of the originality and boldness of his views, the inexhaustible fecundity of his lesser inventions, Law holds an undisputed place among the great imaginative minds.

III

We said above that commerce, in its higher manifestations, is a kind of war.[1] Here, then, would be the place to study the military imagination. The subject cannot be treated save by a man of the profession, so I shall limit myself to a few brief remarks based on personal information, or gleaned from authorities.

Between the various types of imagination hitherto studied we have shown great differences as regards

[1] A general, a former professor in the War College, told me that when he heard a great merchant tell of the quick and sure service of his commercial information, the conception of the whole, and the care in all the details of his operations, he could not keep from exclaiming, "Why, that is war!"

their external conditions. While the so-called forms of pure imagination, whence esthetic, mythic, religious, mystic creations arise, can realize themselves by submitting to material conditions that are simple and not very exacting, the others can become embodied only when they satisfy an *ensemble* of numerous, inevitable, rigorously determined conditions; the goal is fixed, the materials are rigid, there is little choice of the appropriate means. If there be added to the inflexible laws of nature unforeseen human passions and determinations, as in political or social invention, or the offensive combination of opponents, as in commerce and war; then the imaginative construction is confronted with problems of constantly growing complexity. The most ingenious inventor cannot invent an object as a whole, letting his work develop through an immanent logic:—the early plan must be continually modified and readapted; and the difficulty arises not merely from the multiple elements of the problem to be solved, but from ceaseless changes in their positions. So one can advance only step by step, and go forward by calculations and strict examination of possibilities. Hence it results that underneath this thick covering of material and intellectual conditions (calculation, reasoning), spontaneity (the aptness for finding new combinations, "that art of inventing without which we hardly advance"[1]) reveals itself to few clear-sighted persons; but, in spite of everything, this creative power is everywhere,

[1] Leibniz.

flowing like subterranean streams, a vivifying agency.

These general remarks, although not applicable exclusively to the military imagination, find their justification in it, because of its extreme complexity. Let us rapidly enumerate, proceeding from without inwards, the enormous mass of representations that it has to move and combine in order to make its construction adequate to reality, able at a precise moment to cease being a dream:—(1) Arms, engines, instruments of destruction and supply, varying according to time, place, richness of the country, etc. (2) The equally variable human element —mercenaries, a national army; strong, tried troops or weak and new. (3) The general principles of war, acquired by the study of the masters. (4) More personal is the power of reflection, the habitual solving of tactical and strategic problems. "Battles," said Napoleon, "are thought out at length, and in order to be successful it is necessary that we think several times in regard to what may happen." All the foregoing should be headed "science." Advancing more and more within the secret psychology of the individual, we come to art, the characteristic work of pure imagination. (5) Let us note the exact, rapid intuition at the commencement of the opoprtune moments. (6) Lastly, the creative element, the conception, a natural gift bearing the hallmark of each inventor. Thus "the Napoleonic esthetics was always derived from a single concept, based on a principle that may be summed up thus:—

Strict economy wherever it can be done; expenditure without limit on the decisive point. This principle inspires the strategy of the master; it directs everything, especially his battle-tactics, in which it is synthetized and summed up.[1]

Such, in analytical terms, appears the hidden spring that makes everything move, and it is to be attributed neither to experience nor to reasoning, nor to wise combinations, for it arises from the innermost depths of the inventor. "The principle exists in him in a latent state, i. e., in the depths of the unconscious, and unconsciously it is that he applies it, when the shock of the circumstances, of goal and means, causes to flash from his brain the spark stimulating the artistic solution *par excellence,* one that reaches the limits of human perfection."[2]

[1] General Bonnal, *Les Maîtres de la Guerre,* 1899, p. 137. "In him (Napoleon)," says the writer, "there was something of the poet, and one could explain all his acts by means of this singular complex, a medley of imagination, passion, and calculation. The dreams of an Ossian with the positive cast of mind of a mathematician and the passions of a Corsican— such were the heterogeneous elements that clashed in that powerful organization" (p. 151).

[2] *Op. cit.,* p. 6.

CHAPTER VII

THE UTOPIAN IMAGINATION[1]

When the human mind creates, it can use only two classes of ideas as materials to embody its idea, viz.:

(1) Natural phenomena, the forces of the organic and inorganic worlds. In its scientific form, seeking to explain, to know, it ends in the hypothesis, a disinterested creation. In its industrial aspect, aiming towards application and utilization, it ends in practical, interested inventions.

(2) Human, i. e., psychic elements—instincts, passions, feelings, ideas, and actions. Esthetic creation is the disinterested form, social invention is the utilitarian form.

Consequently, we may say that invention in science resembles invention in the fine arts, both being speculative; and that mechanical and industrial invention approaches social invention through a common tendency toward the practical. I shall not insist on this distinction, which, to be definite,

---

[1] This title, as will be seen later, corresponds only in part to the contents of this chapter.

rests only on partial characters; I merely wish to mention that invention, whose rôle in social, political and moral evolution is large, must, in order to be a success, adopt certain processes while neglecting others.   This the Utopians do not do.

The development of human societies depends on a multitude of factors, such as race, geographic and economic conditions, war, etc., which we need neither enumerate nor study.   One only belongs to our topic—the successive appearance of idealistic conceptions that, like all other creations of mind, tend to realize themselves, the moral ideal consisting of new combinations arising from the predominance of one feeling, or from an unconscious elaboration (inspiration), or from analogy.

At the beginning of civilizations we meet semi-historic, semi-legendary persons—Manu, Zoroaster, Moses, Confucius, etc., who were inventors or reformers in the social and moral spheres.   That a part of the inventions attributed to them must be credited to predecessors or successors is probable; but the invention, no matter who is its author, remains none the less invention.   We have said elsewhere, and may repeat, that the expression *inventor* in morals may seem strange to some, because we are imbued with the notion of a knowledge of good and evil that is innate, universal, bestowed on all men and in all times.   If we admit, on the other hand, as observation compels us to do, not a ready-made morality, but a morality in the making, it must be, indeed, the *creation* of an individual or of a group.

Everybody recognizes inventors in geometry, in music, in the plastic and mechanic arts; but there have also been men who, in their moral dispositions, were very superior to their contemporaries, and were promoters, initiators.[1] For reasons of which we are ignorant, analogous to those that produce a great poet or a great painter, there arise moral geniuses who feel strongly what others do not feel at all, just as does a great poet, in comparison with the crowd. But it is not enough that they feel: they must create, they must realize their ideal in a belief and in rules of conduct accepted by other men. All the founders of great religions were inventors of this kind. Whether the invention comes from themselves alone, or from a collectivity of which they are the sum and incarnation, matters little. In them moral invention has found its complete form; like all invention, it is organic. The legend relates that Buddha, possessed with the desire of finding the perfect road of salvation for himself and all other men, gives himself up, at first, to an extravagant asceticism. He perceives the uselessness of this and renounces it. For seven years he meditates, then he beholds the light. He comes into possession of knowledge of the means that give freedom from *Karma* (the chain of causes and effects), and from the necessity of being born again. Soon he renounces the life of contemplation, and during fifty years of ceaseless wanderings preaches, makes con-

---

[1] For facts in support, see the *Psychology of the Emotions,* Second Part, chapter VIII.

verts, organizes his followers. Whether true or
false historically, this tale is psychologically exact.
A fixed and besetting idea, trial followed by failure,
the decisive moment of *Eureka!* then the inner revelation manifests itself outwardly, and through the
labors of the master and his disciples becomes complete, imposes itself on millions of men. In what
respect does this mode of creation differ from others,
at least in the practical order?

Thus, from the viewpoint of our present study,
we may divide ethics into living and dead. Living
ethics arise from needs and desires, stimulate an
imaginative construction that becomes fixed in actions, habits and laws; they offer to men a concrete,
positive ideal which, under various and often contrary aspects, is always happiness. The lifeless
ethics, from which invention has withdrawn, arise
from reflection upon, and the rational codification of,
living ethics. Stored away in the writings of philosophers, they remain theoretical, speculative, without appreciable influence on the masses, mere material for dissertation and commentary.

In proportion as we recede from distant origins
the light grows, and invention in the social and
moral order becomes manifest as the work of two
principal categories of minds—the fantastic, the
positive. The former, purely imaginative beings,
visionaries, utopians, are closely related to poets and
artists. The latter, practical creators or reformers,
capable of organizing, belong to the family of in-

ventors in the industrial-commercial-mechanical order.

I

The chimerical form of imagination, applied to
the social sciences, is the one that, taking account
neither of the external determinism nor of practical
requirements, spreads out freely. Such are the creators of ideal republics, seeking for a lost or to-be-
discovered-in-the-future golden age, constructing, as
their fancy pleases, human societies in their large
outlines and in their details. They are social novelists, who bear the same relation to sociologists that
poets do to critics. Their dreams, subjected merely
to the conditions of an inner logic, have lived only
within themselves, an ideal life, without ever passing through the test of application. It is the
creative imagination in its unconscious form, restrained to its first phase.

Nothing is better known than their names and
their works: The *Republic* of Plato, Thomas More's
Utopia, Campanella's *City of the Sun,* Harrington's
Oceana, Fenelon's *Salente,* etc.[1] However idealistic
they may be, one could easily show that all the
materials of their ideal are taken from the surrounding reality, they bear the stamp of the *milieu,* be it

[1] Our author does not mention Bacon's *New Atlantis,* one of
the best specimens of its kind. "Wisest Verulam," active
and distinguished in so many fields, is not amenable to rules,
and is here found among "idealists," as elsewhere among the
foremost empiricists and iconoclasts. (Tr.)

Greek, English, Christian, etc., in which they lived, and it should not be forgotten that in the Utopians everything is not chimerical—some have been revealers, others have acted as stimuli or ferments. True to its mission, which is to make innovations, the constructive imagination is a spur that arouses; it hinders social routine and prevents stagnation.

Among the creators of ideal societies there is one, almost contemporary, who would deserve a study of individual psychology—Ch. Fourier. If it is a question merely of fertility in pure construction, I doubt whether we could find one superior to him—he is equal to the highest, with the special characteristic of being at the same time exuberant to delirium and exact in details to the least minutiæ. He is such a fine type of the imaginative intellect that he deserves that we stop a moment.

His cosmogony seems the work of an omnipotent demiurge fashioning the universe at will. His conception of the future world with its "counter-cast" creations, where the present ugliness and troubles of animal reign become changed into their opposites, where there will be "anti-lions," "anti-crocodiles," "anti-whales," etc., is one example of hundreds showing his inexhaustible richness in fantastic visions: the work of an imagination that is hot and overflowing, with no rational preoccupation.

On the other hand, his psychogony, based on the idea of metempsychosis borrowed from the Orient, gives itself up to numerical vagaries. Assuming for every soul a periodical rebirth, he assigns it first a

period of "ascending subversion," the first phase
of which lasts five thousand years, the second thirty-
six thousand; then comes a period of completion,
9,000 years; and then a period of "descending subversion," whose first stage is 27,000 years, and the
second 4,000 years—a total of 81,000 years. This
form of imagination is already known to us.[1]

The principal part of his psychology, the theory
of the emotions, questionable in many respects, is
relatively rational. But in the construction of human society, the duality of his imagination—powerful and minute—reappears. We know his methodical organization: the *group,* composed of seven to
nine persons; the *series,* comprising twenty-four to
thirty-two groups; a *phalanx* that includes eighteen
groups, constituting the phalanstery; the small city,
a general center of phalanges; the provincial city,
the imperial capital, the universal metropolis. He
has a passion for classification and ordering; "his
phalanstery works like a clock."

This rare imaginative type well deserved a few
remarks, because of its mixture of apparent exactness and a natural, unconscious utopianism and extravagance. For, beneath all these pulsating inventions of precise, petty details, the foundation is none
the less a purely speculative construction of the
mind. Let us add an incredible abuse of analogy,
that chief intellectual instrument of invention, of
which only the reading of his books can give an

---

[1] See above, Part III, chapter III.

idea.[1]   Heinrich Heine said of Michelet, "He has a Hindoo imagination."   The term would apply still better to Fourier, in whom coexist unchecked profusion of images and the taste for numerical accumulations.   People have tried to explain this abundance of figures and calculation as a professional habit—he was for a long time a bookkeeper or cashier, always an excellent accountant.   But this is taking the effect for cause.   This dualism existed in the very nature of his mind, and he took advantage of it in his calling.   The study of the numerical imagination[2] has shown how it is frequently met with among orientals, whose imaginative development is unquestioned, and we have seen why the idealistic imagination agrees so well with the indefinite series of numbers and makes use of it as a vehicle.

II

With practical inventors and reformers the ideal falls—not that they sacrifice it for their personal interests, but because they have a comprehension of possibilities.   The imaginative construction must be corrected, narrowed, mutilated, if it is to enter into

[1] We recommend to the reader the "Epilogue sur l'Analogie," in *Le Monde Industriel*, pp. 244 ff., where he will learn that the "goldfinch depicts the child born of poor parents; the pheasant represents the jealous husband; the cock is the symbol of the man of the world; the cabbage is the emblem of mysterious love," etc.   There are several pages in this tone, with alleged reasons in support of the statements.

[2] See above, chapter II.

the narrow frame of the conditions of existence, until it becomes adapted and determined. This process has been described several times, and it is needless to repeat it here in other terms. Nevertheless, the ideal—understanding by this term the unifying principle that excites creative work and supports it in its development—undergoes metamorphosis and must be not only individual but collective; the creation does not realize itself save through a "communion of minds," by a co-operation of feelings and of wills; the work of one conscious individual must become the work of a social consciousness.

That form of imagination, creating and organizing social groups, manifests itself in various degrees according to the tendency and power of creators.

There are the founders of small societies, religious in form—the Essenes, the earliest Christian communities, the monastic orders of the Orient and Occident, the great Catholic or Mohammedan congregations, the semi-lay, semi-religious sects like the Moravian Brotherhood, the Shakers, Mormons, etc. Less complete because it does not cover the individual altogether in all the acts of life is the creation of secret associations, professional unions, learned societies, etc. The founder conceives an ideal of complete living or one limited to a given end, and puts it into practice, having for material men grouped of their free choice, or by cooptation.

There is invention operating on great masses— social or political invention strictly so called—ordinarily not proposed but imposed, which, however, despite its coercive power, is subject to requirements even more numerous than mechanical, industrial, or commercial invention. It has to struggle against natural forces, but most of all against human forces —inherited habits, customs, traditions. It must make terms with dominant passions and ideas, finding its justification, like all other creation, only in success.

Without entering into the details of this inevitable determination, which would require useless repetition, we may sum up the rôle of the constructive imagination in social matters by saying that it has undergone a regression—i. e., that its area of development has been little by little narrowed; not that inventive genius, reduced to pure construction in images, has suffered an eclipse, but on its part it has had to make increasingly greater room for experiment, rational elements, calculation, inductions and deductions that permit foresight—for practical necessities.

If we omit the spontaneous, instinctive, semiconscious invention of the earliest ages, that was sufficient for primitive societies, and keep to creations that were the result of reflection and of great pretension, we can roughly distinguish three successive periods:

(1) A very long idealistic phase (Antiquity, Renaissance) when triumphed the pure imagination, and the play of the free fancy that spends itself in social novels. Between the creation of the mind

and the life of contemporary society there was no relation; they were worlds apart, strangers to one another. The true Utopians scarcely troubled themselves to make applications. Plato and More—would they have wished to realize their dreams?

(2) An intermediate phase, when an attempt is made to pass from the ideal to the practical, from pure speculation to social facts. Already, in the eighteenth century, some philosophers (Locke, Rousseau) drew up constitutions, at the request of interested persons. During this period, when the work of the imagination, instead of merely becoming fixed in books, tends to become objectified in acts, we find many failures and some successes. Let us recall the fruitless attempts of the "phalansteries" in France, in Algeria, Brazil, and in the United States. Robert Owen was more fortunate;[1] in four years he reformed New Larnak, after his ideal, and with varying fortune founded short-lived colonies. Saint-Simonism has not entirely died out; the primitive civilization after his ideal rapidly disappeared, but some of his theories have filtered into or have become incorporated with other doctrines.

(3) A phase in which imaginative creation becomes subordinated to practical life: The conception of society ceases to be purely idealistic or con-

---

[1] For an excellent account of the principles of these movements, see Rae, *Contemporary Socialism;* for Owen's ideals, his *Autobiography;* and for an account of some of the trials, Bushee's ''Communistic Societies in the United States,'' *Political Science Quarterly*, vol. XX, pp. 625 ff. (Tr.)

structed *a priori* by deduction from a single principle; it recognizes the conditions of its environment,
adapts itself to the necessities of its development.
It is the passage from the absolutely autonomous
state of the imagination to a period when it sub-
mits to the laws of a rational imperative.   In other
words, the transition from the esthetic to the scientific, and especially the practical, form.   Socialism is a well-known and excellent example of this.
Compare its former utopias, down to about the middle of the last century, with its contemporary forms,
and without difficulty we can appreciate the amount
of imaginative elements lost in favor of an at least
equivalent quantity of rational elements and positive
calculations.

CONCLUSION.

CONCLUSION

I

THE FOUNDATIONS OF THE CREATIVE IMAGINATION

Why is the human mind able to create? In a certain sense this question may seem idle, childish, and even worse. We might just as well ask why does man have eyes and not an electric apparatus like the torpedo? Why does he perceive directly sounds but not the ultra-red and ultra-violet rays? Why does he perceive changes of odors but not magnetic changes? And so on *ad infinitum.* We will put the question in a very different manner: Being given the physical and mental constitution of man such as it is at present, how is the creative imagination a natural product of this constitution?

Man is able to create for two principal reasons. The first, motor in nature, is found in the action of his needs, appetites, tendencies, desires. The second is the possibility of a spontaneous revival of images that become grouped in new combination.

1. We have already shown in detail[1] that the

---

[1] See above, Part I, chapter II.

hypothesis of a "creative instinct," if the expression
is used not as an abbreviated or metaphorical formula but in the strict sense, is a pure chimera, an
empty entity. In studying the various types of imagination we have always been careful to note that
every mode of creation may be reduced, as regards
its beginnings, to a tendency, a want, a special, determinate desire. Let us recall for the last time these
initial conditions of all invention—these desires, conscious or not, that excite it.

The wants, tendencies, desires—it matters not
which term we adopt—the whole of which constitutes the instinct of individual preservation, have
been the generators of all inventions dealing with
food-getting, housing, making of weapons, instruments, and machines.

The need for individual and social expansion or
extension has given rise to military, commercial,
and industrial invention, and in its disinterested
form, esthetic creation.

As for the sexual instinct, its psychic fertility is
in no way less than the physical—it is an inexhaustible source of imagination in everyday life as well as
in art.

The wants of man in contact with his fellows
have engendered, through instinctive or reflective
action, the numerous social and practical creations
regulating human groups, and they are rough or
complex, stable or unstable, just or unjust, kindly
or harsh.

The need of knowing and of explaining, well or

ill, has created myths, religions, philosophical systems, scientific hypotheses.

Every want, tendency or desire may, then, become creative, by itself or associated with others, and into these final elements it is that analysis must resolve "creative spontaneity." This vague expression corresponds to a *sum,* not to a special property.[1] Every invention, then, has a *motor* origin; *the ultimate basis of the constructive imagination is motor.*

2. But needs and desires by themselves cannot create—they are only a stimulus and a spring. Whence arises the need of a second condition—the spontaneous revival of images.

In many animals that are endowed only with memory the return of images is always provoked. Sensation from without or from within bring them

---

[1] It is a postulate of contemporary physiology that all the neurones taken together cannot spontaneously, that is, of themselves, give rise to any movement—they receive from without, and expend their energy outwards. Nevertheless, between the two moments that, in reflex and instinctive actions, seem continuous, a third interposes, which, for the higher psychic acts, may be of long duration. Thus, reasonings in logical form and reflection regarding a decision to be made have a feeble tendency to become changed into acts; their motor effects are indirect, and at a long range. But this intermediate moment is *par excellence* the moment for psychology. It is also the moment of the personal equation: every man receives, transforms, and restores outwards according to his own organization, temperament, idiosyncrasies, character—in a word, according to his personality, of which needs, tendencies, desires, are the direct and immediate expression. So we come back, by another route, to the same definition of spontaneity.

into consciousness under the form, pure and simple, of former experience; whence we have reproduction, repetition without new associations. People of slight imagination and used to routine approach this mental condition. But, as a matter of fact, man from his second year on, and some higher animals, go beyond this stage—they are capable of spontaneous revival. By this term I mean that revival that comes about abruptly, without *apparent* antecedents. We know that these act in a latent form, and consist of thinking by analogy, affective dispositions, unconscious elaboration. This sudden appearance excites other states which, grouped into new associations, contain the first elements of the creative act.

Taken altogether, and however numerous its manifestations, the constructive imagination seems to me reducible to three forms, which I shall call *sketched, fixed, objectified,* according as it remains an internal fancy, or takes on a material but contingent and unstable form, or is subjected to the conditions of a rigorous internal or external determinism.

(a) The *sketched* form is primordial, original, the simplest of all; it is a nascent moment or first attempt. It appears first of all in dreaming—an embryonic, unstable and uncoördinated manifestation of the creative imagination—a transition-stage between passive reproduction and organized construction. A step higher is revery, whose flitting images, associated by chance, without personal intervention, are nevertheless vivid enough to exclude from consciousness every impression of the external world—so much so that the day-dreamer re-enters it only with a shock of surprise. More coherent are the imaginary constructions known as "castles in Spain"—the works of a wish considered unrealizable, fancies of love, ambition, power and wealth, the goal of which seems to be forever beyond our reach. Lastly, still higher, come all the plans for the future conceived vaguely and as barely possible—foreseeing the end of a sickness, of a business enterprise, of a political event, etc.

This vague and "outline" imagination, penetrating our entire life, has its peculiar characters—the unifying principle is *nil* or ephemeral, which fact always reduces it to the dream as a type; it does not externalize itself, does not change into acts, a consequence of its basically chimerical nature or of weakness of will, which reduces it to a strictly internal and individual existence. It is needless to say that this kind of imagination is a permanent and definite form with the dreamers living in a world of ceaselessly reappearing images, having no power to organize them, to change them into a work of art, a theory, or a useful invention.

The "sketched" form is or remains an elementary, primitive, automatic form. Conformably to the general law ruling the development of mind—passage from indefinite to definite, from the incoherent to the coherent, from spontaneity to reflection, from the reflex to the voluntary period—the imagination comes out of its swaddling-clothes, is changed—through the intervention of a teleological act that assigns it an end; through the union of rational elements that subdue it for an adaptation. Then appear the other two forms.

(b) The *fixed* form comprises mythic and esthetic creations, philosophical and scientific hypotheses. While the "outline" imagination remains an internal phenomenon, existing only in and for a single individual, the fixed form is projected outwards, made something else. The former has no reality other than the momentary belief accompanying it; the latter exists by itself, for its creator and for others; the work is accepted, rejected, examined, criticised. Fiction rests on the same level as reality. Do not people discuss seriously the objective value of certain myths, and of metaphysical theories? the action of a novel or drama as though it were a matter of real events? the character of the *dramatis personae* as though they were living flesh and blood?

The fixed imagination moves in an elastic frame. The material elements circumscribing it and composing it have a certain fluidity; they are language, writing, musical sounds, colors, forms, lines. Furthermore, we know that its creations, in spite of the spontaneous adherence of the mind accepting them, are the work of a free will; they could have been otherwise—they preserve an indelible imprint of contingency and subjectivity.

(c) This last mark is rubbed out without disappearing (for a thing imagined is always a personal

thing) in the objectified form that comprises successful practical inventions—whether mechanical, industrial, commercial, military, social, or political.
These have no longer an arbitrary, borrowed reality; they have their place in the totality of physical
and social phenomena. They resemble creations of
nature, subject like them to fixed conditions of
existence and to a limited determinism. We shall
not dwell longer on this last character, so often
pointed out.

In order the better to comprehend the distinction
between the three forms of imagination let us
borrow for a moment the terminology of spiritualism or of the common dualism—merely as a means
of explaining the matter clearly. The "outline"
imagination is a soul without a body, a pure
spirit, without determination in space. The "fixed"
imagination is a soul or spirit surrounded by an
almost immaterial sheath, like angels or demons,
genii, shadows, the "double" or savages, the *pere-
sprit* of spiritualists, etc. The *objectified* imagination is soul and body, a complete organization after
the pattern of living people; the ideal is incarnated,
but it must undergo transformation, reductions and
adaptations, in order that it may become practical—
just as the soul, according to spiritualism, must bend
to the necessities of the body, to be at the same time
the servant of, and served by, the bodily organs.

According to general opinion the great imaginers
are found only in the first two classes, which is,
in the strict sense of the word, true; in the full

sense of the word false. As long as it remains "outline," or even "fixed," the constructive imagination
can reign as supreme mistress. Objectified, it still
rules, but shares its power with competitors; it
avails nought without them, they can do nothing
without it. What deceives us is the fact that we see
it no longer in the open. Here the imaginative
stroke resembles those powerful streams of water
that must be imprisoned in a complicated network
of canals and ramifications varying in shape and
in diameter before bursting forth in multiple jets
and in liquid architecture.[1]

II

THE IMAGINATIVE TYPE.

Let us try now, by way of conclusion, to present
to the reader a picture of the whole of the imaginative life in all its degrees.

If we consider the human mind principally under
its intellectual aspect—i. e., insofar as it knows and
thinks, deducting its emotions and voluntary activity—the observation of individuals distinguishes
some very clear varieties of mentality.

First, those of a "positive" or realistic turn of
mind, living chiefly on the external world, on what

---

[1] Besides these three principal forms, there are intermediate
forms, transitions from one category to another, that are hard
to classify: certain mythic creations are half-sketched, half-
fixed; and we find religious and social and political conceptions,
partly theoretic or fixed, partly practical or objective.

is perceived and what is immediately deducible therefrom—alien or inimical to vain fancy; some of them flat, limited, of the earth earthy; others, men of action, energetic but limited by real things.

Second, abstract minds, "quintescence abstractors," with whom the internal life is dominant in the form of combinations of concepts. They have a schematic representation of the world, reduced to a hierarchy of general ideas, noted by symbols. Such are the pure mathematicians, the pure metaphysicians. If these two tendencies exist together, or, as happens, are grafted one on the other, without anything to counterbalance them, the abstract spirit attains its perfect form.

Midway between these two groups are the imaginers in whom the internal life predominates in the form of combinations of images, which fact distinguishes them clearly from the abstractors. The former alone interest us, and we shall try to trace this imaginative type in its development from the normal or average stage to the moment when evergrowing exuberance leads us into pathology.

The explanation of the various phases of this development is reducible to a well-known psychologic law—the natural antagonism between sensation and image, between phenomena of peripheral origin and phenomena of central origin; or, in a more general form, between the outer and inner life. I shall not dwell long on this point, which Taine has so admirably treated.[1] He has shown in detail how the

[1] Taine, *On Intelligence*, Part I, Book II, ch. I.

image is a spontaneously arising sensation, one that is, however, aborted by the opposing shock of real sensation, which is its reducer, producing on it an arresting action and maintaining it in the condition of an internal, subjective fact. Thus, during the waking hours, the frequency and intensity of impressions from without press the images back to the second level; but during sleep, when the external world is as it were suppressed, their hallucinatory tendency is no longer kept in check, and the world of dreams is momentarily the reality.

The psychology of the imaginer reduces itself to a progressively increasing interchange of rôles. Images become stronger and stronger states; perceptions, more and more feeble. In this movement opposite to nature I note four steps, each of which corresponds to particular conditions: (1) The quantity of images; (2) quantity and intensity; (3) quantity, intensity and duration; (4) complete systematization.

(1) In the first place the predominance of imagination is marked only by the quantity of representations invading consciousness; they teem, break apart, become associated, combine easily and in various ways. All the imaginative persons who have given us their experiences either orally or in writing agree in regard to the extreme ease of the formation of associations, not in repeating past experience, but in sketching little romances.[1] From among many examples I choose one. One of my

[1] See Appendix E.

correspondents writes that if at church, theatre, on a street, or in a railway station, his attention is attracted to a person—man or woman—he immediately makes up, from the appearance, carriage and attractiveness his or her present or past, manner of life, occupation—representing to himself the part of the city he or she must dwell in, the apartments, furniture, etc.—a construction most often erroneous; I have many proofs of it. Surely this disposition is normal; it departs from the average only by an excess of imagination that is replaced in others by an excessive tendency to observe, to analyze, or to criticise, reason, find fault. In order to take the decisive step and become abnormal one condition more is necessary—intensity of the representations.

2. Next, the interchange of place, indicated above, occurs. Weak states (images) become strong; strong states (perceptions) become weak. The impressions from without are powerless to fulfill their regular function of inhibition. We find the simplest example of this state in the exceptional persistence of certain dreams. Ordinarily, our nocturnal imaginings vanish as empty phantasmagorias at the inrush of the perceptions and habits of daily life—they seem like faraway phantoms, without objective value. But, in the struggle occurring, on waking, between images and perceptions, the latter are not always victorious. There are dreams—i. e., imaginary creations—that remain firm in face of reality, and for some time go along parallel with it. Taine was perhaps the first to see the importance

of this fact. He reports that his relative, Dr. Bail-larger, having dreamt that one of his friends had been appointed editor of a journal, announced the news seriously to several persons, and doubt arose in his mind only toward the end of the afternoon. Since then contemporary psychologists have gathered various observations of this kind.[1] The emotional persistence of certain dreams is known. So-and-so, one of our neighbors, plays in a dream an odious rôle; we may have a feeling of repulsion or spite toward him persisting throughout the day. But this triumph of the image, accidental and ephemeral in normal man, is frequent and stable in the imaginers of the second class. Many among them have asserted that this internal world is the only reality. Gérard de Nerval "had very early the conviction that the majority is mistaken, that the material universe in which it believes, because its eyes see it and its hands touch it, is nothing but phantor s and appearances. For him the invisible world, on the contrary, was the only one not chimerical." Likewise, Edgar Allan Poe: "The real things of the world would affect me like visions, and only so; while the wild ideas of the land of dreams became in turn not only the feeding ground of my daily existence but positively the sole and entire existence itself." Others describe their life as "a

---

[1] Sante de Santis, *I Sogni*, chapter X; Dr. Tissie, *Les Rêves*, esp. p. 165, the case of a merchant who dreams of having paid a certain debt, and several weeks afterward meets his creditor, and maintains that they are even, giving way only to proof.

permanent dream." We could multiply examples.
Aside from the poets and artists, the mystics would
furnish copious examples. Let us take an exaggerated instance: This permanent dream is, indeed,
only a part of their existence; it is above all active
through its intensity; but, while it lasts, it absorbs
them so completely that they enter the external
world only with a sudden, violent and painful shock.

(3) If the changing of images into strong states
preponderating in consciousness is no longer an
episode but a lasting disposition, then the imaginative life undergoes a partial systematization that
approaches insanity. Everyone may be "absorbed"
for a moment; the above-mentioned authors are so
frequently. On a higher level this invading supremacy of the internal life becomes a habit. This third
degree is but the second carried to excess.

Some cases of double personality (those of Azam,
Reynolds) are known in which the second state is at
first embryonic and of short duration; then its
appearances are repeated, its sphere becomes extended. Little by little it engrosses the greater part
of life; it may even entirely supplant the earlier self.
The growing working of the imagination is similar
to this. Thanks to two causes acting in unison,
temperament and habit, the imaginative and internal
life tends to become systematized and to encroach
more and more on the real, external life. In an
account by Féré[2] one may follow step by step this

[2] For the complete account, see his *Pathologie des émotions*,
pp. 345-49. (Paris, F. Alcan.)

work of systematization which we abridge here to its chief characteristics.

The subject, M......, a man thirty-seven years old, had from childhood a decided taste for solitude. Seated in an out-of-the-way corner of the house or out of doors, "he commenced from that time on to build castles in Spain that little by little took on a considerable importance in his life. His constructions were at first ephemeral, replaced every day by new ones. They became progressively more consistent. . . . When he had well entered into his imaginary rôle, he often succeeded in continuing his musing in the presence of other people. At college, whole hours would be spent in this way; often he would see and hear nothing." Married, the head of a prosperous business house, he had some respite; then he returned to his former constructions. "They commenced by being, as before, not very durable or absorbing; but gradually they acquired more intensity and duration, and lastly became fixed in a definite form."

"To sum up, here is what this ideal life, lasting almost from his fourth year, meant: M...... had built at Chaville, on the outskirts of the forest, an imaginary summer residence surrounded by a garden. By successive additions the pavilion became a château; the garden, a park; servants, horses, water-fixtures came to ornament the domain. The furnishings of the inside had been modified at the same time. A wife had come to give life to the picture; two children had been born. Nothing was

wanting to this household, only the being true.
. . . One day he was in his imaginary salon at
Chaville, occupied in watching an upholsterer who
was changing the arrangement of the tapestry. He
was so absorbed in the matter that he did not notice
a man coming toward him, and at the question,
'M......, if you please—?' he answered, without
thinking, 'He is at Chaville.' This reply, given in
public, aroused in him a real terror. 'I believe that
I was foolish,' he said. Coming to himself, he
declared that he was ready to do anything to get rid
of his ideas."

Here the imaginative type is at its maximum, at
the brink of insanity without being over it. Associations and combinations of images form the entire
content of consciousness, which remains impervious
to impressions from without. Its world becomes
the world. The parasitic life undermines and cor-
rodes the other in order to become established in its
place—it grows, its parts adhere more closely, it
forms a compact mass—the imaginary systematization is complete.

(4) The fourth stage is an exaggeration of the
foregoing. The *completely* systematized and permanent imaginative life excludes the other. This is
the extreme form, the beginning of insanity, which
is outside our subject, from which pathology has
been excluded.

Imagination in the insane would deserve a special
study, that would be lengthy, because there is no
form of imagination that insanity has not adopted.

In no period have insane creations been lacking in the practical, religious, or mystic life, in poetry, the fine arts, and in the sciences; in industrial, commercial, mechanical, military projects, and in plans for social and political reform. We should, then, be abundantly supplied with facts.[1]

It would be difficult, for, if in ordinary life we are often perplexed to decide whether a man is sane or not, how much more then, when it is a question of an inventor, of an act of the creative faculty, i. e., of a venture into the unknown! How many innovators have been regarded as insane, or as at

[1] Dr. Max Simon, in an article on "Imagination in Insanity" (*Annales médico-psychologiques,* December, 1876), holds that every kind of mental disease has its own form of imagination that expresses itself in stories, compositions, sketches, decorations, dress, and symbolic attributes. The maniac invents complicated and improbable designs; the persecuted, symbolic designs, strange writings, bordering on the horrible; megalomaniacs look for the effect of everything they say and do; the general paralytic lives in grandeur and attributes capital importance to everything; lunatics love the naïve and childishly wonderful.

There are also great imaginers who, having passed through a period of insanity, have strongly regretted it "as a state in which the soul, more exalted and more refined, perceives invisible relations and enjoys spectacles that escape the material eyes." Such was Gérard de Nerval. As for Charles Lamb, he would assert that he should be envied the days spent in an insane asylum. "Sometimes," he said in a letter to Coleridge, "I cast a longing glance backwards to the condition in which I found myself; for while it lasted I had many hours of pure happiness. Do not believe, Coleridge, that you have tasted the grandeur and all the transport of fancy if you have not been insane. Everything seems to me now insipid in comparison." Quoted by A. Barine, *Névrosés,* p. 326.

least unbalanced, visionary! We cannot even invoke success as a criterion. Many non-viable or abortive inventions have been fathered by very sane minds, and people regarded as insane have vindicated their imaginative constructions through success.

Let us leave these difficulties of a subject that is not our own, in order to determine merely the psychological criterion belonging to the fourth stage.

How may we rightly assert that a form of imaginative life is clearly pathologic? In my opinion, the answer must be sought in the nature and degree of belief accompanying the labor of creating. It is an axiom unchallenged by anyone—whether idealist or realist of any shade of belief—that nothing has existence for us save through the consciousness we have of it; but for realism—and experimental psychology is of necessity realistic—there are two distinct forms of existence.

One, subjective, having no reality except in consciousness, for the one experiencing it, its reality being due only to belief, to that first affirmation of the mind so often described.

The other, objective, existing in consciousness and outside of it, being real not only for me but for all those whose constitution is similar or analogous to mine.

This much borne in mind, let us compare the last two degrees of the development of the imaginative life.

For the imaginer of the third stage, the two forms of existence are not confounded. He distinguishes

two worlds, preferring one and making the best of
the other, but believing in both. He is conscious
of passing from one to the other. There is an
alternation. The observation of Féré, although
extreme, is a proof of this.

At the fourth stage, in the insane, imaginative
labor—the only kind with which we are concerned
—is so systematized that the distinction between
the two kinds of existence has disappeared. All the
phantoms of his brain are invested with objective
reality. Occurrences without, even the most extraordinary, do not reach one in this stage, or else are
interpreted in accordance with the diseased fancy.
There is no longer any alternation.[1]

By way of summary we may say: The creative
imagination consists of the property that images
have of gathering in new combinations, through the
effect of a spontaneity whose nature we have attempted to describe. It always tends to realize itself
in degrees that vary from mere momentary belief
to complete objectivity. Throughout its multiple
manifestations, it remains identical with itself in its
basic nature, in its constitutive elements. The
diversity of its deeds depends on the end desired,
the conditions required for its attainment, materials
employed which, as we have seen, under the col-

[1] There has often been cited the instance of certain maniacs
at Charenton, who, during the Franco-Prussian War, despite
the stories that were told them, the papers that they read, and
the shells bursting under the walls of the asylum, maintained
that the war was only imagined, and that all was only a contrivance of their persecutors.

lective name "representations" are very unlike one another, not only as regards their sensuous origin (visual, auditory, tactile, etc.) but also as regards their psychologic nature (concrete, symbolic, affective, emotional-abstract images; generic and schematic images, concepts—each group itself having shades or degrees).

This constructive activity, applying itself to everything and radiating in all directions, is in its early, typical form a mythic creation. It is an invincible need of man to reflect and reproduce his own nature in the world surrounding him. The first application of his mind is thinking by analogy, which vivifies everything after the human model and attempts to know everything according to arbitrary resemblances. Myth-making activity, which we have studied in the child and in primitive man, is the embryonic form whence arise by a slow evolution religious creations—gross or refined; esthetic development, which is a fallen, impoverished mythology; the fantastic conceptions of the world that may little by little become scientific conceptions, with, however, an irreducible residuum of hypotheses. Alongside of these creations, all bordering upon what we have called the fixed form, there are practical, objective creations. As for the latter, we could not trace them to the same mythic source except by dialectic subtleties which we renounce. The former arise from an internal efflorescence; the latter from urgent life-needs; they appear later and are a bifurcation of the early trunk: but the same sap flows in both branches.

The constructive imagination penetrates every part of our life, whether individual or collective, speculative and practical, in all its forms—IT IS EVERYWHERE.

APPENDICES

APPENDIX A

THE VARIOUS FORMS OF INSPIRATION[1]

Among the descriptions of the inspired state found in various authors, I select only three, which are brief and have each a special character.

I. Mystic inspiration, in a passive form, in Jacob Boehme (*Aurora*): "I declare before God that I do not myself know how the thing arises within me, without the participation of my will. I do not even know that which I must write. If I write, it is because the Spirit moves me and communicates to me a great, wonderful knowledge. Often I do not even know whether I dwell in spirit in this present world and whether it is I myself that have the fortune to possess a certain and solid knowledge."

II. Feverish and painful inspiration in Alfred de Musset: "Invention annoys me and makes me tremble. Execution, always too slow for my wish, makes my heart beat awfully, and weeping, and keeping myself from crying aloud, I am delivered of an idea that is intoxicating me, but of which I

---

[1] See Part One, chapter III.

am mortally ashamed and disgusted next morning. If I change it, it is worse, it deserts me—it is much better to forget it and wait for another; but this other comes to me so confused and misshapen that my poor being cannot contain it. It presses and tortures me, until it has taken realizable propor tions, when comes the other pain, of bringing forth a truly physical suffering that I cannot define. And that is how my life is spent when I let myself be dominated by this artistic monster in me. It is much better, then, that I should live as I have imagined living, that I go to all kinds of excess, and that I kill this never-dying worm that people like me modestly term their inspiration, but which I call, plainly, my weakness."[2]

III.   The poet Grillparzer[1] analvzes the condition, thus:

"Inspiration, properly so called, is the concentration of all the faculties and aptitudes on a single point which, for the moment, should include the rest of the world less than represent it.   The strengthening of the state of the soul comes from the fact that its various faculties, instead of being disseminated over the whole world, find themselves contained within the limits of a single object, touch one another, reciprocally upholding, reënforcing, completing themselves.   Thanks to this isolation, the object emerges out of the average level of its

[2] George Sand, *Elle et Lui*, I.

[1] In Oelzelt-Newin, *op, cit.*, p. 49.

milieu, is illumined all around and put in relief—it takes body, moves, lives. But to attain this is necessary the concentration of all the faculties. It is only when the art-work has been a world for the artist that it is also a world for others."

APPENDIX B

ON THE NATURE OF THE UNCONSCIOUS FACTOR

We have seen that in the question of the unconscious there must be recognized a positive part—facts, and an hypothetical part—theories.

Insofar as the facts are concerned, it would be well, I think, to establish two categories—(1) static unconscious, comprising habits, memory, and, in general, all that is organized knowledge. It is a state of preservation, of rest; very relatively, since representations suffer incessant corrosion and change. (2) Dynamic unconscious, which is a state of latent activity, of elaboration and incubation. We might give a multitude of proofs of this unconscious rumination. The well-known fact that an intellectual work gains by being interrupted; that in resuming it one often finds it cleared up, changed, even accomplished, was explained by some psychologists prior to Carpenter by "the resting of the mind." It would be just as valid to say that a traveler covers leagues by lying abed. The author

See Part I, Chapter III.

just mentioned[1] has brought together many observations in which the solution of a mathematical, mechanical, commercial problem appeared suddenly after hours and days of vague, undefinable uneasiness, the cause of which is unknown, which, however, is only the result of an underlying cerebral working; for the trouble, sometimes rising to anguish, ceases as soon as the unawaited conclusion has entered consciousness. The men who think the most are not those who have the clearest and "most conscious" ideas, but those having at their disposal a rich fund of unconscious elaboration. On the other hand, shallow minds have a naturally poor unconscious fund, capable of but slight development; they give out immediately and rapidly all that they are able to give; they have no reserve. It is useless to allow them time for reflection or invention. They will not do better; they may do worse.

As to the nature of the unconscious working, we find disagreement and darkness. One may doubtless maintain, theoretically, that in the inventor everything goes on in subconsciousness and in unconsciousness, just as in consciousness itself, with the exception that a message does not arrive as far as the self; that the labor that may be followed, in clear consciousness, in its progress and retreats, remains the same when it continues unknown to us. This is possible. Yet it must at least be recognized that consciousness is rigorously subject to the con-

---

[1] *Mental Physiology*, Book II, chapter 13.

dition of time, the unconscious is not. This difference, not to mention others, is not negligible, and
could well arouse other problems.

The contemporary theories regarding the nature
of the unconscious seem to me reducible to two
principal positions—one psychological, the other
physiological.

1. The physiological theory is simple and
scarcely permits any variations. According to it,
unconscious activity is simply cerebral; it is an
"unconscious cerebration." The psychic factor,
which ordinarily accompanies the activity of the
nervous centers, is absent. Although I incline
toward this hypothesis, I confess that it is full of
difficulties.

It has been proven through numerous experiments
(Féré, Binet, Mosso, Janet, Newbold, etc.) that
"unconscious sensations"[1] act, since they produce
the same reactions as conscious sensations, and
Mosso has been able to maintain that "the testimony
of consciousness is less certain than that of the
sphygmograph." But the particular instance of
invention is very different; for it does not merely
suppose the adaptation to an end which the physiological factor would suffice to explain; it implies a
series of adaptations, corrections, rational opera-

---

[1] This expression is put in quotation marks because in American and English usage "sensation" is defined in terms of
consciousness, and such an expression as "unconscious sensation" is paradoxical, and would lead to futile discussion. (Tr.)

tions, of which nervous activity alone furnishes us no example.[1]

2. The psychological theory is based on an equivocal use of the word consciousness. Consciousness has one definite mark—it is an internal event existing, not by itself, but for me and insofar as it is known by me. But the psychological theory of the unconscious assumes that if we descend from clear consciousness progressively to obscure consciousness, to the subconscious, to the unconscious that manifests itself only through its motor reactions, the first state thus successively impoverished, still remains, down to its final term, identical in its basis with consciousness. It is an hypothesis that nothing justifies.

No difficulty arises when we bear in mind the legitimate distinction between consciousness of self and consciousness in general, the former entirely subjective, the latter in a way objective (the consciousness of a man captivated by an attractive scene; better yet, the fluid form of revery or of the awaking from syncope). We may admit that this

[1] For the detailed criticism of unconscious cerebration, see Boris Sidis, *The Psychology of Suggestion: A research into the subconscious nature of Man and Society,* New York, Appletons, 1898, pp. 121-127. The author, who assumes the coexistence of two selves—one waking, the other subwaking, and who attributes to the latter all weakness and vice (according to him the unconscious is incapable of rising above mere association by contiguity; it is "stupid," "uncritical," "credulous," "brutal," etc.) would be greatly puzzled to explain its rôle in creative activity.

evanescent consciousness, affective in nature, felt rather than perceived, is due to a lack of synthesis, of relations among the internal states, which remain isolated, unable to unite into a whole.

The difficulty commences when we descend into the region of the subconscious, which allows stages whose obscurity increases in proportion as we move away from clear consciousness, "like a lake in which the action of light is always nearing extinction" (in double coexisting personalities, automatic writing, mediums, etc.). Here some postulate two currents of consciousness existing at the same time in one person without reciprocal connection. Others suppose a "field of consciousness" with a brilliant center and extending indefinitely toward the dim distance. Still others liken the phenomenon to the movement of waves, whose summit alone is lighted up. Indeed, the authors declare that with these comparisons and metaphors they make no pretense of explaining; but certainly they all reduce unconsciousness to consciousness, as a special to a general case, and what is that if not explaining?

I do not intend to enumerate all the varieties of the psychological theory. The most systematic, that of Myers, accepted by Delboef and others, is full of a biological mysticism all its own. Here it is in substance: In every one of us there is a conscious self adapted to the needs of life, and potential selves constituting the subliminal consciousness. The latter, much broader in scope than personal consciousness, has dependent on it the entire vegetative life—

circulation, trophic actions, etc. Ordinarily the conscious self is on the highest level, the subliminal consciousness on the second; but in certain extraordinary states (hypnosis, hysteria, divided consciousness, etc.) it is just the reverse. Here is the bold part of the hypothesis: Its authors suppose that the supremacy of the subliminal consciousness is a reversion, a return to the ancestral. In the higher animals and in primitive man, according to them, all trophic actions entered consciousness and were regulated by it. In the course of evolution this became organized; the higher consciousness has delegated to the subliminal consciousness the care of silently governing the vegetative life. But in case of mental disintegration there occurs a return to the primitive state. In this manner they explain burns through suggestion, stigmata, trophic changes of a miraculous appearance, etc. It is needless to dwell on this conception of the unconscious. It has been vehemently criticised, notably by Bramwell, who remarks that if certain faculties could little by little fall into the domain of subliminal consciousness because they were no longer necessary for the struggle for life, there are nevertheless faculties so essential to the well-being of the individual that we ask ourselves how they have been able to escape from the control of the will. If, for example, some lower type had the power of arresting pain, how could it lose it?

At the foundation of the psychological theory in all its forms is the unexpressed hypothesis that consciousness may be likened to a quantity that forever decreases without reaching zero. This is a postulate that nothing justifies. The experiments of psychophysicists, without solving the question, would support rather the opposite view. We know that the "threshold of consciousness" or minimum perceptible quantity, appears and disappears suddenly; the excitation is not felt under a determinate limit. Likewise in regard to the "summit of perception" or maximum perceptible, any increase of excitation is no longer felt if above a determinate limit. Moreover, in order that an increase or diminution be felt between these two extreme limits, it is necessary that both have a constant relation— differential threshold—as is expressed in Weber's law. All these facts, and others that I omit, are not favorable to the thesis of growing or diminishing continuity of consciousness. It has even been maintained that consciousness "has an aversion for continuity."

To sum up: The two rival theories are equally unable to penetrate into the inner nature of the unconscious factor. We have thus had to limit ourselves to taking it as a fact of experience and to assign it its place in the complex function that produces invention.

The observations of Flournoy (in his book, mentioned above, Part I, chapter III) have a particular interest in relation to our subject. His medium, Helène S......—very unlike others, who are satisfied with forecasts of the future, disclosures of unknown past events, counsel, prognosis, evocation, etc., without creating anything, in the proper sense —is the author of three or four novels, one of which, at least, is invented out of whole cloth— revelations in regard to the planet Mars, its countries, inhabitants, dwellings, etc. Although the descriptions and pictures of Helène S. are found on comparison to be borrowed from our terrestrial globe, and transposed and changed, as Flournoy has well shown, it is certain that in this "Martian novel," to say nothing of the others, there is a richness of invention that is rare among mediums: the creative imagination in its subliminal (unconscious) form encloses the other in its éclat. We know how much the cases of mediums teach us in regard to the unconscious life of the mind. Here we are permitted, as an exceptional case, to penetrate into the dark laboratory of romantic invention, and we can appreciate the importance of the labor that is going on there.

APPENDIX C

Cosmic and Human Imagination[1]

For Froschammer, *Fancy* is the original principle of things. In his philosophical theory it plays
the same part as Hegel's *Idea,* Schopenhauer's *Will,*
Hartmann's *Unconscious,* etc. It is, at first, objective—in the beginning the universal creative power
is immanent in things, just as there is contained in
the kernel the principle that shall give the plant its
form and construct its organism; it spreads out into
the myriads of vegetable and animal existences that
have been succeeded or that still live on the surface
of the Cosmos. The first organized beings must
have been very simple; but little by little the objective imagination increases its energy by exercising
it; it invents and realizes increasingly more complex
images that attest the progress of its artistic genius.
So Darwin was right in asserting that a slow evolution raises up organized beings towards fulness of
life and beauty of form.

Step by step, it succeeds in becoming conscious
of itself in the mind of man—it becomes subjective.

[1] See above, Part One, Chapter IV.

Generative power, at first diffused throughout the organism, becomes localized in the generative organs, and becomes established in sex. "The brain, in living beings, may form a pole opposed to the reproductive organs, especially when these beings are very high in the organic scale." Thus changed, the generative power has become capable of perceiving new relations, of bringing forth internal worlds. In nature and in man it is the same principle that causes living forms to appear—objective images in a way, and subjective images, a kind of living forms that arise and die in the mind.[2]

This metaphysical theory, one of the many varieties of *mens agitat molem,* being, like every other, a personal conception, it is superfluous to discuss or criticise its evident anthropomorphism. But, since we are dealing with hypotheses, I venture to risk a comparison between embryological development in physiology, instinct in psychophysiology, and the creative imagination in psychology. These three phenomena are creations, i. e., a disposition of certain materials following a determinate type.

In the first case, the ovum after fertilization is subject to a rigorously determined evolution whence arises such and such an individual with its specific and personal characters, its hereditary influences,

---

[2] Those who, not having the courage to read the 575 pages of Froschammer's book, want more details, may profitably consult the excellent analysis that Séailles has given (*Rev. Philos.,* March, 1878, pp. 198-220). See also Ambrosi, *Psicologia dell' immaginazione nella storia della filosofia,* pp. 472-498.

etc. Every disturbing factor in this evolution produces deviations, monstrosities, and the creation does not attain the normal. Embryology can follow these changes step by step. There remains one obscure point in any event, and that is, the nature of what the ancients called the *nisus formativus*.

In the case of instinct, the initial moment is an external or internal sensation, or rather, a representation—the image of a nest to be built, in the case of the bird; of a tunnel to be dug, for the ant; of a comb to be made, for the bee and the wasp; of a web to be spun, for the spider, etc. This initial state puts into action a mechanism determined by the nature of each species, and ends in creations of special kinds. However, variations of instinct, its adaptation to various conditions, show that the conditions of the determinism are less simple, that the creative activity is endowed with a certain plasticity.

In the third case, creative imagination, the ideal, a sketched construction, is the quivalent of the ovum; but it is evident that the plasticity of the creative imagination is much greater than that of instinct. The imagination may radiate in several very different ways, and the plan of the invention, as we have seen,[1] may arise as a whole and develop regularly in an embryological manner, or else present itself in a fragmentary, partial form that becomes complete after a series of attractions.

Perhaps an identical process, forming three

[1] See above, Part II, chapter IV.

stages—a lower, middle, and higher—is at the root of all three cases. But this is only a speculative hypothesis, foreign to psychology proper.

APPENDIX D

Evidence in Regard to Musical Imagination[1]

The question asked above,[2] Does the experiencing of purely musical sounds evoke images, universally, and of what nature and under what conditions? seemed to me to enter a more general field—the affective imagination—which I intend to study elsewhere in a special work. For the time being I limit myself to observations and information that I have gathered, picking from them several that I give here for the sake of shedding light on the question. I give first the replies of musicians; then, those of non-musicians.

1. M. Lionel Dauriac writes me: "The question that you ask me is complex. I am not a 'visualizer;' I have infrequent hypnagogic hallucinations, and they are all of the auditory type.

". . . Symphonic music aroused in me no image of the visual type while I remained the amateur that you knew from 1876 to 1898. When that amateur began to reflect methodically on the

[1] See Part Three, Chapter II.
[2] *Ibid.*, IV.

art of his taste, he recognized in music a power of suggesting:

"1. Sonorous, non-musical images—thunder, clock. Example, the overture of *William Tell*.

"2. Psychic images—suggestion of a mental state—anger, love, religious feeling.

"3. Visual images, whether following upon the psychic image or through the intermediation of a programme.

"Under what condition, in a symphonic work, is the visual image, introduced by the psychic image, produced? In the event of a break in the melodic web (see my *Psychologie dans l'Opera,* pp. 119-120). Here are given, without orderly arrangement, some of the ideas that have come to me:

"Beethoven's *symphony in C major* appears to me purely musical—it is of a sonorous design. The *symphony in D major* (the second) suggests to me visual-motor images—I set a ballet to the first part and keep track altogether of the ballet that I picture. The *Heroic Symphony* (aside from the funeral march, the meaning of which is indicated in the title) suggests to me images of a military character, ever since the time that I noticed that the fundamental theme of the first portion is based on notes of perfect harmony—trumpet-notes and, by association, military. The *finale* of this symphony, which I consider superior to other parts, does not cause me to see anything. *Symphony in B flat major*—I see nothing there—this may be said without qualification. *Symphony in C minor*—it is dramatic, although the melodic web is never broken. The first part suggests the image, not of Fate knocking at the gate, as Beethoven said, but of a soul overcome with the crises of revolt, accompanied by a hope of victory. Visual images do not come except as brought by psychic images."

F. G., a musician, always sees—that is the rule, notably in the *Pastoral,* and in the *Heroic Symphony.* In Bach's *Passion* he beholds the scene of the mystic lamb.

A composer writes me: "When I compose or play music of my own composition I behold dancing figures; I see an orchestra, an audience, etc. When I listen to or play music by another composer I do not see anything." This communication also mentions three other musicians who see nothing.

2. D......, so little of a musician that I had some trouble to make him understand the term "symphonic music," never goes to concerts. However, he went once, fifteen years ago, and there remains in his memory very clearly the principal phrase of a minuet (he hums it)—he cannot recall it without seeing people dancing a minuet.

M. O. L...... has been kind enough to question in my behalf sixteen non-musical persons. Here are the results of his inquiry:

Eight see curved lines.

Three see images, figures springing in the air, fantastic designs.

Two see the waves of the ocean.

Three do not see anything.

APPENDIX E

THE IMAGINATIVE TYPE AND ASSOCIATION OF IDEAS[1]

I have questioned a very great number of imaginative persons, well known to me as such, and have chosen preferably those who, not making a profession of creating, let their fancy wander as it wills, without professional care. In all the mechanism is the same, differing scarcely more than temperament and degree of culture. Here are two examples.

B......, forty-six years of age, is acquainted with a large part of Europe, North America, Oceania, Hindoostan, Indo-China, and North Africa, and has not passed through these countries on the run, but, because of his duties, resided there some time. It is worthy of remark, as will be seen from the following observation, that the remembrance of such various countries does not have first place in this brilliant, fanciful personage—which fact is an argument in favor of the very personal character of the creative imagination.

"In a general way, imagination, very lively in

---

[1] See Conclusion, II, above.

me, functions by association of ideas. Memory or the outer world furnishes me some data. On this data there is not always, though there should be, imaginative work proper, and then things remain as they are, without end.

"But when I meet a construction—it matters little whether ancient or in the course of erection—the formula, 'That ought to be fixed,' is one that rises mechanically to my mind in such a case; often it happens that I think aloud and say it, although alone. When going away from the architectural subject[1] under consideration, I make up infinite variations upon it, one after another. Sometimes the things start from a reflex. . . ."

After having noted his preference for the architecture of the Middle Ages, B...... adds (here he touches on the unconscious factor):

"Were I to explain or attempt to explain how the Middle Ages have such an attraction for my mind, I should see therein an atavistic accumulation of religious feeling fixed in my family, on the female side no doubt, and of religiousness in ecclesiastical architecture—these touch.

"Another example illustrating the rôle of association of ideas in the same matter. One Sunday night I left Noumea in the carriage of Dr. F...... who was going to visit a nunnery five leagues from there. At the moment of our arrival the doctor asked what time it was. 'Half-past two,' I said, looking at my watch. As we stopped in the convent-

[1] B... is not an architect.

court in front of the chapel I *heard* the lusty conclusion of a psalm. 'They are singing vespers,' I
remarked to the doctor. He commenced to laugh.
'What time are vespers sung in your town?' 'At
half-past two,' I answered. I opened the chapel
door in order to show the doctor that vespers had
just been held: the chapel was vacant. As I stood
there, somewhat non-plussed, the doctor remarked,
'Cerebral automatism.'

"I may add here, *by association* of ideas. The
doctor had seen through me, and had with fine
insight perceived *why* I had *heard* the end of the
psalm. The incident made a great impression on
me, all the more as ever since the age of eight my
memory testifies to a like hallucination, but of sight
in place of hearing. It was at L...... that on
Good Friday they rang at the cathedral with all
their might. It was the very moment before the
bells remain silent for three days, and it is known
that this silence, ordained in the liturgy, is explained to children by telling them that during these
two days the bells have flown to Rome. Naturally
I was treated to this little tale, and as they finished
telling it, I *saw* a bell flying at an angle that I
could still describe.

"But this transforming power of my imagination
is not present in me to the same extent as regards
all things. It is much more operative in relation to
Romano-Gothic architecture, mystic literature, and
sociological knowledge than in relation, for instance, to my memories of travels. When I see

again, in the mind's eye, the Isle of Bourbon, Niagara, Tahiti, Calcutta, Melbourne, the Pyramids and the Sphinx, the graphic representation is intellectually perfect. The objects live again in all their external surroundings. I feel the *Khamsinn,* the desert wind that scorched me at the foot of Pompey's Column; I hear the sea breaking into foam on the barrier reef of Tahiti. But the image does not lead to evocation of related or parallel ideas.

"When, on the other hand, I take a walk over the Comburg moor, the castle weighs upon me in all its massiveness; the recollections of the *Mémoires d'Outre-tombe* besiege me like living pictures. I see, like Chateaubriand himself, the family of great famished lords in their feudal castle. With Chateaubriand I return in the twinkling of an eye to the Niagara that we have both seen. In the fall of the waters I find the deep and melancholy note that he himself found; and after that I think of that dark cathedral of Dol that evidently suggested to the author his *Génie du Christianisme.*

"In literature, things are very unequally suggestive to me. Classic literature has only few paths outwards for me—Tacitus, Lucretius, Juvenal, Homer, and Saint-Simon excepted. I read the other authors of this class partly for themselves, without making a comparison. On the other hand, the reading of Dante, Shakespeare, St. Jerome's compact verses on the Hebrew, and Middle Age prose excites within me a whole world of ideas, like Wagner's music, *canto-fermo,* and Beethoven. Certain things form a link for me from one order of ideas to another. For example, Michaelangelo and the Bible, Rembrandt and Balzac, Puvis de Chavannes and the Merovingian narratives.

"To sum up: There are in me certain *milieux* especially favorable to imagination. When any circumstance brings me into one of them, it is rare that an imaginative network does not occur; and, if one is produced, association of ideas will perform the work. When I give myself up to serious work, I have to mistrust myself: and in this connection I shall surprise people when I say that in the class of ideas above indicated the subject exciting the most ideas in me is sociology."

M......, sixty years of age, artistic temperament. Because of the necessities of life, he has followed a profession entirely opposite to his bent. He has given me his "confession" in the form of fragmentary notes made day by day. Many are *moral* remarks on the subject of his imagination— I leave them out. I note especially the unconquerable tendency to make up little romances and some details in regard to visual representation, and a dislike for numbers.

"It happens that I experience sharp regret when I see the photograph of a monument, e. g., the Pantheon, the proportions of which I have constructed according to the descriptions of the monument and the idea that I had of the life of the Greeks. The photograph mars my dream.

"From the seen to the unknown. In the S. G.

library. A slender young woman, smartly dressed
—spotless black gloves—between her fingers a small
pencil and a tiny note-book. What business has this
affectation this morning in a classic and dull building, in a common environment of poor workmen?
She is not a servant-maid, and not a teacher. Now
for the solution of the unknown. I follow the
woman to her family, into her home, and it is quite
a task.

"In the same library. I want to get an address
from the *Almanach Bottin*. A young man, perhaps
a student, has borrowed the ridiculous volume.
Bent over it, his hands in his hair, he turns the
leaves with the sage leisure of a scholar looking for
a commentary. From the empty dictionary he often
draws out a letter. He must have received this
letter this morning from the country. His family
advises him to apply to so-and-so. It is a question
of money and employment. He must locate the
people who, provincial ignorance said, are near him.
And so goes the wandering imagination.

"When I feel myself drawn to anyone, I prefer
seeing images or portraits rather than the reality.
That is how I avoid making unforeseen discoveries
that would spoil my model.

"If I make numerical calculations, in the absence
of concrete factors, the imagination goes afield, and
the figures group themselves mechanically, harken-
ing to an inner voice that arranges them in order to
get the sense.

"There may be an imagination devoted to arithmetical calculations—forms, beings intrude, even the outline of the figure 3, for example; and then the addition or any other calculation is ruined.

"I revert to the impossibility of making an addition without a swerve of imagination, because plastic figures are always ready before the calculator. The man of imagination is always constructing by means of plastic images.[1] Life possesses him, intoxicates him, so he never gets tired."

[1] We see that the speaker is a visualizer.

THE END

INDEX.

INDEX.

Invention arises to satisfy a need, 271; Higher forms of, 140 ff.; in morals, 300; in successive parts, 296; of monopolies, 282; Pain of, 51; Spontaneity of, 51; subjected to tradition, 269.

Inventions, Amplifiers of, 270; largely anonymous, 275; Mechanical, neglected by psychologists, 263; Stratification of, 272.

Inventors deified, 269; Oddities of, 72.

James, William, 21, 25, 37, 83, 112.
Janet, 340.
Jealousy, stimulates imagination, 34.
Jordæns, 145.
Joy, 34.

Kant, 248.
Kepler, 246, 247.
Klopstock, 215.
Kühn, 129.

Lagrange, 71.
Lammennais, 73.
Lang, 128, 261.
Language, Origin of, 120.
Laplace, 250.
Larvated epilepsy, 141.
Lavoisier, 246.
Law, 294.
Lazarus, 47.
Leibniz, 73, 74, 146, 253, 296 n.
Lélut, 141.
Leurechon, 277.
Liebig, 244.
Linnæus, 183.
Literal mysticism, 226.
Localization, 65.
Loch Lomond, 58.
Locke, 309.
Lombroso, 141, 142.
Louis XIV, 150.
Love, 34; and hate, 134.
Love-plays, 99.

Machiavelli, 73.
Machines, counterfeits of human beings, 279.

Man and animals, Specific quality of, 273.
Manu, 300.
Mastery, Spirit of, 114.
Materials of imagination, 299.
Maury, A., 6 n.
Mechanic and poet, 279.
Mechanical aptitude, 145.
Mechanical imagination, Ideal of, 268.
Mediate association, 59.
Memory, Predominant tendencies in, 61; untrustworthy, 17.
Men, Great, as makers of history, 150.
Mendelssohn, 145, 213 n., 215, 216.
Mental chemistry, 82.
Merchant sailors, 282.
Metamorphosis, 28; of deities, 129; Regressive, 171.
Metaphysical speculation, 251; thought, Stages of, 252.
Metaphysics, 252 ff.
Methods of invention, 243.
Meynert, 100.
Michelangelo, 145, 148, 149.
Michelet, 186, 306.
Middle Ages, predominantly imaginative, 174.
Military invention, 295; Conditions of, 297.
Mill, John Stuart, 82, 284.
Milton, 73.
Mimicry, 98.
Mind, Varieties of, 320.
Mission, Consciousness of, 148.
Misunderstanding of the new, 151.
Mobility of inventors, 258.
Monadology, 253.
Money, Invention of, 286; sought as an end, 289.
Monge, 237.
Moses, 300.
More, 303, 309.
Morgan, Lloyd, 99.
Mormons, 307.
Monoideism, 87.
Montgolfier, 277.
Moral geniuses, 301.
Moravian brotherhood, 307.

CLASSICS IN PSYCHOLOGY

AN ARNO PRESS COLLECTION

Angell, James Rowland. **Psychology: On Introductory Study of the Structure and Function of Human Consciousness.** 4th edition. 1908

Bain, Alexander. **Mental Science.** 1868

Baldwin, James Mark. **Social and Ethical Interpretations in Mental Development.** 2nd edition. 1899

Bechterev, Vladimir Michailovitch. **General Principles of Human Reflexology.** [1932]

Binet, Alfred and Th[éodore] Simon. **The Development of Intelligence in Children.** 1916

Bogardus, Emory S. **Fundamentals of Social Psychology.** 1924

Buytendijk, F. J. J. **The Mind of the Dog.** 1936

Ebbinghaus, Hermann. **Psychology: An Elementary Text-Book.** 1908

Goddard, Henry Herbert. **The Kallikak Family.** 1931

Hobhouse, L[eonard] T. **Mind in Evolution.** 1915

Holt, Edwin B. **The Concept of Consciousness.** 1914

Külpe, Oswald. **Outlines of Psychology.** 1895

Ladd-Franklin, Christine. **Colour and Colour Theories.** 1929

Lectures Delivered at the 20th Anniversary Celebration of Clark University. (Reprinted from *The American Journal of Psychology,* Vol. 21, Nos. 2 and 3). 1910

Lipps, Theodor. **Psychological Studies.** 2nd edition. 1926

Loeb, Jacques. **Comparative Physiology of the Brain and Comparative Psychology.** 1900

Lotze, Hermann. **Outlines of Psychology.** [1885]

McDougall, William. **The Group Mind.** 2nd edition. 1920

Meier, Norman C., editor. **Studies in the Psychology of Art: Volume III.** 1939

Morgan, C. Lloyd. **Habit and Instinct.** 1896

Münsterberg, Hugo. **Psychology and Industrial Efficiency.** 1913

Murchison, Carl, editor. **Psychologies of 1930.** 1930

Piéron, Henri. **Thought and the Brain.** 1927

Pillsbury, W[alter] B[owers]. **Attention.** 1908

[Poffenberger, A. T., editor]. **James McKeen Cattell: Man of Science.** 1947

Preyer, W[illiam] **The Mind of the Child: Parts I and II.** 1890/1889

The Psychology of Skill: Three Studies. 1973

Reymert, Martin L., editor. **Feelings and Emotions:** The Wittenberg Symposium. 1928

Ribot, Th[éodule Armand]. **Essay on the Creative Imagination.** 1906

Roback, A[braham] A[aron]. **The Psychology of Character.** 1927

I. M. Sechenov: Biographical Sketch and Essays. (Reprinted from *Selected Works* by I. Sechenov). 1935

Sherrington, Charles. **The Integrative Action of the Nervous System.** 2nd edition. 1947

Spearman, C[harles]. **The Nature of 'Intelligence' and the Principles of Cognition.** 1923

Thorndike, Edward L. **Education:** A First Book. 1912

Thorndike, Edward L., E. O. Bregman, M. V. Cobb, et al. **The Measurement of Intelligence.** [1927]

Titchener, Edward Bradford. **Lectures on the Elementary Psychology of Feeling and Attention.** 1908

Titchener, Edward Bradford. **Lectures on the Experimental Psychology of the Thought-Processes.** 1909

Washburn, Margaret Floy. **Movement and Mental Imagery.** 1916

Whipple, Guy Montrose. **Manual of Mental and Physical Tests:** Parts I and II. 2nd edition. 1914/1915

Woodworth, Robert Sessions. **Dynamic Psychology.** 1918

Wundt, Wilhelm. **An Introduction to Psychology.** 1912

Yerkes, Robert M. **The Dancing Mouse** and **The Mind of a Gorilla.** 1907/1926